T0202764

Communications
in Computer and Information Science 2071

Rationale

The CCIS series is devoted to the publication of proceedings of computer science conferences. Its aim is to efficiently disseminate original research results in informatics in printed and electronic form. While the focus is on publication of peer-reviewed full papers presenting mature work, inclusion of reviewed short papers reporting on work in progress is welcome, too. Besides globally relevant meetings with internationally representative program committees guaranteeing a strict peer-reviewing and paper selection process, conferences run by societies or of high regional or national relevance are also considered for publication.

Topics

The topical scope of CCIS spans the entire spectrum of informatics ranging from foundational topics in the theory of computing to information and communications science and technology and a broad variety of interdisciplinary application fields.

Information for Volume Editors and Authors

Publication in CCIS is free of charge. No royalties are paid, however, we offer registered conference participants temporary free access to the online version of the conference proceedings on SpringerLink (http://link.springer.com) by means of an http referrer from the conference website and/or a number of complimentary printed copies, as specified in the official acceptance email of the event.

CCIS proceedings can be published in time for distribution at conferences or as post-proceedings, and delivered in the form of printed books and/or electronically as USBs and/or e-content licenses for accessing proceedings at SpringerLink. Furthermore, CCIS proceedings are included in the CCIS electronic book series hosted in the SpringerLink digital library at http://link.springer.com/bookseries/7899. Conferences publishing in CCIS are allowed to use Online Conference Service (OCS) for managing the whole proceedings lifecycle (from submission and reviewing to preparing for publication) free of charge.

Publication process

The language of publication is exclusively English. Authors publishing in CCIS have to sign the Springer CCIS copyright transfer form, however, they are free to use their material published in CCIS for substantially changed, more elaborate subsequent publications elsewhere. For the preparation of the camera-ready papers/files, authors have to strictly adhere to the Springer CCIS Authors' Instructions and are strongly encouraged to use the CCIS LaTeX style files or templates.

Abstracting/Indexing

CCIS is abstracted/indexed in DBLP, Google Scholar, EI-Compendex, Mathematical Reviews, SCImago, Scopus. CCIS volumes are also submitted for the inclusion in ISI Proceedings.

How to start

To start the evaluation of your proposal for inclusion in the CCIS series, please send an e-mail to ccis@springer.com.

Mohamed Mosbah · Tahar Kechadi ·
Ladjel Bellatreche · Faiez Gargouri ·
Chirine Ghedira Guegan · Hassan Badir ·
Amin Beheshti · Mohamed Mohsen Gammoudi
Editors

Advances in Model and Data Engineering in the Digitalization Era

MEDI 2023 Short and Workshop Papers
Sousse, Tunisia, November 2–4, 2023
Proceedings

Editors
Mohamed Mosbah (iD)
Bordeaux INP
Talence, France

Ladjel Bellatreche (iD)
ENSMA
Chasseneuil-du-Poitou, France

Chirine Ghedira Guegan (iD)
University of Lyon
Villeurbanne, France

Amin Beheshti (iD)
Macquarie University
Sydney, NSW, Australia

Tahar Kechadi (iD)
University College Dublin
Dublin, Ireland

Faiez Gargouri (iD)
University of Sfax
Sfax, Tunisia

Hassan Badir (iD)
ENSA-Tangier, Morocco
Tétouan, Morocco

Mohamed Mohsen Gammoudi
University of Sfax
Manouba, Tunisia

ISSN 1865-0929   ISSN 1865-0937 (electronic)
Communications in Computer and Information Science
ISBN 978-3-031-55728-6   ISBN 978-3-031-55729-3 (eBook)
https://doi.org/10.1007/978-3-031-55729-3

This Springer imprint is published by the registered company Springer Nature Switzerland AG
The registered company address is: Gewerbestrasse 11, 6330 Cham, Switzerland

Paper in this product is recyclable.

Preface

MEDI (the International Conference on Model and Data Engineering) is an annual research conference. It focuses on advances in data management and modeling, including topics such as data models, data processing, ontology, machine learning, model-driven engineering, image processing, natural language processing, optimization, and advanced applications such as healthcare and security.

MEDI was founded by researchers from Euro-Mediterranean countries and has served as a springboard for multiple international projects and collaborations.

The previous editions of MEDI have been held in Egypt, Cyprus, Estonia, France, Greece, Italy, Morocco, Portugal, and Spain. For its 12th edition, MEDI 2023 was held in Sousse, Tunisia, during November 2–4, 2023. A total of 99 submissions were received, from which 27 papers were accepted for full presentation and 12 for a short presentation. This volume contains the 11 short presentation papers, as well as 7 accepted papers from the DEITS 2023 workshop, held at MEDI 2023. Altogether, the 18 papers included in this volume cover a wide range of topics related to the theme of the conference.

DEITS 2023 workshop on Data Engineering in IoT Systems was selected after an open call for workshop proposals and the subsequent evaluation of these proposals by the MEDI workshop co-chairs.

We would like to thank all contributors to the success of MEDI 2023 and DEITS 2023, including authors, organizers, and Program Committee members.

November 2023

Mohamed Mosbah
Tahar Kechadi
Ladjel Bellatreche
Faiez Gargouri
Chirine Ghedira Guegan
Hassan Badir
Amin Beheshti
Mohamed Mohsen Gammoudi

Organization

MEDI General Chairs

Faiez Gargouri   University of Sfax, Tunisia
Ladjel Bellatreche   ISAE-ENSMA Poitiers, France

MEDI Program Committee Chairs

Mohamed Mosbah   LaBRI - Bordeaux INP, France
Tahar Kechadi   University College Dublin, Ireland

MEDI Workshop Chairs

Chirine Ghedira Guegan   University of Lyon, France
Hassan Badir   ENSA-Tangier, Morocco
Amin Beheshti   Macquarie University, Australia
Mohamed Mohsen Gammoudi   University of Manouba, Tunisia

MEDI Program Committee

El Hassan Abdelwahed   University Cadi Ayyad Marrakech, Morocco
Idir Ait Sadoune   Paris Saclay University, France
Moulay Akhloufi   Université de Moncton, Canada
Sanaa Alwidian   Ontario Tech University, Canada
Ikram Amous   MIRACL, Tunisia
Heba Aslan   Nile University, Egypt
Christian Attiogbé   Université de Nantes, France
Ahmed Awad   University of Tartu, Estonia
Narjès Bellamine Ben Saoud   University of Manouba, Tunisia
Ladjel Bellatreche   LIAS/ENSMA, France
Orlando Belo   Universidade do Minho, Portugal
Antonio Corral   University of Almería, Spain
Sahraoui Dhelim   University College Dublin, Ireland
Karima Dhouib   University of Sfax, Tunisia

Tai Dinh	Kyoto College of Graduate Studies for Informatics, Japan
Georgios Evangelidis	University of Macedonia, Greece
Flavio Ferrarotti	Software Competence Centre Hagenberg, Austria
Mamoun Filali-Amine	IRIT, France
Philippe Fournier-Viger	Shenzhen University, China
Jaroslav Frnda	University of Zilina, Slovakia
Enrico Gallinucci	University of Bologna, Italy
Faiez Gargouri	University of Sfax, Tunisia
Raju Halder	Indian Institute of Technology Patna, India
Ahmed Hassan	Nile University, Egypt
Irena Holubova	Charles University, Prague, Czech Republic
Luis Iribarne	University of Almería, Spain
Mohamed Jmaiel	University of Sfax, Tunisia
Jérôme Rocheteau	ICAM site de Nantes, France
Pinar Karagoz	Middle East Technical University, Turkey
Regine Laleau	Paris Est Creteil University, France
Yves Ledru	Université Grenoble Alpes, France
Ben Ayed Leila	ENSI, Tunisia
Ivan Luković	University of Belgrade, Serbia
Sofian Maabout	University of Bordeaux, France
Yannis Manolopoulos	Open University of Cyprus, Cyprus
Walaa Medhat	Nile University, Egypt
Dominique Mery	Université de Lorraine, France
Mohamed Mhiri	University of Sfax, Tunisia
Mohamed Mosbah	Bordeaux INP, France
Chokri Mraidha	CEA LIST, France
Ahlem Nabli Chakroun	University of Sfax, Tunisia
Mourad Nouioua	Hunan University, China
Samir Ouchani	CESI Lineact, France
Milu Philip	University College Dublin, Ireland
Jaroslav Pokorný	Charles University, Prague, Czech Republic
Giuseppe Polese	University of Salerno, Italy
Elvinia Riccobene	University of Milan, Italy
Oscar Romero	Universitat Politècnica de Catalunya, Spain
Milos Savic	University of Novi Sad, Serbia
Arsalan Shahid	University College Dublin, Ireland
Neeraj Singh	INPT-ENSEEIHT/IRIT, University of Toulouse, France
Benkrid Soumia	ESI, Algeria
Goce Trajcevski	Iowa State University, USA

Mohamed Turki	Higher Institute of Computer Science and Multimedia of Sfax (ISIMS), Tunisia
Javier Tuya	Universidad de Oviedo, Spain
Panos Vassiliadis	University of Ioannina, Greece
Hala Zayed	Benha University, Egypt

Additional Reviewers

Hamza Alshawabkeh	Frédéric Gervais
Abdelhakim Baouya	Imed Ghnaya
Bernardo Breve	Tahar Kechadi
Loredana Caruccio	Amine Khaldi
Stefano Cirillo	Sabri Khamari
Domenico Desiato	Hannes Sochor
Soha Eid	Aimilia Tasidou
Bernhard Fischer	Ahmed Hassan Mohamed Yousef

DEITS Program Committee Chairs

| Abderrazak Jemai | University of Carthage, Tunisia |
| Takoua Abdellatif | University of Carthage, Tunisia |

DEITS Program Committee

Walid Gaaloul	SAMOVAR, Polytechnic Institute of Paris, France
Sami Yangui	LAAS-CNRS, INSA Toulouse, France
Wided Souidene	SERCOM Polytechnic School of Tunisia, Tunisia
Ines Bousnina	SERCOM Polytechnic School of Tunisia, Tunisia
Olfa Besbes	Isitcom Sousse, Tunisia
Asma Mansour	Horizon Sousse, Tunisia
Nawal Bayar	Horizon Sousse, Tunisia
Aymen Yahyaoui	Military Academy of Tunisia, Tunisia
Imen Jegham	Horizon Sousse, Tunisia
Imen Boudali	SERCOM Polytechnic School of Tunisia, Tunisia
Feten Slimeni	Military Academy of Tunisia, Tunisia
Sonia Kotel	Horizon Sousse, Tunisia
Wided Ben Abid	Horizon Sousse, Tunisia

Contents

Machine Learning and Optimization

A Comparative Analysis of Time Series Transformers and Alternative Deep Learning Models for SSVEP Classification

Heba Ali[1,2]([✉]) [iD], Adel Elzemity[3] [iD], Amir E. Oghostinos[3] [iD],
and Sahar Selim[1,2] [iD]

[1] Center for Informatics Science, Nile University, Sheikh Zayed City 12588, Egypt
h.ali2137@nu.edu.eg
[2] School of Information Technology and Computer Science,
Sheikh Zayed City 12588, Egypt
[3] School of Engineering, Nile University, Sheikh Zayed City 12588, Egypt
https://nu.edu.eg/index.php

Abstract. Steady State Visually Evoked Potentials (SSVEPs) are intrinsic responses to specific visual stimulus frequencies. When the retina is activated by a frequency ranging from 3.5 to 75 Hz, the brain produces electrical activity at the same frequency as the visual signal, or its multiples. Identifying the preferred frequencies of neurocortical dynamic processes is a benefit of SSVEPs. However, the time consumed during calibration sessions limits the number of training trials and gives rise to visual fatigue since there is significant human variation across and within individuals over time, which weakens the effectiveness of the individual training data. To address this issue, we propose a novel cross-subject-based classification method to enhance the robustness of SSVEP classification by employing cross-subject similarity and variability. Through an efficient time-series transformer, we compared Time Series Transformers (TST) with different deep learning approaches in the literature. We utilized the TST to speed up calibration processes and improve classification precision for new users. Then we compare this technique to other techniques: EEGNet, FBtCNN, and C-CNN. Our suggested framework's outcomes are validated using two datasets with two different time window lengths. The experimental results suggest that cross-subject time-series transformers and EEGNet achieve better performance with specific subjects than state-of-the-art techniques when compared to other techniques that have high potential for building high-speed BCIs.

Keywords: Brain Computer Interface · SSVEP · Time Series Transformer (TST) · EEGNet · C-CNN

The first two authors contributed equally to this work.

M. Mosbah et al. (Eds.): MEDI 2023, CCIS 2071, pp. 3–16, 2024.
https://doi.org/10.1007/978-3-031-55729-3_2

1   Introduction

One of the most commonly used control signals in Brain-Computer Interface (BCI) systems is steady-state visual evoked potential (SSVEP) [17]. However, traditional spatial filtering algorithms for SSVEP classification rely significantly on subject-specific calibration data. Calibration data is required for the creation of spatial filters and templates. As a result, the calibration process is typically complicated and time-consuming, limiting the utility of BCIs in a real-world situation. Many studies have attempted to apply transfer-learning algorithms to speed up the calibration process without losing classification accuracy [17]. Methods to reduce the demand for calibration data are desperately needed. Developing techniques that can be employed in inter-subject categorization [5] scenarios has arisen as a possible new discipline in recent years [8].

Recent studies used transfer learning algorithms to find SSVEPs with limited training data. As mentioned in [17], different individuals might share a common SSVEP template; they developed SSVEP templates for new subjects using the overall average of SSVEP data from all prior subjects. Study [8] proposes collecting a large amount of existing user data, each of which must include EEG data at all stimulus frequencies. As a result, each existing user must examine each stimulus target in turn while concurrently recording their EEG. SSVEP templates from current themes that have been spatially screened [3]. Transformer, a well-known deep learning model, performed well in EEG signal categorization tests. There has recently been an explosion of transformer-based solutions for the Long-Term Time Series Forecasting (LTSF) problem. Transformers, in particular, are arguably the most effective way to find the semantic links between the components of a long sequence. In time series modeling, the temporal links in an ordered collection of continuous points must be retrieved. During this investigation, a Time Series Transformer (TST) was employed to extract valuable features from the data and classify them according to the correct flickering frequency [18]. As a result, this article assesses the Transformer Time Series classification accuracy, and the architecture hyperparameters are tuned to get the best classification accuracy.

This study intends to employ the TST to enhance the efficiency of calibration procedures and the accuracy of the classification of steady-state visual evoked potential (SSVEP)-based brain-computer interfaces (BCIs) using two different time window lengths (1 s and 0.5 s) and two different datasets. The experimental findings indicate that the utilization of cross-subject analysis in conjunction with time-series transformers and EEGNet yields better results for specific subjects in comparison to state-of-the-art methods. The paper was organized into three sections: methods, results, and discussion.

2   Methods

In this section, we will provide a detailed description of the utilized dataset and the pre-processing pipeline employed for each.

2.1   Dataset Description

The proposed approach and other previously published methods were assessed and compared on two datasets: Dataset 1 [10] and a benchmark dataset - Dataset 2 [16].

Dataset 1. A public repository was used to download the offline SSVEP dataset taken from ten healthy participants [10]. All participants sat in a comfortable chair 0.6 m from an LCD monitor. Twelve flashing stimuli with the following flicker frequencies appeared on the monitor: 9.25 Hz, 9.75 Hz, 10.25 Hz, 10.75 Hz, 11.25 Hz, 11.75 Hz, 12.25 Hz, 12.75 Hz, 13.25 Hz, 13.75 Hz, 14.25 Hz, and 14.75 Hz. The stimuli were organized in a 4×3 grid of $6\,\text{cm} \times 6\,\text{cm}$ squares that looked like a numeric keypad.

The BioSemi ActiveTwo EEG (Biosemi B.V., Netherlands) equipment was used to collect the EEG data, which had a sampling rate of 2048 Hz. Over the occipito-parietal regions, eight active electrodes were implanted. A red square cue guided the participant's sight to a specific stimulus on the screen at the start of each session. The cue time was one second. The subject was instructed to concentrate on the specific stimulus for 4 s. One block included 12 trials, one for each of the 12 stimuli on the screen. They were shown in random order. A total of 15 blocks were shown, resulting in 180 trials.

Dataset 2 [16]. The dataset included 40 visual target stimuli that were shown on an LCD panel. The 40 targets were encoded using the joint frequency and phase modulation (JFPM) approach, with target stimulation frequencies ranging from 8 Hz to 15.8 Hz in 0.2 Hz steps and phases beginning at 0 in 0.5 steps. The investigation included 35 people with normal or corrected-to-normal vision, eight of whom had previous experience with SSVEP-based experiments.

The experiment was divided into six blocks for each subject. The subjects stared at 40 targets in random order according to the prompts in each block, for a total of 40 trials. Each trial was 6 s long. The subjects were instructed to move the realization to the target stimulus position according to the prompt for the first 0.5 s, then fixate on the target stimulus for 5 s, and lastly, the monitor was blank for 0.5 s. EEG data were collected using Synamps2 EEG equipment (Neuroscan, Inc.) at 1000 Hz and downsampled to 250 Hz. Finally, to remove power frequency interference, a 50 Hz notch filter was utilized.

2.2   Pre-processing

Since the SSVEP data was four-dimensional, we began our preprocessing pipeline by reshaping the data to two dimensions, as shown in Fig. 1. Each dataset's preprocessing was done separately. For Dataset 1, the signals were pre-processed for comparison using the steps mentioned in [10]. This dataset's eight channels were all used. To filter the data, a 4th-order Butterworth band-pass filter with a frequency range of 6 to 80 Hz was utilized, as described in [10]. Each of the

four trials was divided into non-overlapping 0.5- and 1-s windows. The data for
Dataset 2 were segmented using stimulus markers that specified the start and
end of the flickering. A band-pass filter with cutoff frequencies of 6 and 80 Hz was
applied to the data to remove the trend and high-frequency abnormalities, such
as power line noise, from the segmented data. As SSVEPs are not sensitive to low-
frequency artifacts such as eye or body movements, no further artifact reduction
procedure was applied, and the trials were separated into non-overlapping 0.5 s
and 1 s time windows.

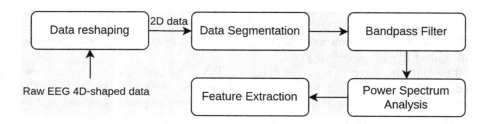

Fig. 1. Preprocessing pipeline

Feature Extraction Using FB-TRCA. Our approach for Feature extraction is the use of Filterbank-Task Related Component Analysis or ensemble-
TRCA. TRCA extracts signal components that are reproducible across trials, as
it is known that EEG signals demonstrate a considerable amount of variability
across different trials for a given subject and target frequency. The extracted
components capture the highest covariance between a single trial and the other
trials, and the remaining components are discarded. The filterbank modification
extracts features that improve classification accuracy by dividing the EEG signal
into sub-bands. Each sub-band is TRCA-processed then the resulting combination of signals gives a better representation of the original EEG [19].

The FB-TRCA works by finding the covariance between all pairs of trials
and finds Coefficients for (classes, channels) that maximize reproducibility of
signal across several trials for a given target (class) as shown in Fig. 2. The set
of coefficients constitute the "Spatial Filter" [14].

3   Classification Techniques

Multiple experiments were performed to get the best classification accuracy by
testing the subjects with Time Series Transformer, and EEGNet, then comparing
it with FBtCNN and C-CNN.

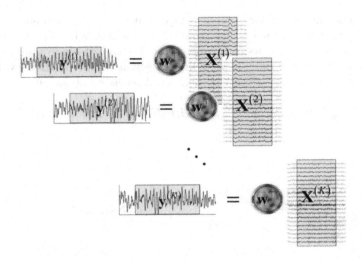

Fig. 2. Feature Extraction using FB-TRCA. The test signal is passed through the spatial filter of each class, and the correlation coefficient is calculated for possible combinations of spatially-filtered test data and train data classes [13]

3.1 Time Series Transformer (TST)

A transformer encoder, as detailed in the original transformer work by study [6], is at the heart of our methodology. However, we do not use the decoder portion of the architecture. Figure 3 displays a schematic diagram of the generic portion of our approach, which is applicable to all tasks under consideration.

For a thorough explanation of the transformer model, we direct the reader to the original work. Here, we offer the suggested adjustments that allow it to be used with multivariate time series data rather than a set of discrete word indices. However, only predictions on the masked values are taken into account in the Mean Squared Error loss [6].

First, the initial feature vectors xt are normalized (for each dimension, we subtract the mean and divide by the variance across the training set samples), and then they are linearly projected onto a d-dimensional vector space, where d is the dimension of the transformer model sequence element representations (commonly referred to as the model dimension):

$$\mathbf{u_t} = \mathbf{W_p}\mathbf{x_t} + \mathbf{b_p} \tag{1}$$

where the model input vector 1, matches the NLP transformer's word vectors. These will be multiplied by the respective matrices, added to the positional encodings, and then constitute the queries, keys, and values of the self-attention layer.

Although we only test our method on multivariate time series in the context of this study, the aforementioned formula covers the univariate time series situation, i.e., $m = 1$. Because the computational complexity of the model scales as

O(w2) and the number of parameters as O(w) with the input sequence length w, we also note that the input vectors ut need not essentially be acquired from the (transformed) feature vectors at a time step t. Instead, if the granularity (temporal resolution) of the data is very fine, one may utilize a 1D-convolutional layer with 1 input and d output channels and kernels Ki of size [6]:

$$u_t^i = u(t, i) = \sum_j \sum_h x(t + j, h) K_i(j, h), \quad i = 1, \ldots, d \tag{2}$$

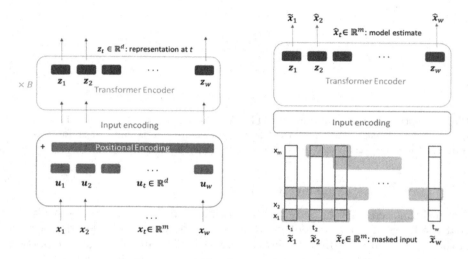

Fig. 3. The TST Encoder architecture. The (Left) block: shows a generic model architecture that all tasks share. The first self-attention layer receives the feature vector xt at each time step t and linearly projects it to a vector ut with the same dimensionality (d) as the internal representation vectors of the model to create the keys, queries, and values after encoding the positions. The (Right) block: The unsupervised pre-training task's training setup [20].

Hyperparameter Tuning. The TSAI library was utilized to tune the hyperparameters and implement data augmentation methods to achieve higher accuracy [11]. Then identify the fittest learning rate using a function built by the Fast.ai library.

The TST architecture has been used with the default hyperparameter configurations set up by the TSAI library [20], except for the dropout rates. They are calibrated to reduce overfitting on the training data. There are two dropout rates for this architecture to be set up: dropout and fc dropout. "Dropout" is the amount of residual dropout applied in the encoder, and "fc dropout" is the dropout applied to the final fully connected layer. Dropout is set to 0.5 and fc dropout is set to 0.8 after applying the Gaussian hyperparameter tuning method to identify the best combination of both.

Data Augmentation. Attention-based architectures need vast amounts of data to reach higher accuracy; thus, data augmentation techniques are used in this paper to maximize the efficiency of the training process by providing more data. The following techniques are used in this training interchangeably:

- TSShuffleSteps: Randomly shuffles consecutive sequence data points in batch
- TSGaussianNoise: Applies additive or multiplicative Gaussian noise

The resulting classification accuracy has improved due to the introduction of these data augmentation techniques compared to the original dataset only.

3.2   EEGNet

EEGNet is a small CNN architecture for EEG-based BCIs that can be used with different BCI paradigms, trained with little data, and make features that can be understood neurophysiologically. Utilizing the Adam optimizer and the given default settings, we fitted the model with the goal of reducing the categorical cross-entropy loss function. We execute validation pausing after 300 training iterations (epochs) and save the model weights that resulted in the most minor validation set loss. Bias units are not used in any of the convolutional layers. Even though convolutions are always one-dimensional, we utilize two-dimensional convolution functions because they are simpler to implement in software [7]. The EEGNet architecture has the following parameters: C = channels, T = time points, F1 = temporal filters, D = depth multiplier (number of spatial filters), F2 = pointwise filters, and N = classes. We have chosen p = 0.25 for classification across subjects for the Dropout layer [7].

4   Results

The experimental findings of the TST will be presented for each dataset individually, followed by a comparison with three different deep learning models documented in the literature.

4.1   Dataset 1 Analysis

Table 1 shows the average classification accuracies of all methods across 10 participants for Dataset 1 at time window 1 s, and Table 2 shows the classification methods ranked from highest to lowest at time window 0.5 s, as follows: EEGNet, C-CNN, FBtCNN, and TST. Among all categorization approaches, EEGNet outperformed TST. The investigation was carried out on two distinct temporal window lengths in order to assess the relationships between window lengths and classification algorithms. Both the EEGNet and C-CNN algorithms outperformed TST in subject 3 and 4. There was also a substantial variation in accuracy at smaller windows ranging at 0.5 S. The average accuracies of the various approaches for 1 s window length were as follows: EEGNet: 80.782%, FBtCNN: 75.265%, C-CNN: 77.156 %, TST: 73.89%.

Table 1. The evaluation of the model's classification accuracy was conducted on Dataset 1, using a temporal window length of 1 s. The values denoted in bold represent the utmost level of accuracy.

Subject	EEGNet [12]	FBtCNN [12]	C-CNN [12]	TST
S1	52.34	46.09	**57.81**	42.78
S2	44.53	**40.62**	36.72	35.00
S3	**66.41**	44.53	60.94	54.44
S4	**96.88**	92.19	95.31	91.11
S5	89.06	**89.94**	60.62	82.78
S6	**95.31**	88.28	**95.31**	94.44
S7	93.75	85.16	89.84	**93.89**
S8	**97.66**	96.09	96.88	83.33
S9	87.5	92.19	**97.66**	90.00
S10	**84.38**	77.56	80.47	71.11
Mean	**80.782**	75.265	77.156	73.89

Table 2. The evaluation of the model's classification accuracy was conducted on Dataset 1, using a temporal window length of 0.5 s. The values denoted in bold represent the utmost level of accuracy.

Subject	EEGNet [12]	FBtCNN [12]	C-CNN [12]	TST
S1	34.89	27.89	30.78	**35.00**
S2	**22.56**	17	17.22	18.89
S3	**45.78**	28.33	40.89	45.56
S4	**79.44**	68.89	71.78	67.22
S5	**72.11**	70.78	71.78	61.11
S6	**80.33**	74.33	75.11	74.44
S7	81.22	72.67	74	**81.67**
S8	79.33	73.89	**78.78**	57.22
S9	64.56	57.44	**65.89**	42.77
S10	57.22	**52.78**	50.44	44.44
Mean	**61.744**	54.4	57.667	52.83

4.2   Dataset 2 Analysis

As demonstrated in Table 3, the C-CNN and TST algorithms outperform EEG-Net and FBtCNN reverse Dataset 1. C-CNN had an average accuracy of 81.878%, EEGNet had an accuracy of 80.781%, and TST had an accuracy of 62.21%. At S2, S3, and S7, the TST model outperformed EEGNet and C-CNN. At time window 0.5 S, the EEGNet algorithm and C-CNN performed much better than TST and FBtCNN AS, as demonstrated in Table 4.

Table 3. The evaluation of the model's classification accuracy was conducted on Dataset 2, using a temporal window length of 1 s. The values denoted in bold represent the utmost level of accuracy.

Subject	EEGNet [12]	FBtCNN [12]	C-CNN [12]	TST
S1	93.75	**100**	96.88	72.08
S2	60.94	51.56	54.69	**67.08**
S3	68.75	46.88	67.19	**86.67**
S4	68.75	**87.5**	73.44	29.17
S5	87.5	95.31	**98.44**	71.25
S6	95.31	**98.44**	93.75	52.92
S7	75	73.44	76.56	**93.89**
S8	**82.81**	76.56	81.25	65.83
S9	**81.25**	78.12	**81.25**	49.17
S10	93.75	87.5	**95.31**	63.75
Mean	80.781	79.531	**81.876**	62.21

Table 4. The evaluation of the models' classification accuracy was conducted on Dataset 2, using a temporal window length of 1 s. The values denoted in bold represent the utmost level of accuracy.

Subject	EEGNet [12]	FBtCNN [12]	C-CNN [12]	TST
S1	82.67	**84**	80.67	40.83
S2	39	30.67	40.67	**42.5**
S3	53.67	33	57.33	**62.5**
S4	**71**	66	**71**	8.75
S5	81	**89**	85.33	37.92
S6	73.67	70.67	**79.33**	22.49
S7	66	59	**64.67**	27.92
S8	56.33	**59.67**	56	17.92
S9	65.33	**71.33**	68	20.00
S10	**89**	58	80	31.25
Mean	67.767	62.134	**68.3**	31.21

5 Discussion

We handled the data for the classification task; the data has been randomly split between training and validation sets, as shown in Fig. 4 with data distribution.

5.1 Classification

Due to the nonstationary and nonlinear nature of electroencephalogram (EEG) data, it is still very hard to make high-performance algorithms for Brain-

Fig. 4. Data distribution with random selection for data points after splitting for training/validation sets.

Computer Interface (BCI) systems. In the field of SSVEP data analysis, numerous conventional and deep learning techniques have been suggested and have made significant advancements over the years. Examples of these methods include Canonical Correlation Analysis (CCA), Task-Related Component Analysis (TRCA) [4], and EEGNET, among others. The TRCA methods require calibration data, which can be a time-consuming and labor-intensive process to gather. Hence, the topic of lowering the duration of data collection, namely the time required for gathering data from a patient, has gained significant attention in the field of brain-computer interfaces in recent years. One such approach is to utilize the available data from pre-existing participants in order to train a model that is tailored to a particular sub-discipline. Deep learning technologies have garnered growing interest in the development of design schemes. In the present study, it has been observed that deep learning (DL) methods have superior performance compared to methods such as TRCA, particularly in the context of inter-subject categorization. This can be attributed to the substantial variations that exist between participants. In this research, a comparative analysis was conducted with the aim of enhancing the accuracy of classification outcomes in SSVEP-based BCI systems. The study focused on both 12-class and 4-class paradigms. The C-CNN, TST, and EEGNet demonstrated superior performance relative to other state-of-the-art (SOTA) techniques across several evaluation scenarios, suggesting their potential to decrease the required calibration duration. To perform the classification, we used the TST encoder architectures then trained and tuned them to achieve maximum accuracy and compare them with three other models from the literature. When looking at the performance of each individual architecture and analyzing the process of hyperparameter tuning for each one, the learning rate is calculated for each architecture separately and differs for each.

EEGNet utilizes depthwise and separable convolutions to classify EEG signals and demonstrate how to build an EEG-specific model that incorporates well-known EEG feature extraction ideas [7]. EEGNet has achieved poor classification accuracy for subjects 1, 2, and 10 in Dataset 1 and subject 4, 10 in Dataset 2. However, when comparing the same subjects across different architectures, the performance seems lower than the other subjects. That indicates having noisy data in these subjects, which is also confirmed in the literature [2, 9].

Due to the transformer's strong capacity to capture long-term dependence, it has been demonstrated to be useful in various time series classification problems. The majority of classification transformers use a straightforward encoder structure, where self-attention levels carry out representation learning and feed-forward layers provide class probabilities.

When it comes to the classification accuracy of the Time Series Transformer, it has better performance on specific subjects compared to EEGNet across all subjects. According to Table 2, the accuracy for subjects 1, 2, and 10 is poor but relatively higher than EEGNet. However, when comparing the performance of transformers on other data types and different use cases, the overall performance is poor on this dataset.

Is the amount of training data currently available a constraint for Time Series Transformers? Some may contend that the tiny sizes of the benchmark datasets are to blame for the subpar performance of Transformer-based solutions. It is challenging to scale up the training data amount for Time Series Transformer since it uses collected time series, unlike computer vision or natural language processing applications. In actuality, the model's performance would be significantly impacted by the magnitude of the training data [15]. To overcome this issue, data augmentation methods are implemented to improve the model's performance by providing more data for training. After implementing the strategies highlighted in the methods section for data augmentation, the classification accuracy of the TST has noticeably improved, as shown in the following Table 1.

The EEGNet architecture may, in general, produce higher performance since it has the best average accuracy across all subjects in dataset 1, and C-CNN achieves the highest accuracy on dataset 2. For instance, when comparing subject 8's accuracy across all architectures, the highest model has the highest accuracy 97.66%. The transformer reaches stable accuracy after 50 epochs.

The findings derived from the analysis of both datasets demonstrate that the TST approach had the least favorable performance when compared to the other methods on specific subjects. One plausible explanation for this phenomenon is that, in the present investigation, the SSVEP data underwent asynchronous processing, wherein the training trials were divided into segments using a predetermined window and step size, and the data was not synchronized with any specific phase. Prior research utilizing the Temporal Response Classification Analysis (TRCA) technique has predominantly employed synchronous Steady-State Visual Evoked Potential (SSVEP) paradigms. These studies have consistently utilized fixed data windows that are perfectly aligned with the stimulus. In a previous study conducted by [1], it was noted that the combined-CCA technique exhibited suboptimal performance when applied to SSVEP data that was processed asynchronously. Hence, it is suggested that future research endeavors should focus on exploring the potential applicability of asynchronous steady-state visually evoked potential (SSVEP) paradigms.

Also, all the models achieve better performance with time window 1 s compared to 0.5 s, as shown in Tables 1, 2, 3, and 4, which give us intuition about the effect of window length on improving the classification accuracies. The current study employed TST, which was compared with FBtCNN, EEGNet, and C-CNN from the existing literature, as shown in Fig. 5. The comparison results are shown in Tables 1, 2, 3, and 4. In the present investigation, we have endeavored to impartially compare our methodologies with other techniques proposed in the literature.

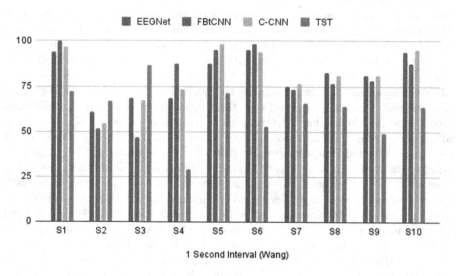

Fig. 5. The analysis of model accuracy reveals that EEGNet, FBtCNN, C-CNN, and TST exhibit varying performance when applied to Dataset 2 with a temporal window of 1 s.

6   Conclusion

The objective of this study was to enhance the calibration process while maintaining classification accuracy by employing the TST method. The Steady State Visual Evoked Potential (SSVEP) benchmark dataset was used to compare TST to other methods. The goal was to get more accurate results than in previous studies. This improvement in accuracy would have implications for the application of SSVEP as a frequently utilized control signal. In the preliminary analysis, it was shown that EEGNet and TST were better at classifying specific participants than FBtCNN and C-CNN. Furthermore, it has been shown that the performance of FB-TRCA in the task of feature extraction is exceptionally high and exhibits a high level of accuracy. Additionally, our findings indicate that the TST model effectively addresses the intricate issue of determining the optimal timing for extracting crucial information from time series data. Also, we recommend using time window length 1 s, as it performs better than 0.5 s. The results of this study have the potential to enhance future investigations into the classification of steady-state visually evoked potentials (SSVEPs) by including more intricate experimental designs. In future endeavors, it is imperative to contemplate enhancing the preprocessing pipeline in order to get superior performance with TST. Additionally, it is advisable to modify the architecture to optimize performance.

Data Availibility Statement. The dataset - 1 for this study can be found in the following link here and dataset - 2 here.

References

1. Cecotti, H.: A time-frequency convolutional neural network for the offline classi-fication of steady-state visual evoked potential responses. Pattern Recogn. Lett. **32**(8), 1145–1153 (2011)
2. Chen, X., Wang, Y., Gao, S., Jung, T.P., Gao, X.: Filter bank canonical correlation analysis for implementing a high-speed SSVEP-based brain-computer interface. J. Neural Eng. **12**(4), 046008 (2015)
3. Chiang, K.J., Wei, C.S., Nakanishi, M., Jung, T.P.: Boosting template-based SSVEP decoding by cross-domain transfer learning. J. Neural Eng. **18**(1), 016002 (2021)
4. Deng, Y., Sun, Q., Wang, C., Wang, Y., Zhou, S.K.: TRCA-net: using TRCA filters to boost the SSVEP classification with convolutional neural network. J. Neural Eng. **20**(4), 046005 (2023)
5. Fahimi, F., Zhang, Z., Goh, W.B., Lee, T.S., Ang, K.K., Guan, C.: Inter-subject transfer learning with an end-to-end deep convolutional neural network for EEG-based BCI. J. Neural Eng. **16**(2), 026007 (2019)
6. Kaiser, L., et al.: One model to learn them all. arXiv preprint arXiv:1706.05137 (2017)
7. Lawhern, V.J., Solon, A.J., Waytowich, N.R., Gordon, S.M., Hung, C.P., Lance, B.J.: EEGNet: a compact convolutional neural network for EEG-based brain-computer interfaces. J. Neural Eng. **15**(5), 056013 (2018)
8. Liu, Q., Chen, K., Ai, Q., Xie, S.Q.: Recent development of signal processing algorithms for SSVEP-based brain computer interfaces. J. Med. Biol. Eng. **34**(4), 299–309 (2014)
9. Nakanishi, M., Wang, Y., Chen, X., Wang, Y.T., Gao, X., Jung, T.P.: Enhancing detection of SSVEPs for a high-speed brain speller using task-related component analysis. IEEE Trans. Biomed. Eng. **65**(1), 104–112 (2017)
10. Nakanishi, M., Wang, Y., Wang, Y.T., Jung, T.P.: A comparison study of canon-ical correlation analysis based methods for detecting steady-state visual evoked potentials. PLoS ONE **10**(10), e0140703 (2015)
11. Oguiza, I.: tsai-a state-of-the-art deep learning library for time series and sequential data. Github, San Francisco (2022)
12. Pan, Y., Chen, J., Zhang, Y., Zhang, Y.: An efficient CNN-LSTM network with spectral normalization and label smoothing technologies for SSVEP frequency recognition. J. Neural Eng. **19**(5), 056014 (2022)
13. Tanaka, H.: Group task-related component analysis (gTRCA): a multivariate method for inter-trial reproducibility and inter-subject similarity maximization for EEG data analysis. Sci. Rep. **10**(1), 84 (2020)
14. Tanaka, H., Katura, T., Sato, H.: Task-related component analysis for functional neuroimaging and application to near-infrared spectroscopy data. Neuroimage **64**, 308–327 (2013)

15. Tang, W., Long, G., Liu, L., Zhou, T., Blumenstein, M., Jiang, J.: Omni-scale CNNs: a simple and effective kernel size configuration for time series classification. arXiv preprint arXiv:2002.10061 (2020)
16. Wang, Y., Chen, X., Gao, X., Gao, S.: A benchmark dataset for SSVEP-based brain-computer interfaces. IEEE Trans. Neural Syst. Rehabil. Eng. **25**(10), 1746–1752 (2016)
17. Yuan, P., Chen, X., Wang, Y., Gao, X., Gao, S.: Enhancing performances of SSVEP-based brain-computer interfaces via exploiting inter-subject information. J. Neural Eng. **12**(4), 046006 (2015)
18. Zeng, A., Chen, M., Zhang, L., Xu, Q.: Are transformers effective for time series forecasting? In: Proceedings of the AAAI Conference on Artificial Intelligence, vol. 37, pp. 11121–11128 (2023)
19. Zerafa, R., Camilleri, T., Falzon, O., Camilleri, K.P.: To train or not to train? a survey on training of feature extraction methods for SSVEP-based BCIs. J. Neural Eng. **15**(5), 051001 (2018)
20. Zerveas, G., Jayaraman, S., Patel, D., Bhamidipaty, A., Eickhoff, C.: A transformer-based framework for multivariate time series representation learning. In: Proceedings of the 27th ACM SIGKDD Conference on Knowledge Discovery & Data Mining, pp. 2114–2124 (2021)

MixUp Data Augmentation for Handwritten Arabic Mathematical Symbols Recognition

Ibtissem Hadj Ali[1]([✉]), Anouar Ben Khalifa[1,2], and Mohamed Ali Mahjoub[1]

[1] Université de Sousse, Ecole Nationale d'Ingénieurs de Sousse, LATIS- Laboratory of Advanced Technology and Intelligent Systems, 4023 Sousse, Tunisia
`ibtissemhadjali@gmail.com`
[2] Université de Jendouba, Institut National des Technologies et des Sciences du Kef, 7100 Le Kef, Tunisia

Abstract. Handwritten mathematical expression and symbol recognition is a subfield of document image analysis that aims to convert images of handwritten mathematical formulas into a machine-readable format. Despite decades of research, recognition of handwritten mathematical expressions and symbols, particularly those written in Arabic, remains a challenging problem. To address this issue, we propose a Deep Neural Network (DNN)-based approach for Handwritten Arabic Mathematical Symbol Recognition. DNNs are powerful tools for data analysis and image classification, but they are susceptible to overfitting. Additionally, there are limited large-scale databases available for Arabic mathematical symbol recognition. To overcome this, we propose using MixUp data augmentation to increase the diversity of available data. MixUp involves training a CNN on convex combinations of pairs of examples and their corresponding labels. Furthermore, we integrate our new framework with both Cross Entropy loss and triplet loss on the augmented samples, which significantly improves the classification accuracy. The experimental results conducted on the Handwritten Arabic Mathematical Dataset (HAMF) [1] demonstrate that our proposed framework yields a significant improvement in accuracy compared to the standard CNN.

Keywords: Handwritten Arabic Mathematical symbols · MixUp augmentation · Triplet Network · Cross Entropy Loss · Triplet Loss

1 Introduction

Handwritten mathematical expression recognition (HMER) is an active research area in the field of computer vision and pattern recognition [2,3]. The recognition of mathematical expressions is a fundamental task in document analysis and it has various applications, such as intelligent education, assignment grading, digital library service, and office automation. The aim of HMER is to generate the math expression sequence in LATEX or MATHML format in accordance with

M. Mosbah et al. (Eds.): MEDI 2023, CCIS 2071, pp. 17–30, 2024.
https://doi.org/10.1007/978-3-031-55729-3_3

the handwritten math expression image [3]. HMER is a challenging task due to the complex two-dimensional structures of formulas, the enormous ambiguity and variability of mathematical symbols, the variations in writing styles, and the difficulty of segmentation symbols in the expression.

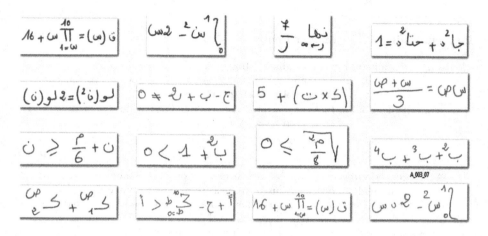

Fig. 1. Examples of different Arabic handwritten mathematical expressions.

Recently, the advent and advancement of machine learning and deep learning techniques, have made great progress in mathematical expression recognition handwritten in Latin. However, it is still a challenge for existing methods to process and recognize Arabic handwritten mathematical expressions and symbols due to several issues including the large number of symbols used in Arabic mathematics such as Arabic and Latin numbers, the Arabic alphabet, arithmetic operators, Arabic function names, equality operators, etc. makes certain expressions extremely difficult to recognize even for a human Fig. 1 shows several examples of different Arabic handwritten mathematical expressions.

The visually similar symbols like the Arabic digit one and the Arabic letter Alif or like digit nine and the Arabic letter Waw. Also, most Arabic characters have similar shapes but differ in the position and number of dots. Ambiguity arises not only because of the large number of similar symbols but also due to the different styles and imprecision in human writing which engenders inter-class similarity and intra-class variance problems. For example, the same symbol can be written in different ways and some different symbols can have strong similarities, all depending on the writing style. Figure 2 gives some examples of ambiguity. the lack of large training data is another challenge facing the recognition of Arabic mathematical symbols.

Although Latin mathematical symbol recognition has attracted much attention and has achieved promoted recognition performance thanks to the availability of large annotated datasets and the development of deep learning models. In contrast, the recognition of Arabic mathematical symbols suffers from a shortage of interest and much more research is still needed. The lack of sufficient training data for learning the high variability and ambiguity between symbols is one of the most important problems.

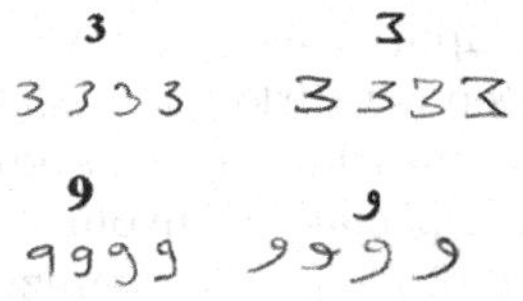

Fig. 2. Examples of ambiguity among symbols.

In this paper, we address the recognition of handwritten Arabic mathematical symbols. We propose variations of MixUp [5] based augmentation to generate new samples from a linear combination of samples during mini-batch training. The main concept of our method is to alleviate the lack of training data and reduce class imbalance by mixing the training samples. In addition, our framework is strengthened by incorporating both the softmax loss and triplet loss. Specifically, the softmax loss is computed directly on the MixUp feature space, while the triplet loss is trained on the positive, negative, and mixed features of the triplets.

The rest of the paper is organized as follows. Section 2 presents a review of the related work in the field of handwritten mathematical expressions and symbol recognition. Section 3 describes the proposed approach in detail, including the architecture of the CNN-based recognition model the data augmentation techniques used for the training dataset, and the proposed new loss function. Section 4 presents the experimental results and analysis. Finally, Sect. 5 concludes the paper and discusses future directions of research in the field.

2 Related Work

The recognition of handwritten mathematical expressions [6–8] has attracted the interest of the research community for decades. Since the first works in the 1960s [9], the research in HMER has significantly improved but the accuracy of different methods is still limited due to the enormous challenge of the problem. Mathematical symbol recognition is the fundamental task in the process of HMER, which causes most of the ambiguities. Labeling the symbols [10] and allocating them proper symbol class is performed in this phase [11]. It associates a label to each found symbol in the segmentation step, then the structural analysis determines the relationships between the symbols and proposes a valid interpretation of the mathematical expression using appropriate grammar.

Several approaches have been proposed for the recognition of handwritten mathematical symbols, including feature extraction and classification [12,13], template matching [14,15], and deep learning techniques [3,11]. Feature extraction and classification methods use handcrafted features such as the histogram of oriented gradients (HOG) features and Shape Context [12] to represent the symbols and rely on traditional classifiers such as support vector machines (SVM) [16], k-nearest neighbors (k-NN), HMM [4,17] and Random forest [18]. Template matching methods match the input image with a predefined template to recognize the symbols. Currently, deep networks reach state-of-the-art performance in many fields, such as image classification, image segmentation, object detection, and human action recognition. Especially Convolutional Neural Networks (CNN) [19,20], have shown remarkable progress in recognizing handwritten mathematical expressions and symbols. Deep CNNs typically estimate their parameters by minimizing the empirical loss computed on the training data. Due to the high number of parameters involved, regularization techniques are usually employed. Furthermore, the prediction accuracy of a trained deep CNN tends to decrease significantly when presented with samples that lie outside the training data distribution. To address this issue, in [21] authors proposed data augmentation, a technique that generates additional training samples through transformations of existing samples, thereby enriching the training data and improving the model's generalization ability for out-of-distribution samples.

Several data augmentation techniques have been proposed for handwritten symbol recognition, including rotation, scaling, translation, shearing, and noise injection [25]. These techniques have been used to generate additional samples for handwritten character recognition because the labels should be invariant to such perturbations. One can also integrate invariance directly into a classification function. Another approach involves virtually generating perturbations by introducing additive noises into the hidden layers of neural networks [22]. MixUp is a recently proposed data augmentation technique [5] that has shown promising results in various computer vision tasks. MixUp generates synthetic data by linearly interpolating between pairs of samples in the training data, creating a convex combination of the images and their corresponding labels. Empirically, Mixup is helpful for robust representation learning, and it alleviates the overconfident problems and the failure of distribution shift settings as well as the in-distribution accuracy [26].

3   Proposed Method

In the handwritten symbols recognition task, obtaining a robust and discriminative representation of a shape is crucial for obtaining good performance. The goal of a discriminative representation is to maximize the inter-class similarity and minimize the intra-class similarity, so that samples from different classes are more easily distinguishable from each other, while samples within the same class are grouped together more tightly. We use a Triplet Network to learn our feature space. A triplet network consists of three identical base sub-networks of CNN that share parameters. Usually, the network [23] takes in three inputs: an anchor image, a positive image, and a negative image. The anchor and positive images are images of the same object or symbol, while the negative image is an image of a different object or symbol. The goal of the network is to learn a feature representation that maps each image to a point in a high-dimensional space, such that the distance between the anchor and positive images is minimized, while the distance between the anchor and negative images is maximized.

The overall architecture of our proposed framework is depicted in Fig. 3, the input data of this network consists of a triplet of samples (x_1, x_2, x') where x_1 and x_2 are two random samples and x' is a virtual example Constructed with the MixUp technique. The triplet samples will proceed with CNN in parallel. The trained CNN is expected to map symbols images from image space to feature space $F(x)$ defined by $F : \mathbb{R}^{n \times n} \longrightarrow \mathbb{R}^n$ that directly maps the input image $x \in \mathbb{R}^{n \times n}$ to a low-dimensional embedding space $F(x) \in \mathbb{R}^n$. For training two branches are used: the Softmax branch optimized by a softmax loss with the aim to determine the class samples and the triplet branch based on metric learning (triplet loss). The objective of triplet loss is to optimize the network to extract improved representations by decreasing the intra-class distance while increasing the inter-class distance.

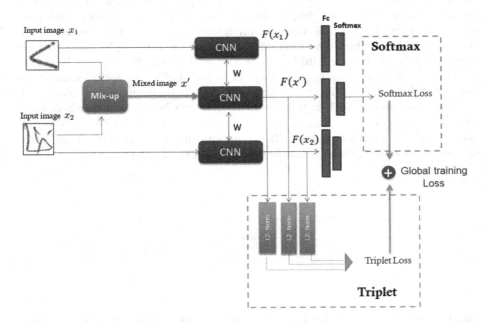

Fig. 3. Overall architecture of the proposed framework based on MixUp data augmentation

3.1 Mix-Up

Hongyi Zhang et al. [5] proposed MixUp as a data augmentation technique that involves training a deep neural network (DNN) on convex combinations of pairs of examples and their corresponding labels. This involves creating new samples by taking a weighted average of two different training examples. According to the authors, this straightforward approach has been shown to achieve state-of-the-art performance on various datasets. Let x_1 and x_2 be two randomly selected images from the training samples, and y_1 and y_2 are their corresponding labels. The new image x' and its corresponding label y' are generated by:

$$x' = \lambda x_1 + (1 - \lambda)x_2 \qquad (1)$$

$$y' = \lambda y_1 + (1 - \lambda)y_2 \qquad (2)$$

In this expression, $\lambda \in [0, 1]$ is a random number generated from a Beta distribution ($\lambda \sim Beta(\alpha, \alpha)$) and having parameters α ($\alpha > 0$). The random number λ is generated for each training pair. An example of Mixup implementation on symbol images is illustrated in Fig. 4.

Thus, MixUp is a method that expands the training distribution by leveraging the prior knowledge that linear interpolations of feature vectors should result in linear interpolations of associated targets. This technique regularizes the deep neural network (DNN) during training to encourage linear behavior between training examples, leading to improved generalization and performance of the model. Additionally, implementing MixUp training is simple and only adds minimal computational overhead. In our implementation, we apply the mixup to each mini-batch. In fact each batch $\mathcal{B}_l$ contains K examples $\mathcal{B}_i = [(x_{i1}, y_{i1}), (x_{i2}, y_{i2}), \ldots, (x_{ik}, y_{ik})]$, we shuffle the samples to get a new batch $\mathcal{B}_j = [(x_{j1}, y_{j1}), (x_{j2}, y_{j2}), \ldots, (x_{jk}, y_{jk})]$ then we Mixup samples at the same position in both batches and we obtain a batch with k mixed samples $\mathcal{B}' = [mix((x_{i1}, x_{j1}), (y_{i1}, y_{j1})), \ldots, mix((x_{ik}, x_{jk}), (y_{ik}, y_{jk}))]$. Finally, the batch $\mathcal{B}'$ will be used for training, the samples in this new mixed batch are more diverse which improves the generalization capability of our network.

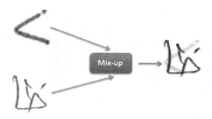

Fig. 4. Example of mixing images to construct a virtual example with the Mixup technique

3.2 Network Architecture for Features Extraction

In this section, we provide an overview of the deep CNNs (Convolutional Neural Networks) used in our work. Our deep CNNs based on DenseNet [27] blocks are applied for feature extraction and distance metric learning. DenseNet has various appealing benefits: it addresses the issue of vanishing gradients, promotes the reuse of features, enhances feature propagation, and significantly reduces the parameter count. These advantages contribute to making the network easier to train. Hence, we have constructed our network using DenseNet blocks. The used network primarily comprises four densely connected blocks, each of which is accompanied by a transition layer. The final transition layer is subsequently followed by a fully-connected layer. Figure 5 provides a schematic representation of our DenseNet architecture.

In each dense block, direct connections from each layer to its subsequent layers are built. The data stream in one dense block is depicted in Fig. 6. Consequently, the l-th layer receives the feature maps of all preceding layers, $X_0, \ldots, X_{l-1}$, as input:

$$X_l = \mathcal{H}_l([X_0, \ldots, X_{l-1}]) \tag{3}$$

$[X_0, \ldots, X_{l-1}]$ refers to the concatenation of the feature maps produced in layers $0, 1, \ldots, l-1$. $\mathcal{H}_l(.)$ is a function composed of three consecutive operations: batch normalization (BN) [28], followed by a ReLU [29] and a 3×3 convolution (Conv). The feature map size remains unchanged within each block. However, it is subsampled by the transition layers, which perform convolution and pooling operations. In our experiments, the transition layers comprise a batch normalization layer, a 1×1 convolutional layer, and a 2×2 average pooling layer. Finally, we utilize a dropout layer and a fully-connected layer to map the final feature maps to a unit vector.

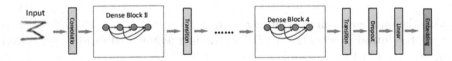

Fig. 5. The architecture of our task's network. The input of the network is a math symbol image, it is initially passed through four consecutive densely connected dense blocks, each of which is followed by a transition layer. Following the last transition layer is a dropout layer, and then a fully-connected layer with an output size of 128.

3.3   Proposed Loss Function

During training, we jointly minimize the sum of cross entropy and triplet loss:

$$\mathcal{L}_{total} = \mathcal{L}_{ce} + \beta \mathcal{L}_{trp} \tag{4}$$

$\mathcal{L}_{ce}$ refers to the cross-entropy loss that aims to minimize classification errors, while $\mathcal{L}_{trp}$ is the triplet loss that serves as a regularization term for learning a more effective feature representation. The parameter β is a trade-off between the two losses. For our experiments, we fixed the value of β at 0.1.

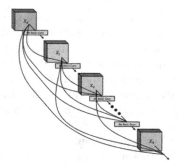

Fig. 6. The dense block consists of 9 layers and a growth rate of 6 and each of all the internal features $X_1, X_2 \ldots, X_9$ have 6 channels. The output of this dense block which is the concatenation of $X_0, X_1, \ldots, X_9$ is then fed into the transition layer.

Classification Loss

The most commonly used loss function for classification and recognition tasks is the cross-entropy loss, also known as the softmax loss. This loss is used during the training of the network with the goal of minimizing the classification error. For a classification problem, the categorical cross-entropy is defined as follows:

$$\mathcal{L}_{ce} = -\sum_{i=1}^{C} y_i' \log(\hat{y_i'}) \tag{5}$$

where:

- C is the number of mixed training samples
- y_i' is the mixed ground truth label of the i-th augmented sample x_i'. x_i' and y_i' are given in Eq. (1) and (2).
- $\hat{y_i'}$ is the predicted probability of the mixed sample generated by the softmax branch as presented in Fig. 3.

As seen in Fig. 3, only mixup samples were used in this loss. Thus, the cross entropy loss function measures the average difference between the predicted probability distribution and the true distribution of labels overall mixed samples in the training set. The goal of the optimization process is to minimize this loss function by adjusting the weights and biases of the neural network. The model is encouraged to learn from the augmented images which can improve its ability to generalize to new data.

Triplet Loss

The triplet loss [24] is a training method that operates on a set of triplets $\{\mathbf{a}^{(i)}, \mathbf{p}^{(i)}, \mathbf{n}^{(i)}\}$, where $\mathbf{a}^{(i)}$ is an anchor sample in the i-th triplet, $\mathbf{p}^{(i)}$ is a positive sample of the same class with $\mathbf{a}^{(i)}$, and $\mathbf{n}^{(i)}$ is a negative sample of a different class with $\mathbf{a}^{(i)}$. The aim of the triplet loss is to encourage $\mathbf{a}^{(i)}$ to be closer to $\mathbf{p}^{(i)}$ than to $\mathbf{n}^{(i)}$. The formulation of the triplet loss is as follows:

$$\mathcal{L}_{\text{trp}} = \sum_{i=1}^{N} \left[\left\| f(\mathbf{a}^{(i)}) - f(\mathbf{p}^{(i)}) \right\|_2^2 - \left\| f(\mathbf{a}^{(i)}) - f(\mathbf{n}^{(i)}) \right\|_2^2 + \alpha \right]_+ \qquad (6)$$

where N is the number of triplets in the training set, $[\cdot]+$ denotes the hinge function, and $f(a^{(i)})$, $f(p^{(i)})$, $f(n^{(i)})$ refer to the features of three input images processed using the architecture model described in Sect. 3.2. Typically, during training, these features are properly normalized with the L2 normalization layer. The threshold α is a margin parameter that separates positive and negative pairs.

4 Experiments

In this section, we first introduce the dataset used to evaluate our approach. Then we elaborate on the implementation details and the evaluation metrics of our experiments. Finally, the experimental results of our method are given in detail.

4.1 Dataset

This study uses the publicly available dataset of the Handwritten Arabic Mathematical (HAMF) [1]. The HAMF database consists of two subsets, the first contains 4238 images of handwritten Arabic mathematical formulas written by 66 different writers, and the second is formed by 20300 isolated symbols images. In our experiments, The second subset is used. This dataset contains 49 different classes of isolated mathematical symbols divided into seven different sets: Arabic characters, Latin digits, arithmetic operators, comparison operators, elastic operators, function names, and others like π and ∞ symbols. All images of the dataset are grayscale and resized to 32×32 with zero paddings. The intensity values of images are normalized to the range $[0, 1]$. We randomly divide the instances into a training set and a test set. each class has 80% instances for training and 20% for testing.

4.2 Implementation Details

All experiments are implemented on the Pytorch framework and are enhanced through the utilization of an NVIDIA GTX 1080 GPU for acceleration. The batch size is empirically set to 64, and the training process lasts for 200 epochs. Additionally, we employ the early stopping strategy in a way the training process will stop early when validation loss does not decrease over the last 20 training epochs. For optimization, SGD optimizer with the adaptive learning rate strategy is adopted to further improve the performance of our architecture. The network training will stop early if the validation loss does not decrease during the last 20 training epochs. We also employ the adaptive learning rate strategy to further improve the performance of our network. Initially, the learning rate is set at 0,001 and it will be divided by 10 when the validation loss does not decrease during 10 epochs. The α in triplet loss is 0.2 in accordance with [24].

4.3 Evaluation Metrics

Our evaluation criteria have been chosen according to performance measures that are particularly applied to classification systems. For the evaluation of our models, we make use of two different performance metrics: i) Total Accuracy, and ii) Average Accuracy (mean diagonal of the normalized confusion matrix). Total accuracy is the most widely used evaluation metric in classification, which reports the percentage of correct predictions among the total number of predictions defined as:

$$\text{Total}_{\text{accuracy}} = \frac{1}{T} \sum_{c=1}^{C} n_c \tag{7}$$

where T is the total number of test images, C is the total number of classes and n_c represents the number of correctly classified images of class c However total accuracy is not preferred in imbalanced data distribution because it can be dominated by the majority classes. Therefore, to have a superior insight, we should take into account an additional metric. The Average Accuracy is reported, since it gives equal importance to each class, in contrast to total Accuracy which gives equal importance to each sample, thus favoring majority classes. Average Accuracy is defined as:

$$\text{Average}_{\text{accuracy}} = \frac{1}{C} \sum_{c=1}^{C} \frac{n_c}{t_c} \tag{8}$$

In this equation, C represents the number of total classes, t_c is the number of test images of class c, and n_c represents the number of correctly classified images of class c.

4.4 Experimental Results

We investigate the role mixup plays during training, and demonstrate the impact of using triplet loss combined with cross-entropy loss. Initially, we conducted experiments on different architectures of convolutional neural networks with softmax layer to select a possible backbone for extracting features for our proposed architecture. In these experiments, the network weights were initialized randomly. We compare the different backbones with and without the use of Mixup augmentation. The mixup value λ of Eq. (1) was selected randomly from the distribution $Beta(0.1, 0.1)$. Considering the results of Table 1 we can see that the Densenet architecture adopted in this paper and optimized with cross-entropy obtained the best performance of 96.86%. Looking also at this table, we can infer that the addition of an augmentation strategy based on the MixUp method always increases the performance of all networks tested in this experiment. The model trained with Mixup outperforms by at least 2% in all studied evaluation metrics the model trained without Mixup. For example, by using Densnet, MixUp improves total accuracy and average accuracy by 3.30% and 2.05%. To effectively compare our method with the softmax layer-based method we conduct experiments with only the softmax branch as a baseline, then, we apply the architecture composed of two branches softmax and triplet. Results reported in Table 2 prove that our proposed method outperforms the softmax layer-based method and allows us to underline that the majority of the models benefit from the mixup data augmentation technique. To evaluate the impact of hyperparameter α on our proposed architecture we adopt several values of α, $\alpha \in \{0.1, 0.2, 0.6, 1\}$ during training of our model composed of the softmax branch and triplet. The results are recorded in the table and it can be concluded that the best results across all metrics have been obtained when $\alpha = 0.1$. Let us note that large values of the hyperparameter ($\alpha > 4$) in Mixup lead to underfitting and not good network performance (Table 3).

Table 1. Performance of different backbones architectures for extracting features trained with and without MixUp

Network	Mixup	Total.Accu	Average.Accu
DenseNet	Yes (Ours)	**96.86%**	**94.28%**
	No	93.56%	92.23%
VGG13	Yes	92.98%	91.34%
	No	90.22%	89.73%
VGG19	Yes	94.14%	92.78%
	No	90.97%	90.38%
ResNet18	Yes	95.32%	94.09%
	No	92.18%	91.29%
ResNet50	Yes	96.07%	94.19%
	No	92.98%	92.17%

Table 2. Comparison of classification results of different models on HAMF dataset

Model	Total.Acc	Average.Acc
Baseline	93.56%	92.23%
Baseline +Triplet	96.21%	95.87%
Baseline +Triplet+MixUp	97.66%	96.76%

Table 3. Impact of hyperparameter α on classification results

MixUp	Total.Acc	Average.Acc
$\alpha = 0,1$	97.56%	96.56%
$\alpha = 0,2$	96.21%	95.87%
$\alpha = 0,6$	97.26%	95.56%
$\alpha = 1$	94.23%	93.12%

5 Conclusion

In this paper, at first, we examine the effectiveness of Mixup with triplet loss for the recognition of handwritten mathematical Arabic symbols. Mixup is a data augmentation strategy in which a Deep Network is trained on convex combinations of pairs of examples and their corresponding labels. The triplet loss function is incorporated to supervise the backbone network and to encourage the learning of more compact representations within the same class, while simultaneously promoting larger distances between different classes. We have conducted a large experimental study on the database of handwritten Arabic mathematical symbols HAMF. The experimental results demonstrate that the MixUp augmentation method improves the performances of DNN architectures and its combination with the triplet loss improves the accuracy further. In future work, we plan to improve metric learning by selecting better triplets and we will consider the generative adversarial networks as an augmentation strategy to oversample minority classes.

References

1. Hadj Ali, I., Mahjoub, M.A.: Database of handwritten Arabic mathematical formula images. In: 2016 13th International Conference on Computer Graphics, Imaging and Visualization (CGiV), pp. 145–149. IEEE (2016)
2. Li, Z., Wang, X., Liu, Y., et al.: Improving handwritten mathematical expression recognition via similar symbol distinguishing. IEEE Trans. Multimed. (2023)
3. Zhang, J., Du, J., Zhang, S., et al.: Watch, attend and parse: an end-to-end neural network-based approach to handwritten mathematical expression recognition. Pattern Recogn. **71**, 196–206 (2017)
4. Alvaro, F., Sánchez, J.-A., Benedí, J.-M.: Recognition of on-line handwritten mathematical expressions using 2D stochastic context-free grammars and hidden Markov models. Pattern Recogn. Lett. **35**, 58–67 (2014)
5. Zhang, H., Cisse, M., Dauphin, Y.N., et al.: MixUp: beyond empirical risk minimization. arXiv:1710.09412 (2017)
6. Zanibbi, R., Blostein, D., Cordy, J.R.: Recognizing mathematical expressions using tree transformation. IEEE Trans. Pattern Anal. Mach. Intell. **24**(11), 1455–1467 (2002)
7. Hadj Ali, I., Mahjoub, M.A.: Structure relationship classification for the recognition of mathematical expression handwritten in Arabic. In: 2020 5th International Conference on Advanced Technologies for Signal and Image Processing (ATSIP), pp. 1–6. IEEE (2020)
8. Yuan, Y., Liu, X., Dikubab, W., et al.: Syntax-aware network for handwritten mathematical expression recognition. In: Proceedings of the IEEE/CVF Conference on Computer Vision and Pattern Recognition, pp. 4553–4562 (2022)
9. Anderson, R.H.: Syntax-directed recognition of hand-printed two-dimensional mathematics. In: Symposium on Interactive Systems for Experimental Applied Mathematics, pp. 436–459. Association for Computing Machinery Inc. (1967)
10. Awal, A.-M., Mouchère, H., Viard-Gaudin, C.: Towards handwritten mathematical expression recognition. In: 2009 10th International Conference on Document Analysis and Recognition, pp. 1046–1050. IEEE (2009)

11. Zhang, J., Du, J., Dai, L.: Multi-scale attention with dense encoder for handwritten mathematical expression recognition. In: 2018 24th International Conference on Pattern Recognition (ICPR), pp. 2245–2250. IEEE (2018)
12. Ali, I.H., Mahjoub, M.A.: Dynamic random forest for the recognition of Arabic handwritten mathematical symbols with a novel set of features. Int. Arab J. Inf. Technol. **15**(3A), 565–575 (2018)
13. Álvaro, F., Sánchez, J.A.: Comparing several techniques for offline recognition of printed mathematical symbols. In: 2010 20th International Conference on Pattern Recognition, pp. 1953–1956. IEEE (2010)
14. Hirata, N.S.T., Honda, W.Y.: Automatic labeling of handwritten mathematical symbols via expression matching. In: Jiang, X., Ferrer, M., Torsello, A. (eds.) GbRPR 2011. LNCS, vol. 6658, pp. 295–304. Springer, Heidelberg (2011). https://doi.org/10.1007/978-3-642-20844-7_30
15. Chan, K.-F., Yeung, D.-Y.: Elastic structural matching for online handwritten alphanumeric character recognition. In: Proceedings of Fourteenth International Conference on Pattern Recognition (Cat. No. 98EX170), pp. 1508–1511. IEEE (1998)
16. Keshari, B., Watt, S.: Hybrid mathematical symbol recognition using support vector machines. In: Ninth International Conference on Document Analysis and Recognition (ICDAR 2007), pp. 859–863. IEEE (2007)
17. Hu, L., Zanibbi, R.: HMM-based recognition of online handwritten mathematical symbols using segmental k-means initialization and a modified pen-up/down feature. In: 2011 International Conference on Document Analysis and Recognition, pp. 457–462. IEEE (2011)
18. Ali, I.H., Mahjoub, M.A.: Random forests for the recognition of handwritten Arabic mathematical symbols (2017)
19. Le, A.D., Indurkhya, B., Nakagawa, M.: Pattern generation strategies for improving recognition of handwritten mathematical expressions. Pattern Recogn. Lett. **128**, 255–262 (2019)
20. Shams, M., Elsonbaty, A., Elsawy, W., et al.: Arabic handwritten character recognition based on convolution neural networks and support vector machine. arXiv preprint arXiv:2009.13450 (2020)
21. Krizhevsky, A., Sutskever, I., Hinton, G.E.: ImageNet classification with deep convolutional neural networks. Commun. ACM **60**(6), 84–90 (2017)
22. Sabri, M., Kurita, T.: Effect of additive noise for multi-layered perceptron with autoencoders. IEICE Trans. Inf. Syst. **100**(7), 1494–1504 (2017)
23. Hoffer, E., Ailon, N.: Deep metric learning using triplet network. In: Feragen, A., Pelillo, M., Loog, M. (eds.) SIMBAD 2015. LNCS, vol. 9370, pp. 84–92. Springer, Cham (2015). https://doi.org/10.1007/978-3-319-24261-3_7
24. Schroff, F., Kalenichenko, D., Philbin, J.: FaceNet: a unified embedding for face recognition and clustering. In: Proceedings of the IEEE Conference on Computer Vision and Pattern Recognition, pp. 815–823 (2015)
25. Shorten, C., Khoshgoftaar, T.M.: A survey on image data augmentation for deep learning. J. Big Data **6**(1), 1–48 (2019)
26. Thulasidasan, S., Chennupati, G., Bilmes, J.A., et al.: On mixup training: improved calibration and predictive uncertainty for deep neural networks. In: Advances in Neural Information Processing Systems, vol. 32 (2019)
27. Huang, G., Liu, Z., van der Maaten, L., et al.: Densely connected convolutional networks. In: Proceedings of the IEEE Conference on Computer Vision and Pattern Recognition, pp. 4700–4708 (2017)

28. Ioffe, S., Szegedy, C.: Batch normalization: accelerating deep network training by reducing internal covariate shift. In: International conference on machine learning, pp. 448–456. PMLR (2015)
29. Glorot, X., Bordes, A., Bengio, Y.: Deep sparse rectifier neural networks. In: Proceedings of the Fourteenth International Conference on Artificial Intelligence and Statistics. JMLR Workshop and Conference Proceedings, pp. 315–323 (2011)

Natural Language Processing

Towards an Open Domain Arabic Question Answering System: Assessment of the Bert Approach

Chaimae Azroumahli[1(✉)], Yacine El Younoussi[2], and Hassan Badir[3]

[1] Laboratory of Intelligent Systems and Applications (LSIA), Moroccan School of Engineering Sciences (EMSI), Tangier, Morocco
c.azroumahli@emsi.ma

[2] SIGL, ENSA Tetuan, Abdelmalek Essaadi University, Tétouan, Morocco

[3] IDS-Team, ENSA Tangier, Abdelmalek Essaadi University, Tanger, Morocco

Abstract. Recently, deep learning-based contextualized word representations have made substantial advancements in enhancing the efficiency of various natural language processing (NLP) applications. However, only limited efforts have been dedicated to employing these representations for the development of Arabic open-domain question-answering (QA) systems, which are an indispensable component of conversational agents such as ChatGPT. In this study, we address this gap by delving into the Bert architecture to create a pre-trained Arabic Bert model. Furthermore, we assess the performance of this model in constructing a QA system by comparing its performance with that of a multilingual Bert model. The experimental results show that our *AraQA_Bert_SL* model, fine-tuned on the weights of a single-language pre-trained model, outperforms existing systems, boasting an F1 score of 90.6% and a pRR score of 93.7%. This achievement surpasses the performance of the *AraQA_Bert_ML* model, which relies on a multilingual pre-trained model. Notably, our approach significantly reduces the computational costs associated with the process of Bert fine-tuning.

Keywords: Arabic NLP · Contextualized word representations · Transformers · Question Answering · Bert

1 Introduction

In recent years, the task of QA has gained a growing interest from the NLP research community. It presents a subfield of Information Retrieval Systems used to create chatbots like ChatGPT [1, 2]. They are versatile intelligent conversational agents that can interact with users by answering their questions using natural language [3]. However, Answering an open-domain question is considered one of the notable challenges in NLP [2]. This task generally requires retrieving several documents relevant to the question and utilizing them to create an elaborate paragraph-length response in the same natural language as the question.

M. Mosbah et al. (Eds.): MEDI 2023, CCIS 2071, pp. 33–46, 2024.
https://doi.org/10.1007/978-3-031-55729-3_4

Due to natural languages' semantic and syntactic peculiarities, the word sense ambiguity makes creating an open domain QA system a challenging task, especially for languages with complex morphology like Arabic [2, 4]. For instance, in general, words in Arabic follow the form of prefixes, stems and Suffixes (e.g., "will you remember us" translates to one word in Arabic: أ - سـتـَ - تـ - ذَكّرُ - ونَ ـنَا). Furthermore, the majority of Modern Standard Arabic (MSA) content – The most common variety of Arabic used on the web – does not include diacritics, when diacritics play the important role of vowels that alter the pronunciation of phoneme, thus, distinguishing between words of similar spelling. All of these challenges lead to many challenges for Arabic QA System development.

Many NLP applications such as the task of Part of Speech Tag, and Named Entity Recognition, benefited from linguistic approaches. These approaches rely on a word's features exported manually by linguistic experts [5]. Nonetheless, for applications with a major semantic component like Sentiment Analysis and QA, machine learning and deep learning-based approaches are more beneficial [6]. The use of Word Embeddings majorly benefited the performance of many NLP applications [7], it introduced deep learning to the distributional hypothesis of the traditional word representations, thus capturing the word's semantic and syntactic features. There are several architectures used to create Word Embeddings like Word2Vec [8], GloVe [9] and FastText [10], where a corpus containing a large amount of unlabeled data is used to learn real-valued vectors called Word Embeddings. Though using the words' contexts leads the generated Word Embeddings to learn the semantic and syntactic features automatically, they are generally context-independent. More specifically, each word is associated with its vectorized representation combining all the word's features, without considering the word position while training, so, one word will have one unique representation regardless of the possibility of it having multiple meanings [7]. Bert [11], ELMO [12] and XLNET are groundbreaking contextual Word Embedding models that have revolutionized the performance of several NLP tasks. Literature shows that they presented an improvement on the "traditional" contextualized word representations created using architectures like Word2Vec [13].

In this paper, we adopt the Bert Word Embeddings approach to create our QA system. Bert is based on the transformer architecture that allows the generated Word Embeddings to handle the word's contexts and dependencies effectively [14]. Moreover, during pre-training, Bert is a masked language model (MLM) that learns bidirectional contextual embeddings by randomly masking words in a sentence. The decision to use this architecture is based on several arguments. For instance, Bert doesn't just provide the Word Embeddings model, but it incorporates an approach that allows the NLP application to be fine-tuned as an integrated task-specific architecture. This feature is very beneficial since it can reduce a model's complexity, consequently, it will cut down the use of another tool to optimize the performance of the system. In addition, due to its bi-directionality, Bert excels in a variety of NLP tasks, which is one of its main strengths. Indeed, the authors of [15] the creators of the Bert model demonstrated in their paper that Bert outperformed human results by 2.0%.

In this work, we obtain massive Arabic content by crawling the web and pre-train the Bert model on unlabeled open-domain Wikipedia content. In addition, we use the publicly available Bert multilingual[1] pre-trained model as a baseline model. Then while fine-tuning we add a classification layer after the layers of the pre-trained model to predict and rewrite an answer using its start and end position within its context. The objective of this work is twofold: (1) Building an efficient Arabic QA model using various labelled Arabic QA datasets and Bert pre-trained models. (2) Investigating the performance of two pre-trained Bert models on the application of QA.

The rest of this paper is structured as follows: Sect. 2 discusses related works on the task of Arabic QA. Section 3 describes the crawled unlabeled pre-training data, and gives an overview of the created models *AraQA-Bert-ML* and *AraQA-Bert-SL* with their additional features, the training hyper-parameters and the computational cost. Section 4 presents the experiment results. Finally, Sect. 5 concludes the work of this paper.

2 Related Works

Considering the growing interest in developing QA systems for Arabic, researchers have explored various methods to robust their performance. To characterize the current state of research in Arabic QA systems, we summarize the most important works related to Arabic QA systems. Early works on Arabic QA were mainly rule-based approaches, where they relied on manually created linguistic resources to undertake the Arabic morphology and syntax complexity.

In [16], the authors introduced a QA system called QASAL implanted with the Nooj linguistic engine [17] to extract the main target of a question using its lexical patterns. Their system includes a morphological analyzer, an automatic annotator a linguistic research tool and an electronic dictionary. Another work on the Arabic QA system created using a rule-based approach was presented by the authors of [18]. The main objective of their system was the comprehension test of all types of questions to create answers of all types including the why and how questions. The answer is typically found by extracting several rules from the question adding up the score of each answer and selecting the answer with the highest score. The system was tested on 75 documents and 335 questions crawled from Wikipedia and achieved an F1 score of 62.22%.

In [19], the authors proposed a rule-based method for classifying Arabic questions. They adopted a taxonomy based on the semantic interpretation of the answer type. This taxonomy can be deployed before classifying the questions in a structured architecture. The authors used TREC and CLEF systems for testing, these datasets contain open-domain questions with various interrogative forms, however, they didn't cover all the possible domains. They tested their system using 2300 questions, and they claim that they achieved an accuracy of 78%.

Other works used ontologies concepts like Arabic WordNet to create their Arabic QA systems. One of which is the work described in [20] where the authors described how they designed a system for answering why and how questions. Their system followed the approach of classifying a question into two classes Person and manner, and the WordNet was applied to query expansion. Then, they used the TF-IDF weighting to retrieve relevant documents to the questions. As for the evaluation, they used a dataset containing

---

[1] https://github.com/google-research/Bert.

500 documents extracted from Arabic Wikipedia and 40 how and why questions. Their system reported a mean performance of 60% F1 score on how and why questions.

Even though there have been various works done using the rule-based approach to create Arabic QA systems, these approaches faced limitations in achieving state-of-the-art performance under the scarcity of large-scale annotated Arabic QA datasets. Later on, and due to the rise of deep learning and pre-trained language models, more research activities focused on techniques based on machine learning and deep learning which led to significant advancements in Arabic QA systems. The authors of [21] proposed a hybrid approach that implements semantic query expansion for retrieving information in Arabic. They based their method on Word embedding, AWN and term frequency to calculate the weight of each term in the input question. The contextual representation of ELMO was used in [12] to create various NLP applications including an Arabic QA system. The creators of ELMO pre-trained a large corpus with Bidirectional Language Models (bi-LM) to learn word representations. They reported an F1 score of 85% on the QA application using SQUAD, a dataset that contains a large collection of questions and contexts written in various languages including Arabic.

In [22], an open domain Arabic QA called SOQAL system was created. It was composed of a machine reading comprehension module where they find the exact answers in a context given using QA-Net and BERT. Their system achieved an F1 score of 27.6%. Another work creating an Arabic QA system using BERT was described in [23] where the authors introduced their system pre-trained model Ara-BERT that achieved state-of-the-art results on several tasks. The QA task was used as an evaluation metric for their pre-trained model where it achieved an F1 score of 62.7% using the SQUAD database. Subsequently, the same authors of [19], developed another system for classifying Arabic questions where they used machine learning approaches instead of the rule-based their work was described in [24]. Their approach compared the implementations of SVM, Decision Tree and Naïve Bayes. Again, they used TREC and CLEF systems for the evaluation while in this work they utilized the 'bag of words' as a feature extractor. Their most accurate system was created by SVM where it achieved an accuracy of 84% on the task of question classification.

Despite the growth of using Machine Learning approaches to improve the accuracy of domain-specific and open-domain Arabic QA systems, challenges remain. The need for methods that handle dialectal variations, more extensive datasets and incorporating domain-specific knowledge are some of the adjustments that must be considered to improve the performance of such systems. These requirements can be solved by the use of pre-trained contextual word embedding models such as ELMO and BERT which have led to significant advancement for a variety of Arabic NLP applications [13]. These pre-trained models are known for utilizing transfer learning that showed promising results in their ability to handle intrinsic ambiguities and context reliance of the Arabic language.

3 Methodology

3.1 Overview of the Architecture of Bert

Bidirectional Encoder Representations from Transformers or Bert presents a potent app-roach to building and pre-train deep bidirectional contextualized word representations by pre-training a large non-annotated corpus as a language model. It resulted in the most cutting-edge performances in various NLP applications. Compared to other contextual presentation models, Bert is deeper and contains many more parameters, thus possess-ing more contextual features. In particular, instead of providing word Embeddings as features it can be incorporated in the downstream NLP application and gets fine-tuned as a task-specific integrated architecture.

Bert is a stack of multi-layer bidirectional Transformer encoders-decoders that adopted transfer learning and tunable language models for building NLP applications. The Transformers replaced the LSTM layers and contained a stack of encoders, a stack of decoders and a self-attention layer. The attention decides the context of words that can contribute to the word representation of a specific word. It outputs the weighted sum value Vector V using a matrix of the queries Q and a matrix of Keys K:

$$Attention(Q, K, V) = softmax\left(\frac{QK^T}{\sqrt{d_k}}\right)V \qquad (1)$$

Figure 1 illustrates the architecture of the transformers used by Bert; On one hand, the input of the lowest encoder is the word Embeddings that gets fed to the self-attention layer while considering the word's context, and, the output is a layer that goes through a feed-forward neural network. On the other hand, the input of the decoder gets fed to the self-attention layer, the encoder-decoder attention layer and the feed-forward neural network as illustrated in Fig. 2 [11]. The process of adopting the Bert approach to create an NLP application involves pre-training models on unlabeled data and fine-tuning the pre-trained models' parameters using the labelled dataset for the NLP application. Pre-training Bert models can include two sub-tasks; The application of the MLM and the next sentence prediction (NSP). The MLM trains deep bidirectional representations by trying to predict 15% of the input tokens that were masked randomly. NSP pre-trains the binarized representations by choosing a pair of random sentences A and B for each training example, thus, the possibility of A following B is 50%, while the remaining 50% is a random sentence from the corpus.

Fine-tuning Bert follows a straightforward fine-tuning approach where a classifica-tion layer is added to a pre-trained model. Thus, not all the downstream NLP parameters $W \in \mathbb{R}^{K \times H}$ are learned from the ground up but fine-tuned according to the number of classifier labels K. In this step, the output of the transformer is considered the first token in the input sequence. The token of every sequence is annotated as the vector $C \in \mathbb{R}^H$ that represent the classification embeddings, and H presents the hyper-parameters of Bert. The NLP parameters W and the parameters of Bert are fine-tuned in the added classification layer to maximize the log-probability of the correct labels $P \in \mathbb{R}^K$ using a standard Softmax activation function (2).

$$P = \text{softmax}\left(C \cdot W^T\right) \qquad (2)$$

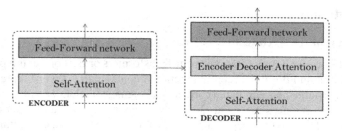

Fig. 1. The architecture of Bert's Transformers

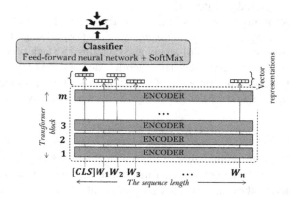

Fig. 2. Transformer blocs in Bert Architecture

3.2 Bert for a Question Answering System

The creation of QA systems generally follows the standard architecture illustrated in Fig. 3 with different implementations for each one of the three components; Question Analysis (QA), Passage Retrieval (PR) and Answer Extraction (AE). The QA component identifies the interest of the user's question and creates and classifies the query to predict the anticipated answer type. In some QA systems, the step of question classification is crucial to eliminate the answer's ambiguities. The PR component is the task of information retrieval that extracts and ranks the relevant documents to the questions that were classified. The final AE component identifies and parses the answers from ordered paragraphs outputted by the PR component, afterwards, it extracts the correct answer for the question's generated query, and then it validates the possible correct answers following the different possible implementations.

The contribution of this paper lies in building an Arabic QA system following two main steps. The first step is creating contextual word representations using the architecture of Bert to map the questions and their answer into a vector space. The second step is building and comparing the different classifiers on the QA task. The architecture of the followed approach is illustrated in Fig. 4. Our approach follows the two traditional main steps of using Bert in NLP: Pre-training and Fine-Tuning. For the Pre-training we

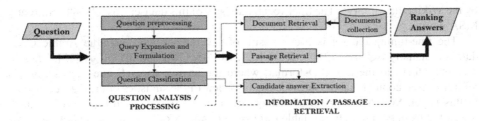

Fig. 3. The architecture of a standard question-answering system.

implemented the Bert Architecture to create an Arabic pre-trained model using the pre-training dataset described in the next section. However, for the Fine-tuning, we keep the word piece embeddings generated from the pre-trained model, but we tweak the positional and the segmentation embeddings to adapt the pre-trained Bert model to perform the specific task of QA based on a given context from the training dataset.

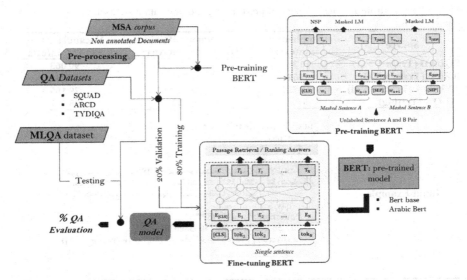

Fig. 4. Arabic QA system using Bert Architecture

3.3 Datasets Description

As was explained in the previous section, to implement our Arabic QA system, we used two different datasets; a pretraining dataset that contains a large amount of non-annotated Arabic texts, and a fine-tuning dataset containing questions, answers and their context. The pre-training dataset was collected and preprocessed in a previous work [5] and Wikipedia was the main web source wherein the dataset was collected. We crawled over 810k Arabic articles written in MSA by employing a function-based method provided by the Wikipedia Library[2]. The final vocabulary size of this dataset was 325544 different MSA words.

The fine-tuning dataset is a composite of several publicly available Arabic QA datasets, namely SQUAD [25], ARCD [22], MLQA [26], and TYDIQA [25]. These datasets adhere to the SQUAD format, where the answer to each question is found within a given context. Table 1 provides an overview of the statistics of the datasets used in this paper. SQUAD consists of $48k$ question-answer pairs based on $10k$ contexts, translated from the publicly available English SQUAD. ARCD is an Arabic QA dataset comprising 1395 question-answer pairs derived from 464 contexts crawled from 155 Wikipedia articles. TyDiQA, another Arabic QA dataset, contains approximately 16 k question-answer pairs. As for the final utilized dataset, MLQA was employed for testing purposes only, as we separated the fine-tuning dataset into training and validation sets, excluding the test portion. Ultimately, all datasets were combined, resulting in a total of 65465 instances, which were subsequently split into the usual 80% for training (52373 instances) and 20% for validation (13093 instances).

Table 1. The statistics of pre-training and fine-tuning datasets

Source	Number Of contexts	Number of pair Questions and Answer	Vocabulary Size in the Contexts
SQUAD (Train + Val)	10 364	48 344	90 063
ARCD (Train + Val)	464	1 395	14 049
TYDIQA (Train + Val)	15 726	16 425	29 185
MLQA (Testing)	5 085	5 852	98 047

Input Example	{
	'title': 'Internet_Service_Provider',
	'paragraphs':
	[{
	'context':
	'مزود خدمة الإنترنت ISP هو منظمة تقدم خدمات للوصول إلى الإنترنت واستخدامه. قد يتم تنظيم مزودي خدمة الإنترنت بأشكال مختلفة، مثل التجارية أو المملوكة للمجتمع أو غير الربحية أو المملوكة للقطاع الخاص.',
	'qas': [
	{'question': 'ماذا يرمز ISP؟',
	'id': '56dfb9227aa994140058e079',
	'answers': [{'text': 'مزود خدمة الإنترنت', 'answer_start': 0}]},
	...]
	}, ...]
	}		

3.4 Model Structure

Pre-train Details. After the pre-training procedure of BERT [15], we generate the.tfrecord file using Modern Standard Arabic (MSA) contexts sourced from Wikipedia. We adopt the implementation of both the MLM and the NSP task. We set the MLM probability to be 0.15 and 77 as the maximum number of masked LM predictions per

---

[2] https://pypi.org/project/wikipedia/.

sequence. Moreover, for the data pipeline configuration to create training instances, we opted for a sequence length of 512, a training batch size of 32, $10k$ training steps, 100 warmup steps, and a learning rate of $2e^5$ [13].

Regarding the base configuration, we opted for the bidirectional transformer pre-training, adhering to the ensuing setup: a dropout ratio of 0.1 for attention probabilities, employment of the "Gulu" non-linear activation function, a dropout probability of 0.1 for all fully connected layers within embeddings, encoder, and pooler components. Encoder layers were established at a dimensionality of 768, while weight matrices were initialized with a deviation of 0.02. The feed-forward layer of the transformer encoder featured a dimensionality of 3072. To accommodate potential usage scenarios, a maximum sequence length of 2048 was defined. Each attention layer within the transformer encoder comprised 12 attention heads, and the transformer encoder consisted of a total of 12 hidden layers. With regards to token IDs, a vocabulary size of 2 was set, while the pre-trained model's vocabulary size, was set at 156226.

Fine-Tuning for QA. Fine-tuning Bert for a QA system includes retraining the pre-trained Bert models to the specific task of answering questions based on a provided context. To elaborate, within the scope of this study, the fine-tuning process for QA consisted of three primary phases: Data Preprocessing, the creation of the QA models using BERT-Base and BERT-MSA models, and ultimately, the validation of the resulting QA models; *AraQA-Bert-ML*, created with Bert-Base, and *AraQA-Bert-SL* with Bert-MSA.

Data Preprocessing. This phase involves the meticulous preparation of data, entailing the combination of the various Arabic QA datasets and their adaptation for the QA task. The new format of the finetuning dataset included the contexts, the questions, the answers and their respective identifiers. Furthermore, the text within questions, answers, and their associated contexts required tokenization. However, conventional word tokenization is inadequate for QA, as QA systems deviate from traditional classification tasks. This specialized tokenization process aligns the inputs into the format compatible with Bert's finetuning, adding the special tokens [CLS] and [SEP] at the beginning and end of a sentence, respectively. After adding the tokens, the next step involved partitioning our dataset into the standard training and validation. During the fine-tuning process of the QA model for each epoch, the validation subset played a crucial role in computing the Loss function. Conversely, for testing purposes, a distinct dataset, MLQA, was employed. Notably, this dataset was entirely separate from the training and validation data, ensuring that it remained untouched during those phases. Its main purpose was to evaluate the performance of the generated model.

Models Creation. In this phase, the initial step involves initializing Bert by loading the pre-trained models where its weights are retained to preserve the pre-existing knowledge. This approach is particularly valuable due to our primary objective of developing an open-domain QA system. The pre-trained model draws from extensive, non-annotated corpora encompassing a diverse array of subjects. Typically, the architecture of Bert Pretrained models contains multiple transformer layers. After the Bert pre-trained models have been successfully loaded, the next step is fine-tuning.

During this step, Bert models are trained on the preprocessed QA dataset, where the initial weights are adapted through the conventional Deep Learning approach, aiming to minimize the loss between the predicted answer and the answer stipulated within the annotated QA dataset. After the fine-tuning, particularly for the QA task, we add a classification layer using a 2D convolution before the Linear building block. This newly added layer functions as a prediction module that outputs the start and the end positions of an answer within a context. The answer prediction within a context is possible since we included the start answers' identifiers in the training. Table 2 summarizes the architecture of our models' output, including the input sizes and parameters used for each layer, except for the bias which was consistent across all the dense layers.

4 Results and Discussion

To properly assess the training process of *AraQA_Bert_SL* and *AraQA_Bert_ML*, we examine the loss variation for 100 epochs. Figure 5 illustrates the curves of losses for both training and validation throughout the training cycle of both models. The loss curves for training and validation demonstrate that the training is in an optimal state.

Table 2. The architecture of *AraQA_Bert_SL* after fine-tuning

	AraQA_Bert_SL **Building Blocks**	
Bert Model	**Embeddings**: BertEmbeddings	(word_embeddings): Embedding(32000, 768) (position_embeddings): Embedding(512, 768) (token_type_embeddings): Embedding(2, 768) (LayerNorm): LayerNorm((768,), eps=$1e^{-12}$) (dropout): Dropout(p=0.1, inplace=False)

	Encoder: BertEncoder (12 module Lists)	(**attention**): BertAttention(
		   (self): BertSelfAttention(
		     (query): Linear(in_features=768, out_features=768)
		     (key): Linear(in_features=768, out_features=768)
		     (value): Linear(in_features=768, out_features=768)
		     (dropout): Dropout(p=0.1, inplace=False)
		   )
		   (output): BertSelfOutput(
		     (dense): Linear(in_features=768, out_features=768)
		     (LayerNorm): LayerNorm((768,), eps=$1e^{-12}$)
		     (dropout): Dropout(p=0.1, inplace=False)
		   ))
		 (**Intermediate**): BertIntermediate(
		   (dense): Linear(in_features=768, out_features=3072)
		   (intermediate_act_fn): GELUActivation()
		)
		 (**output**): BertOutput(
		   (dense): Linear(in_features=3072, out_features=768)
		   (LayerNorm): LayerNorm((768,), eps=$1e^{-12}$))
		   (dropout): Dropout(p=0.1, inplace=False)
		)

QA Outputs	**Conv2d**(in_features=768, out_features=768, bias=True) **Linear**(in_features=768, out_features=2, bias=True)	

For the beginning of the two models' training, the loss did not exhibit a consistent downward trend, despite starting with a lower learning rate of 0.001. Nevertheless,

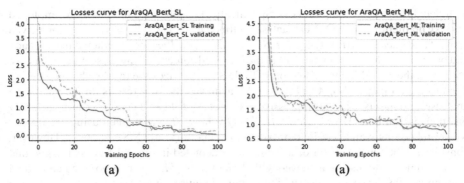

Fig. 5. The Training Loss Curve for 100 epochs. (a) Losses for *AraQA_Bert_ML*. (b) Losses for *AraQA_Bert_SL*.

following the initial 50 epochs, the validation loss was ultimately reduced to 1.27 for *AraQA_Bert_ML* and 0.47 for *AraQA_Bert_SL*. As expected, and due to the distinct characteristics of the pre-trained model weights employed for the system creation, there is a noticeable difference in the achieved values for the final epochs. The last loss value attained for *AraQA_Bert_SL* was stabilized at 0.00169, which is deemed optimal for training. Conversely, for *AraQA_Bert_ML*, it yielded a more modest loss value of 1.2741, indicating that *AraQA_Bert_ML* requires additional training epochs to attain a diminished loss and consequently enhance its performance.

To further assess the performance of *ARA_QA_Bert_SL* and *ARA_QA_Bert_ML*, we evaluate the generated models using three metrics; the F1 score, Exact Matches (EM) and the partial Reciprocal Rank (pRR). The F1 score is a widely recognized evaluation metric extensively employed in QA applications. The F1 score is calculated using:

$$F1 = 2.\frac{pPrecision * pRecall}{pPrecision + pRecall}; pPrecision = \frac{\sum_{r \in R} m_r}{|A|}; pRecall = \frac{\sum_{r \in R} m_r}{|R|} \quad (3)$$

where, for the returned $|R|$ answers and the $|A|$ gold answers, m_r presents the answer matching score. With this formula, the F1 score computes the proportion of shared words between the correct answer and the top-ranked predicted answers.

The EM metric, on the other hand, assigns values of 1 or 0 for each question-answer pair in the validation and testing dataset based on whether the predicted answer matches exactly the correct answer. Furthermore, given that QA is considered more of a ranking task rather than a classification task, we also incorporated pRR:

$$pRR(R) = \frac{m_{r_k}}{k}; k = \min\{k | m_{r_k} > 0\} \quad (4)$$

where m_{r_k} is the matching score of the answer at the rank position k of the first answer with a matching score higher than 0. This metric is used to acknowledge the answers that may not exactly match the correct answer but exhibit some similarity with the top-ranked answers [27].

Once the two models were created, and to properly evaluate their performances, we introduced an additional evaluation step using a separate dataset that had not been included during the training process. Specifically, the generated models were employed to make predictions on the MLQA dataset outlined in Sect. 3.3. Consequently, for a given context and question, *ARA_QA_Bert_SL* and *ARA_QA_Bert_ML* predicted the start and end positions of the answer span within the provided context. Using these predictions, we computed the F1, EM, and pRR scores. Table 3 summarizes the results obtained during this evaluation phase. The *AraQA_Bert_SL* achieved the best results on the validation and testing datasets with an impressive pRR score of 93%. This outcome is arguably justified since unlike *AraQA_Bert_ML*, *AraQA_Bert_SL* was created using pre-trained word Embedding weights trained on a dataset containing only MSA contents. However, considering the final segment of the loss curve depicted in Fig. 5(b), we can argue that this outcome could also be achieved with *AraQA_Bert_ML* by incorporating additional training epochs. Therefore, employing a single language pre-trained model for Arabic has the potential to considerably reduce the computational cost associated with creating Arabic NLP applications.

Regarding the results obtained from testing on the MLQA dataset, naturally, we notice a significant decrease in comparison to the outcomes from the validation dataset. These findings can be rationalized by the similarity between the domains of the validation dataset and the training dataset. However, there is a slight divergence for the MLQA testing dataset, as discussed in Sect. 3.3. Nonetheless, upon comparing the results of *ARA_QA_Bert_SL* to the literature, it is evident that there is substantial improvement.

Table 3. Evaluation Metrics retrieved by the different pre-trained on the validation and testing dataset

Model	Evaluation	pRR	Exact Matches	F1 Score
AraQA_Bert_SL	On the Validation dataset	0.937	10082/13093	0.906
AraQA_Bert_ML		0.875	9535/13093	0.858
AraQA_Bert_SL	MLQA: The Testing dataset after the training	0.814	2036/5852	0.786
AraQA_Bert_ML		0.743	1020/5852	0.681

5   Conclusion

In this paper, we create and compare the performances of two QA systems: *ARA_QA_Bert_SL* and *ARA_QA_Bert_ML*. These systems are created by fine-tuning distinct pre-trained Bert models, following the Bert methodology. In which, a classification layer is introduced to rank answers and predict the correct response to a given question within its context. Our study yielded two key findings. Firstly, beyond the application of Bert fine-tuning, the incorporation of a tailored fully connected layer as part of the classification process atop the pre-trained model offers a notable enhancement in extracting the most pertinent features from words. Consequently, this improvement contributes to the construction of better NLP applications, including QA systems. Secondly, opting for single-language models instead of multi-language pre-trained models can significantly decrease the computational cost associated with the fine-tuning process. Besides, the outcomes can be further enhanced for an open-domain QA system by either expanding the range of the employed QA dataset or fine-tuning the resultant model itself to encompass a broader spectrum of domains.

A promising research direction is to assess ELMO's effectiveness in building an Arabic QA system and to compare it with large language models like Llama. Additionally, exploring the integration of ELMO representations with Bert is valuable, given Bert's tendency to miss dependencies between masked positions, which could lead to inconsistencies between pretraining and fine-tuning stages.

References

1. Ray, P.P.: ChatGPT: a comprehensive review on background, applications, key challenges, bias, ethics, limitations and future scope. Internet Things Cyber-Phys. Syst. **3**, 121–154 (2023). https://doi.org/10.1016/j.iotcps.2023.04.003
2. Alkhurayyif, Y., Sait, A.R.W.: A comprehensive survey of techniques for developing an Arabic question answering system. PeerJ Comput. Sci. **9**, 1–21 (2023). https://doi.org/10.7717/peerj-cs.1413
3. Luo, B., Lau, R.Y.K., Li, C., Si, Y.W.: A critical review of state-of-the-art chatbot designs and applications. Wiley Interdiscip. Rev. Data Min. Knowl. Discov. **12**, 1–26 (2022). https://doi.org/10.1002/widm.1434
4. Azroumahli, C., El Younoussi, Y., Achbal, F.: An overview of a distributional word representation for an arabic named entity recognition system. In: Abraham, A., Haqiq, A., Muda, A.K., Gandhi, N. (eds.) SoCPaR 2017. AISC, vol. 737, pp. 130–140. Springer, Cham (2018). https://doi.org/10.1007/978-3-319-76357-6_13
5. Chaimae, A., El Younoussi, Y., Moussaoui, O., Zahidi, Y.: An Arabic dialects dictionary using word embeddings. Int. J. Rough Sets Data Anal. **6**, 18–31 (2019). https://doi.org/10.4018/IJRSDA.2019070102
6. Garrido-Merchan, E.C., Gozalo-Brizuela, R., Gonzalez-Carvajal, S.: Comparing BERT against traditional machine learning models in text classification. J. Comput. Cogn. Eng. (2023). https://doi.org/10.47852/bonviewJCCE3202838
7. Chaimae, A., Rybinski, M., Yacine, E.Y., Montes, J.F.A.: Comparative study of Arabic word embeddings: evaluation and application. Int. J. Comput. Inf. Syst. Ind. Manag. Appl. **12**, 349–362 (2020). ISSN 2150-7988
8. Mikolov, T., Chen, K., Corrado, G., Dean, J.: Efficient estimation of word representations in vector space. CrossRef List Deleted DOIs **1**, 4069–4076 (2013). https://doi.org/10.48550/arXiv.1301.3781
9. Pennington, J., Socher, R., Manning, C.: Glove: global vectors for word representation. In: Proceedings of the 2014 Conference on Empirical Methods in Natural Language Processing (EMNLP), pp 1532–1543 (2014)
10. Bojanowski, P., Grave, E., Joulin, A., Mikolov, T.: Enriching word vectors with subword information. Anal Methods **5**, 729–734 (2016). https://doi.org/10.48550/arXiv.1607.04606
11. Devlin, J., Chang, M.-W., Lee, K., Toutanova, K.: BERT: pre-training of deep bidirectional transformers for language understanding. In: NAACL HLT 2019 - 2019 Conference of the North American Chapter of the Association for Computational Linguistics: Human Language, Proceedings Conference, vol. 1, pp. 4171–4186 (2018). arXiv:1810.04805
12. Peters, M.E., Neumann, M., Iyyer, M., et al.: Deep contextualized word representations. In: Proceedings of the 2018 Conference of the North American Chapter of the Association for Computational Linguistics: Human Language Technologies, pp. 2227–2237 (2018)

13. Chaimae, A., Yacine, E.Y., Rybinski, M., Montes, J.F.A.: BERT for Arabic named entity recognition. In: 2020 International Symposium on Advanced Electrical and Communication Technologies (ISAECT), pp. 1–6. IEEE (2020)
14. Li, X., Zhang, H., Zhou, X.H.: Chinese clinical named entity recognition with variant neural structures based on BERT methods. J. Biomed. Inform. **107**, 103422 (2020). https://doi.org/10.1016/j.jbi.2020.103422
15. Devlin, J., Chang, M.-W., Lee, K., Toutanova, K.: BERT: pre-training of deep bidirectional transformers for language understanding. arXiv Prepr arXiv:1811.03600v2 (2018)
16. Brini, W., Ellouze, M., Mesfar, S., Belguith, L.H.: An Arabic question-answering system for factoid questions. In: 2009 International Conference on Natural Language Processing and Knowledge Engineering, pp. 1–7. IEEE (2009)
17. Silberztein, M.: Formalizing Natural Languages. Wiley, Hoboken (2016)
18. Akour, M., Abufardeh, S., Magel, K., Al-Radaideh, Q.: QArabPro: a rule-based question answering system for reading comprehension tests in Arabic. Am. J. Appl. Sci. **8**, 652–661 (2011). https://doi.org/10.3844/ajassp.2011.652.661
19. Lahbari, I., Ouatik, S.E.A., Zidani, K.A.: A rule-based method for Arabic question classification. In: Proceedings of 2017 International Conference on Wireless Networks Mobile Communication, WINCOM 2017 (2017). https://doi.org/10.1109/WINCOM.2017.8238208
20. Ahmed, W., Babuanto, P.: Answer extraction for how and why questions in question answering systems, pp. 18–22 (2016)
21. ALMarwi, H., Ghurab, M., Al-Baltah, I.: A hybrid semantic query expansion approach for Arabic information retrieval. J. Big Data, **7**, 1–19 (2020). https://doi.org/10.1186/s40537-020-00310-z
22. Mozannar, H., El Hajal, K., Maamary, E., Hajj, H.: Neural Arabic question answering. In: ACL 2019 - 4th Arabic Natural Language Processing Workshop WANLP 2019 - Proceedings Workshop, pp. 108–118 (2019). https://doi.org/10.18653/v1/w19-4612
23. Antoun, W., Baly, F., Hajj, H.: AraBERT: transformer-based model for Arabic language understanding (2020)
24. Panicker, A.D., Athira, U., Venkitakrishnan, S.: Question classification using machine learning approaches. Int. J. Comput. Appl. **48**, 1–4 (2012). https://doi.org/10.5120/7405-0101
25. Rajpurkar, P., Zhang, J., Lopyrev, K., Liang, P.: SQuad: 100,000+ questions for machine comprehension of text. In: EMNLP 2016 - Conference on Empirical Methods in Natural Language Processing Proceedings, pp. 2383–2392 (2016). https://doi.org/10.18653/v1/d16-1264
26. Lewis, P., Oguz, B., Rinott, R., et al.: MLQA: evaluating cross-lingual extractive question answering. In: Proceedings of Annual Meeting of the Association for Computational Linguistics, pp. 7315–7330 (2020). https://doi.org/10.18653/v1/2020.acl-main.653
27. Malhas, R., Elsayed, T.: AyaTEC: building a reusable verse-based test collection for Arabic question answering on the Holy Qur'an. ACM Trans. Asian Low-Resource Lang. Inf. Process. **19**, 1–21 (2020). https://doi.org/10.1145/3400396

Multi-lingual Scene Text Detection Containing the Arabic Scripts Using an Optimal then Enhanced YOLO Model

Houssem Turki[1,4], Mohamed Elleuch[2,3,4(✉)], and Monji Kherallah[3,4]

[1] National Engineering School of Sfax (ENIS), University of Sfax, Sfax, Tunisia
turkihoussem@gmail.com

[2] Higher Institute of Computer Science and Management of Kairoun (ISIGK), University of Kairoun, Kairoun, Tunisia
elleuch.mohameds@gmail.com

[3] Faculty of Sciences, University of Sfax, Sfax, Tunisia
monji.kherallah@fss.usf.tn

[4] Advanced Technologies for Environment and Smart Cities (ATES Unit), University of Sfax, Sfax, Tunisia

Abstract. In the past few years, notable progress has been achieved in the field of deep learning, particularly in the realm of identifying text within images of natural scenes, owing to the advancements in machine learning and artificial intelligence. The effectiveness of deep learning and text detection in the wild, especially when dealing with Arabic language, is frequently hindered by the scarcity of diverse datasets encompassing multiple languages and scripts, which poses an additional challenge. Despite significant advancements, this shortage continues to be a limiting factor. The YOLO (You Only Look Once) deep learning neural network has gained widespread popularity for its adaptability in tackling various machine learning tasks, notably in the field of computer vision. The YOLO algorithm has garnered growing recognition for its remarkable capability to address intricate issues when dealing with images taken in natural environments, managing noisy data, and surmounting the diverse challenges encountered in the wild. Our experiments provide a concise evaluation of text detection algorithms centered around convolutional neural networks (CNNs). Specifically, we concentrate on different versions of the YOLO models, applying identical data augmentation methods to both the SYPHAX dataset and the ICDAR MLT-2019 dataset, both of which encompass Arabic scripts within images of natural scenes. The objective of this article is to pinpoint the most efficient YOLO algorithm for recognizing Arabic script in the wild, and subsequently, to improve upon the best-performing model. Additionally, we aim to investigate potential research directions that can further enhance the capabilities of the most robust architecture in this domain.

Keywords: Text detection in the wild · Natural Scene images · Multi-lingual script · Arabic script · YOLO · Optimal model · enhanced architecture · Computer Vision · Deep Learning

M. Mosbah et al. (Eds.): MEDI 2023, CCIS 2071, pp. 47–61, 2024.
https://doi.org/10.1007/978-3-031-55729-3_5

1 Introduction

In the realm of computer vision, text detection holds a pivotal position, and it is imperative to utilize a variety of machine learning and deep learning models to augment the effectiveness of text detection and associated tasks. Text detection in natural scenes poses numerous difficulties, including the occurrence of multiple languages, intricate character designs, and a broad array of image degradations like variations in size, shape, orientation, noise, blur, and more. These difficulties become especially notable when addressing multilingual scripts that incorporate Arabic language [1, 2]. The mentioned difficulties, particularly related to Arabic scripts, are specific to the "SYPHAX dataset" [3] and the ICDAR MLT-2019 dataset [4], as illustrated in Fig. 1. In the experimental portion of our research, we will extensively utilize these datasets. Furthermore, the detection of text in natural scene images has evolved into a crucial element in numerous applications that encompass a wide range of domains, including multilingual text conversion, geolocation, efficient data retrieval, road safety for navigation, and autonomous driving systems for vehicles, among various others. Among the many algorithms employed for object and text detection, the YOLO framework has attracted considerable interest [5] owing to its noteworthy characteristics of exceptional speed, accuracy, and precise identification of objects in images of natural scenes. Throughout its development in the realm of text detection, the YOLO algorithm family has experienced numerous enhancements. With each iteration, it strives to address limitations and attain better performance to effectively tackle the task of detecting scripts in the wild. This progression ranges from YOLOv5 to YOLOv7. This impetus leads us to opt for three consecutive iterations of YOLO and assess their detection capabilities within various neural network architectures when employed for text detection in the wild. This evaluation is conducted using the "SYPHAX dataset" [3] and the ICDAR MLT-2019 dataset [4].

We choose the three YOLO models based on their status as state-of-the-art approaches and the promising results they have exhibited. In this research, we put forth three pivotal contributions:

Initially, our primary contribution involves presenting a fresh, openly accessible dataset sourced from Tunisia [3]. This dataset encompasses images of natural environments featuring a blend of Arabic and Latin scripts. Secondly, our contribution extends to the careful selection and application of distinct data augmentation methods, meticulously designed for images captured in the wild, featuring text. These techniques are devised with a keen focus on preserving the unique characteristics associated with Arabic scripts, including punctuation marks, multi-level baselines, intersecting letters, skewed letters, intra-word spacing, inter-word spacing, and line spacing, among others (as illustrated in Fig. 2). Finally, we will conduct an extensive comparative examination of the main outcomes achieved by employing various YOLO models with the aim of enhancing the efficacy of the most effective algorithm identified.

The paper is structured into four sections, which are detailed as follows: Sect. 2 provides a synopsis of diverse related studies along with their methodologies, highlighting the commonly employed techniques. Section 3 outlines the methodology and showcases the experimental assessment. Lastly, Sect. 4 provides the paper's conclusion.

(a)   images from SYPHAX dataset

(b)   images from MLT-2019 dataset

Fig. 1. Samples of images from SYPHAX dataset [3] and MLT-2019 dataset [4] containing the Arabic script

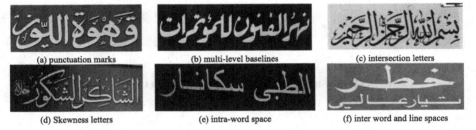

(a) punctuation marks   (b) multi-level baselines   (c) intersection letters

(d) Skewness letters   (e) intra-word space   (f) inter word and line spaces

Fig. 2. Samples of Arabic scripts properties from SYPHAX dataset (top row) and MLT-2019 dataset (down row)

2 Related Work

Many applications utilize the potential of deep learning and computer vision algorithms to enhance the learning process in text detection [6]. Object detection involves the process of recognizing particular objects within images, videos, or real-time applications. This encompasses the identification of text scripts in the wild [7]. YOLO has become a widely embraced technology for a variety of applications in object and text detection [8]. YOLO streamlines the detection process by partitioning the input image into a grid, allowing it to predict bounding boxes and class probabilities for each grid cell. This method greatly expedites and enhances object detection. Thanks to its straightforward architecture, minimal complexity, ease of implementation, and speed, YOLO has risen to prominence as one of the most frequently employed models for object detection [9]. The YOLO architecture is structured into three primary components: the Backbone, Neck, and a Prediction Head responsible for generating detailed predictions (see Fig. 3). The pretrained network, referred to as the backbone, is used to extract comprehensive feature representations from images. This process involves reducing the image's spatial resolution while improving its feature (channel) resolution. The model's neck component is employed to extract feature pyramids, enhancing the model's ability to effectively generalize to objects of varying sizes and scales. The model's head is utilized for the final stage tasks, placing anchor boxes on feature maps and producing the ultimate output, which includes class information, objectivity scores, and bounding boxes.

The abbreviation YOLO, which stands for "You Only Look Once," indicates the capacity to execute the detection task in a single pass through the network. In a solitary analysis of the image, a convolutional neural network forecasts the bounding boxes and their corresponding locations. By making use of the information contained in the bounding boxes, this algorithm proficiently detects objects and precisely establishes their spatial positions [10]. Our objective is to offer a thorough examination of the progression of the YOLO framework, ranging from version five (YOLOv5) to version seven (YOLOv7). This review aims to illuminate the notable innovations, distinctions, and improvements introduced in each iteration, along with the recent application of these three versions in text detection within natural scenes.

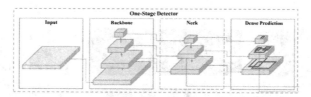

Fig. 3. Stage Detector Architecture of YOLO [11]

2.1 The Evolution of the Framework from YOLOv5 to YOLOv7

Soon after the launch of YOLOv4 in 2020, Glenn Jocher introduced YOLOv5 [12]. YOLOv5 is an accessible open-source solution known for its ease of implementation. It provides five distinct scaled versions, offering flexibility for adjusting the model's size and applying data augmentation methods. The architecture of YOLOv5 is trained and assessed using the MS COCO dataset [12, 13]. Subsequent works [14–16] have utilized and improved upon YOLOv5. The Meituan Vision AI Department published YOLOv6 on ArXiv in September 2022 [17]. Like YOLOv5, it comprises multiple models of varying sizes tailored for industrial purposes. Nevertheless, unlike its predecessors, YOLOv6 embraces an anchor-free detection approach, aligning with the prevailing trend of anchor point-based methods [18]. YOLOv6's architecture is trained and assessed using the MS COCO dataset [13]. Subsequent works [19, 20] have both applied and improved upon YOLOv6. In July 2022, YOLOv7 was unveiled on ArXiv [21]. Unlike its predecessors, YOLOv7 underwent training solely on the MS COCO dataset [13], without the use of pre-trained backbones. This version brought about several structural adjustments and integrated a set of bag-of-freebies (BoF) techniques. These improvements led to enhanced accuracy without compromising inference speed or substantially extending the training duration. YOLOv7 has been both applied and enhanced in subsequent works [22, 23].

2.2 Datasets Employed for Detecting Text in the Wild

Many datasets containing images captured in natural scene are commonly utilized in research related to computer vision and image processing. These datasets encompass images obtained from various environments. Here are a few popular databases of natural scene images:

- COCO-text [24]: created in 2016, this dataset is widely recognized as one of the largest and most extensive repositories for text detection. It comprises over 63,000 images and encompasses approximately 173,000 annotated text regions, encompassing a diverse array of text orientations.
- ICDAR 2015 [25]: The Incidental Scene Text dataset primarily focuses on text in the Latin script. It consists of a set of 1,670 images, covering a total of 17,548 annotated regions.
- RRC-MLT datasets [4]: These datasets are integral parts of the ICDAR 2017 and ICDAR 2019 Robust Reading Challenge, with a specific focus on multi-lingual scene text detection and script identification. The images within the ICDAR MLT-2019 Dataset of Real Images are natural scene images featuring embedded text, such as street signs, street advertisements, shop names, passing vehicle labels, and user photos from microblogs. This dataset consists of 20,000 images containing text in 10 different languages, with 2,000 images per language. While most images include text in multiple languages, each language is represented in at least 2,000 images. The ten languages covered are Arabic, Bangla, Chinese, Devanagari, English, French, German, Italian, Japanese, and Korean.
- SYPHAX dataset [3]: This dataset was collected in the Tunisian city of "Sfax," which is the second-largest city in the country, following the capital. It includes a total of 2,008 images, with 80% of the dataset (1,607 images) designated for training, while the remaining 20% (401 images) is reserved for testing. The dataset is divided into 16 distinct sections, spanning a distance of roughly 365 km. The images in the dataset predominantly feature text, encompassing both Arabic and Latin scripts.
- ARASTI [26]: The dataset consists of 374 Arabic scene text images taken in authentic situations, without specific regard for environmental conditions. Additionally, it contains an Arabic word image dataset, encompassing 1,280 isolated word images extracted from scene texts.

These datasets provide annotated images that serve as valuable resources for researchers and developers to train and evaluate algorithms related to scene text detection and similar tasks. However, there is a limited number of databases in this field that support multiple languages, particularly those containing Arabic scripts. Additionally, as the YOLO framework continues to evolve, most researchers primarily focus on "object detection" rather than "text detection". Given this context, we have decided to take on the new challenge and apply YOLO to two datasets: the SYPHAX dataset [3], which introduces a novel challenge of multilingual text detection, encompassing 100% of its images featuring Arabic scripts, and the ICDAR MLT-2019 dataset [4], which includes Arabic scripts in 10% of its total images.

2.3   Applications of YOLO in Different Text Detection Domains

The YOLO algorithm, well-known for its prowess in object detection, finds diverse applications in various domains, including text detection. Employing YOLO for text detection involves the process of training the algorithm to recognize and pinpoint text regions within an image. Below are a few instances of how YOLO is used for text detection in different fields, particularly in natural scenes. YOLO can be employed to detect text within images of real-world scenes [10]. This application holds significant importance in domains such as autonomous driving, where the ability to identify and recognize text on road signs, billboards, and traffic signals is vital for navigation and decision-making. In the realm of video surveillance, YOLO can be harnessed within video surveillance systems to achieve text detection in real-time [27]. This use case proves advantageous for recognizing text within surveillance videos, encompassing tasks such as identifying license plates [28], vehicle identification numbers, recognizing traffic signs [29], or detecting text on suspicious objects. By aiding in security and forensic analysis, YOLO plays a pivotal role in augmenting the overall capabilities of surveillance. In the context of Augmented Reality (AR), YOLO finds application in detecting text within AR applications [30]. It adeptly identifies text in real-time captured frames, facilitating the smooth integration of virtual content with the identified text areas. This capability holds significance in a range of applications, including text translation, information overlay, and interactive experiences, thereby enhancing the overall interactive AR experiences. In the field of Document Analysis, YOLO can be applied to document analysis tasks [31], which entail extracting text from scanned documents, forms, or invoices. Through the training of YOLO using annotated document images, the algorithm gains the ability to recognize and pinpoint text areas within the document. This streamlines document processing workflows by enabling automated text extraction and analysis. By employing suitably annotated datasets designed specifically for text detection, YOLO can be trained to effectively identify and locate text regions within images or videos. This capacity opens the door to automating text-related tasks across various domains, offering numerous opportunities for streamlined and efficient text processing.

3   Methodology

This research encompasses a series of experiments with the objective of refining the most effective iteration of YOLO for optimal text detection in images of natural scenes featuring Arabic scripts. The investigation is grounded in the latest developments in the field and relies on the SYPHAX dataset [3] and the ICDAR MLT-2019 Dataset of Real Images [4]. In the initial phase, following the implementation of a specific data augmentation techniques on both datasets, various iterations of YOLO models, spanning from version 5 to version 7, were subject to experimentation. In the subsequent phase, we will enhance the architecture of the identified optimal YOLO version. The nature of this enhancement will be contingent on the chosen version, and further rounds of experimentation will be conducted to explore these improvements.

3.1 A Specific Data Augmentation Techniques

Utilizing optimal data augmentation techniques proves advantageous when training YOLO-based models for text detection in the wild. These techniques augment the variety and quantity of training data, thereby enhancing the models' capacity to generalize to real-world situations. The choice of a suitable augmentation technique holds significance as it should closely mirror the traits of authentic images encountered in natural scenes and align with the attributes of the selected dataset. By employing text detection methods in this fashion, we can attain favorable outcomes. We have chosen four data augmentation techniques (as shown in Fig. 4) that encompass basic image alterations [32]. To begin with, we decided to utilize geometric transformations via rigid transformations [33] to create two additional skew angles that closely mimic demanding camera shooting perspectives, one to the right and one to the left. Secondly, we introduced a horizontal directional blur effect to replicate the capture of moving images from a camera. Thirdly, we utilized color space transformations through white balance adjustments. This method allowed us to create two different variations in color temperature and brightness, symbolizing different times of the day. Finally, we introduced a noise injection sourced from a Gaussian distribution, along with a 20% augmentation of contrast, histogram equalization, and sharpening.

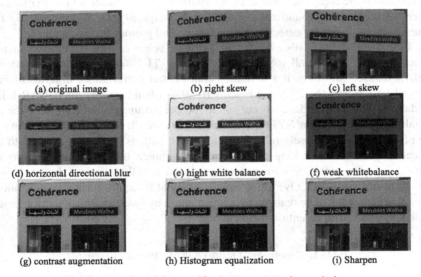

Fig. 4. Samples of the specific data augmentation techniques

3.2 Experiments and Results

Highlighting the significance of the matter, it should be noted that the effectiveness of text detection algorithms using YOLO can fluctuate based on the particular version utilized, the attributes of the dataset employed, and the training techniques employed. Hence, in our study, the documented precision, recall, and F-scores exhibit variations due to the diverse YOLO architectures employed, the inclusion of multilingual text featuring the Arabic script, and the utilization of specific data augmentation methods. The assessment criteria encompass precision, recall, and F-score, which are described as follows:

$$Precision = \frac{\sum_i^N \sum_j^{|D^i|} M_D\left(D_j^i, G^i\right)}{\sum_i^N |D^i|} \tag{1}$$

$$Recall = \frac{\sum_i^N \sum_j^{|G^i|} M_G\left(G_j^i, D^i\right)}{\sum_i^N |G^i|} \tag{2}$$

$$F-score = 2 \times \frac{Precision \times Recall}{Precision + Recall} \tag{3}$$

N represents the complete count of images within a given dataset. $|D^i|$ and $|G^i|$ are the number of detection and ground true rectangles in i^{th} image. $M_D(D_j^i, G^i)$ and $M_G(G_j^i, D^i)$ are the matching scores for detection rectangles D^j and ground true rectangle G^j.

In Table 1 and Table 2, it's evident that YOLOv5 achieves superior results in terms of Precision (74.5%), Recall (68.4%), and F-score (71.3%) when working with the SYPHAX dataset. Similarly, it also demonstrates better performance in terms of Precision (70.1%), Recall (62.2%), and F-score (65.9%) when handling the ICDAR MLT-2019 dataset. The YOLOv5 stands out as the top-performing model for both datasets, especially excelling with the SYPHAX dataset. This dataset, characterized by a limited range of languages and closely related script features, aligns particularly well with the architecture of YOLOv5, making it the most suitable choice. It is evident that the metrics do not exhibit consistent improvement across successive YOLO versions. In conclusion, while the results from YOLOv5 are promising, they still require further enhancement. These enhancements will be realized in the next phase by incorporating a reinforcement module known as "The Attention Mechanism".

Table 1. Experimental result on the SYPHAX Dataset

YOLO version	Precision (%)	Recall (%)	F score (%)
YOLOv5	**74.5**	**68.4**	**71.3**
YOLOv6	68.6	62	65.1
YOLOv7	70.2	66	68

Table 2. Experimental result on the ICDAR MLT-2019 Dataset

YOLO version	Precision (%)	Recall (%)	F score (%)
YOLOv5	**70.1**	**62.2**	**65.9**
YOLOv6	61.3	55.4	58.2
YOLOv7	63.5	60.3	61.9

3.3 Enhancement of the Optimal YOLO Model Obtained (YOLOv5)

3.3.1 The Attention Mechanism

The purpose of the attention mechanism is to extract crucial information by directing attention towards significant areas within input images. In practical terms, various implementations of the attention mechanism exist, tailored to specific applications. ECA-Net [35] represents a highly efficient channel attention mechanism capable of capturing insights into inter-channel connections, meaning the interdependence among channels. This mechanism leads to a substantial improvement in performance. Simultaneously, CBAM [36] is a commonly employed, resource-efficient attention mechanism that integrates both spatial and channel attention. In the first enhancement of the architecture, we exclusively employ the channel attention mechanism (ECA-Net). In the second architecture improvement, we incorporate both the first enhancement and the spatial attention mechanism (CBAM). Lastly, we compare the outcomes of these two approaches.

3.3.2 The Channel Attention Mechanism

The YOLOv5 model consists of three primary elements: a backbone segment tasked with feature extraction, a neck segment for merging these features, and an output segment specifically designed for text detection. The backbone employs a convolutional neural network (CNN) to generate feature maps of different sizes by processing the input image using a sequence of convolution and pooling operations [34]. This backbone network yields four sets of feature maps with dimensions of 152×152 pixels, 76×76 pixels, 38×38 pixels, and 19×19 pixels. By utilizing these feature maps of diverse dimensions, the neck component combines the feature maps extracted from various levels to capture improved contextual information and reduce the loss of relevant data. The goal of the attention mechanism is to extract vital information by focusing on important regions within the input image. In the wild, a range of attention mechanism implementations are employed across various applications. We choose ECA-Net [35], which is a powerful channel attention mechanism that can capture interactions between channels, specifically, the dependencies among channels. This results in a significant improvement in performance. After applying global average pooling at the channel level without dimension reduction, ECA-Net examines the interactions among channels by analyzing each channel in conjunction with its K adjacent channels. To improve the YOLOv5 detection method for the identification of multi-scale and small text in images, we augment it by integrating the ECA-Net attention mechanism [35]. This adjustment better suits the attributes of Arabic scripts, resulting in a decrease in model complexity, effective management of output feature channels with different weights, and the successful extraction of authentic image features. As indicated in Table 3, the ultimate outcomes exhibit improvements while remaining quite promising.

Table 3. Experimental result using ECA-Net

Dataset	Precision (%)	Recall (%)	F score (%)
SYPHAX	**79**	**72.5**	**75.6**
MLT-2019	73	63.3	67.8

3.3.3 The Spatial Attention Mechanism

CBAM [36] combines both spatial and channel attention mechanisms. Channel attention involves the learning of weights for various channels and multiplying these weights with the respective channels to amplify focus on the crucial channel domain. The spatial attention mechanism concentrates on the positional details of text within the images and selectively consolidates the spatial characteristics of each region by using a weighted sum of spatial features. To enhance the representation of text information in the images, we introduce attention modules within the feature fusion layers. These attention modules are realized as a fusion of both ECA-Net and CBAM. To clarify, the channel attention component is adopted from ECA-Net [35], while the spatial attention component is sourced from CBAM [36]. The ECA module initially undergoes learning on the features post-global average pooling (GAP) using 1D convolution. It then multiplies the modified weights with the input feature map to produce a fresh feature map. The feature map produced by the ECA module serves as the input for CBAM's spatial attention module. This module generates a spatial attention feature map, which is then added to the original feature map to mimic the structure of a residual block. Ultimately, the final feature map is obtained by applying the ReLU activation function to the combined feature map (refer to Fig. 5). These modifications lead to promising results, as shown in Table 4.

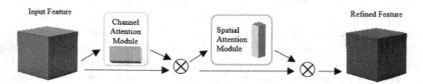

Fig. 5. The structure of the combined attention modules

Table 4. Experimental result using CBAM

Dataset	Precision (%)	Recall (%)	F score (%)
SYPHAX	**81.5**	**75.2**	**78.2**
MLT-2019	75	64.8	69.5

3.4 Discussion

Within the realm of YOLOv5, a systematic investigation has been conducted across multiple facets of the algorithm, with particular emphasis on enhancements and integration of the attention mechanism. In our study, these efforts have yielded promising results in terms of detection performance when applied to two datasets, each presenting unique challenges: images in natural scenes and those featuring Arabic scripts. We observe that YOLOv5 provides versatility in choosing models, as even its smaller variants yield impressive outcomes. Although YOLOv5 maintains consistent network architecture, it places a particular emphasis on text detection across diverse scales, making it capable of handling text in different sizes effectively. In contrast, YOLOv6 utilizes increased levels of parallelism within its backbone when compared to YOLOv5. However, in our specific case, these modifications have led to less favorable results compared to the previous version. YOLOv7 incorporates a novel classification approach with fewer associated losses, resulting in promising outcomes. It also reduces the number of box predictions. However, it still exhibits a slightly lower level of efficiency when compared to YOLOv5 (Figs. 6 and 7).

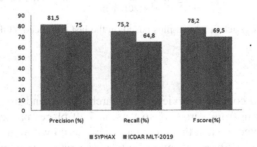

Fig. 6. Metrics of the final experimental results

(a) Successful text detection samples using the enhanced YOLOv5 from SYPHAX dataset (top row)
and ICDAR MLT-2019 (down row)

(b) Failed text detection samples using the enhanced YOLOv5 from SYPHAX dataset (right) and
ICDAR MLT-2019 (left)

Fig. 7. Text detection samples based on the last enhanced YOLOv5

4   Conclusion

This paper provides a concise overview of the architecture and uses of three distinct YOLO models, ranging from version 5 to version 7. It places particular emphasis on their application in detecting text that includes Arabic script within images from natural scenes. Moreover, it gives more prominence to comparative implementations, specifically investigating text detection across various iterations of YOLO frameworks for multilingual scripts. It pays special attention to the Arabic language within the SYPHAX dataset and the ICDAR MLT-2019 dataset. The findings demonstrate that the best results are obtained with version 5. Subsequently, we enhanced YOLOv5 by incorporating attention modules, and this modification also yielded favorable results.

The YOLO series of algorithms has room for further development by implementing specific enhancements to improve its text detection capabilities. This could involve modifications to the network structure, fine-tuning training methodologies, or integrating innovative approaches to tackle challenges unique to text detection. Considering their relatively recent emergence, the YOLO models still offer significant potential for future research and investigation. However, they currently encounter specific constraints, especially when addressing the complexities associated with text detection in diverse natural scenes images involving multilingual scripts, as opposed to their more general application in object detection tasks. Future research efforts can fine-tune the best-performing architectures for text detection and work towards elevating the overall effectiveness of text detection algorithms, particularly for the Arabic language. This approach will better equip them to tackle a diverse range of challenges.

References

1. Bai, X., Yang, M., Lyu, P., Xu, Y., Luo, J.: Integrating scene text and visual appearance for fine-grained image classification. IEEE Access **6**, 66322–66335 (2018)
2. Abdelaziz, I., Abdou, S., Al-Barhamtoshy, H.: A large vocabulary system for Arabic online handwriting recognition. Pattern Anal. Appl. **19**, 1129–1141 (2016). https://doi.org/10.1007/s10044-015-0526-7
3. Turki, H., Elleuch, M., Kherallah, M.: SYPHAX dataset. IEEE Dataport (2023). https://doi.org/10.21227/ydqd-2443
4. Nayef, N., et al.: ICDAR2019 robust reading challenge on multi-lingual scene text detection and recognition—RRC-MLT-2019. In: 2019 International conference on document analysis and recognition (ICDAR), pp. 1582–1587. IEEE (2019)
5. Sultana, F., Sufian, A., Dutta, P.: A review of object detection models based on convolutional neural network. In: Mandal, J.K., Banerjee, S. (eds.) Intelligent Computing: Image Processing Based Applications. AISC, vol. 1157, pp. 1–16. Springer, Singapore (2020). https://doi.org/10.1007/978-981-15-4288-6_1
6. Turki, H., Halima, M.B., Alimi, A.M.: Text detection based on MSER and CNN features. In: 2017 14th IAPR international conference on document analysis and recognition (ICDAR), vol. 1, pp. 949–954. IEEE (2017)
7. Amrouche, A., Bentrcia, Y., Hezil, N., Abed, A., Boubakeur, K.N., Ghribi, K.: Detection and localization of Arabic text in natural scene images. In: 2022 First International Conference on Computer Communications and Intelligent Systems (I3CIS), pp. 72–76. IEEE (2022)
8. Redmon, J., Divvala, S., Girshick, R., Farhadi, A.: You only look once: unified, real-time object detection. In: Proceedings of the IEEE Conference on Computer Vision and Pattern Recognition, pp. 779–788 (2016)
9. Ravi, N., El-Sharkawy, M.: Real-time embedded implementation of improved object detector for resource-constrained devices. J. Low Power Electron. Appl. **12**(2), 21 (2022)
10. Diwan, T., Anirudh, G., Tembhurne, J.V.: Object detection using YOLO: challenges, architectural successors, datasets and applications. Multimed. Tools Appl. **82**(6), 9243–9275 (2023). https://doi.org/10.1007/s11042-022-13644-y
11. Bochkovskiy, A., Wang, C.Y., Liao, H.Y.M.: Yolov4: optimal speed and accuracy of object detection. arXiv preprint arXiv:2004.10934 (2020)
12. Jocher, G., Nishimura, K., Mineeva, T., Vilarino, R.: Yolov5 by ultralytics. Disponível em (2020). https://github.com/ultralytics/yolov5
13. Redmon, J., Farhadi, A.: Yolov3: an incremental improvement. arXiv preprint arXiv:1804.02767 (2018)
14. Latha, R.S., et al.: Text detection and language identification in natural scene images using YOLOv5. In: 2023 International Conference on Computer Communication and Informatics (ICCCI), pp. 1–7. IEEE (2023)

15. Xu, Q., Zheng, G., Ren, W., Li, X., Yang, Z., Huang, Z.: An efficient and effective text spotter for characters in natural scene images based on an improved YOLOv5 model. In: International Conference on Artificial Intelligence, Virtual Reality, and Visualization (AIVRV 2022), vol. 12588, pp. 64–68. SPIE (2023)
16. Luo, Y., Zhao, C., Zhang, F.: Research on scene text detection algorithm based on modified YOLOv5. In: International Conference on Mechatronics Engineering and Artificial Intelligence (MEAI 2022), vol. 12596, pp. 620–626. SPIE (2023)
17. Li, C., et al.: YOLOv6: a single-stage object detection framework for industrial applications. arXiv preprint arXiv:2209.02976 (2022)
18. Ge, Z., Liu, S., Wang, F., Li, Z., Sun, J.: Yolox: exceeding yolo series in 2021. arXiv preprint arXiv:2107.08430 (2021)
19. Norkobil Saydirasulovich, S., Abdusalomov, A., Jamil, M.K., Nasimov, R., Kozhamzharova, D., Cho, Y.I.: A YOLOv6-based improved fire detection approach for smart city environments. Sensors 23(6), 3161 (2023)
20. Gupta, C., Gill, N.S., Gulia, P., Chatterjee, J.M.: A novel finetuned YOLOv6 transfer learning model for real-time object detection. J. Real-Time Image Proc. 20(3), 42 (2023). https://doi.org/10.1007/s11554-023-01299-3
21. Wang, C.Y., Bochkovskiy, A., Liao, H.Y.M.: YOLOv7: trainable bag-of-freebies sets new state-of-the-art for real-time object detectors. In: Proceedings of the IEEE/CVF Conference on Computer Vision and Pattern Recognition, pp. 7464–7475 (2023)
22. Negi, A., Kesarwani, Y., Saranya, P.: Text based traffic signboard detection using YOLO v7 architecture. In: Singh, M., Vipin Tyagi, P.K., Gupta, J.F., Ören, T. (eds.) Advances in Computing and Data Sciences: 7th International Conference, ICACDS 2023, Kolkata, India, April 27–28, 2023, Revised Selected Papers, pp. 1–11. Springer, Cham (2023). https://doi.org/10.1007/978-3-031-37940-6_1
23. Moussaoui, H., El Akkad, N., Benslimane, M.: Arabic and Latin license plate detection and recognition based on YOLOv7 and image processing methods (2023)
24. Veit, A., Matera, T., Neumann, L., Matas, J., Belongie, S.: Coco-text: dataset and benchmark for text detection and recognition in natural images. arXiv preprint arXiv:1601.07140 (2016)
25. Karatzas, D., et al.: ICDAR 2015 competition on robust reading. In: 2015 13th International Conference on Document Analysis and Recognition (ICDAR), pp. 1156–1160. IEEE (2015)
26. Tounsi, M., Moalla, I., Alimi, A.M.: ARASTI: a database for Arabic scene text recognition. In: 2017 1st International Workshop on Arabic Script Analysis and Recognition (ASAR), pp. 140–144. IEEE (2017)
27. Ashraf, A.H., et al.: Weapons detection for security and video surveillance using CNN and YOLO-v5s. CMC-Comput. Mater. Contin. 70, 2761–2775 (2022)
28. Chen, R.C.: Automatic license plate recognition via sliding-window darknet-YOLO deep learning. Image Vis. Comput. 87, 47–56 (2019)
29. Dewi, C., Chen, R.C., Jiang, X., Yu, H.: Deep convolutional neural network for enhancing traffic sign recognition developed on Yolo V4. Multimed. Tools Appl. 81(26), 37821–37845 (2022). https://doi.org/10.1007/s11042-022-12962-5
30. Zhang, L., Xu, F., Liu, Y., Zhang, D., Gui, L., Zuo, D.: A posture detection method for augmented reality–aided assembly based on YOLO-6D. Int. J. Adv. Manuf. Technol. 125(7–8), 3385–3399 (2023). https://doi.org/10.1007/s00170-023-10964-7
31. Zhang, D., Mao, R., Guo, R., Jiang, Y., Zhu, J.: YOLO-table: disclosure document table detection with involution. Int. J. Doc. Anal. Recognit. (IJDAR) 26(1), 1–14 (2023). https://doi.org/10.1007/s10032-022-00400-z
32. Shorten, C., Khoshgoftaar, T.M.: A survey on image data augmentation for deep learning. J. Big Data 6(1), 1–48 (2019)
33. Schaefer, S., McPhail, T., Warren, J.: Image deformation using moving least squares. In: ACM SIGGRAPH 2006 Papers, pp. 533–540 (2006)

34. Zeiler, M.D., Taylor, G.W., Fergus, R.: Adaptive deconvolutional networks for mid and high level feature learning. In: Proceedings of the 2011 International Conference on Computer Vision, Barcelona, Spain, 6–13 November 2011, pp. 2018–2025 (2011)
35. Wang, Q., Wu, B., Zhu, P., Li, P., Zuo, W., Hu, Q.: ECA-Net: efficient channel attention for deep convolutional neural networks. In: Proceedings of the Conference on Computer Vision and Pattern Recognition (CVPR), 14 June 2020, Seattle, WA, USA (2020)
36. Woo, S., Park, J., Lee, J.-Y., Kweon, I.S.: CBAM: convolutional block attention module. In: Ferrari, V., Hebert, M., Sminchisescu, C., Weiss, Y. (eds.) ECCV 2018. LNCS, vol. 11211, pp. 3–19. Springer, Cham (2018). https://doi.org/10.1007/978-3-030-01234-2_1

Transfer Learning Model for Cyberbullying Detection in Tunisian Social Networks

Sahar Ben Bechir$^{(\boxtimes)}$ ⓘ, Asma Mekki ⓘ, and Mariem Ellouze ⓘ

ANLP Research Group, MIRACL Lab., University of Sfax, Sfax, Tunisia
saharbenbechir2018@gmail.com, mariem.ellouze@fsegs.usf.tn

Abstract. Due to the proliferation of smartphones connected to the Internet, many individuals, particularly young people in Arab society, have widely embraced social media platforms as the primary means of communication, interaction, and friendship formation. Technological advancements in smartphones and communication have enabled young people to stay in touch and join massive social networks worldwide. However, such networks expose young individuals to cyberbullying and offensive content, endangering their safety and emotional well-being. Although numerous solutions have been proposed for automatically detecting cyberbullying, most existing solutions have been designed for English-speaking users. Morphologically rich languages, such as Arabic, specifically the Tunisian dialect, present challenges of data scarcity. As a result, solutions developed for another language prove ineffective when applied to Arabic content. With this in mind, this study aims to enhance the effectiveness of existing cyberbullying detection models for Arabic content by designing and developing a cyberbullying detection model. A diverse set of heterogeneous classifiers derived from traditional machine learning and deep learning and transformer learning techniques were trained using annotated Arabic cyberbullying datasets collected from three different platforms (Facebook, Twitter, and YouTube). The results demonstrate the efficacy of the proposed model compared to other examined classifiers. The overall improvement achieved by the proposed model reaches 85% compared to the best-trained classifier.

Keywords: Cyberbullying · Social media · Machine learning · Arabic dialect · Tunisian dialect

1 Introduction

The widespread proliferation of social networks has a substantial impact on individuals and communities, enabling people to become more connected and engaged with vast networks of relatives, friends, followers, and other individuals. Social networks facilitate close relationships, enhance communication skills, language proficiency, writing abilities, and the sharing of ideas, talents, and

M. Mosbah et al. (Eds.): MEDI 2023, CCIS 2071, pp. 62–75, 2024.
https://doi.org/10.1007/978-3-031-55729-3_6

experiences. Unfortunately, some users exploit this digital world by spreading offensive content with the intention of embarrassing or harming others, leading to what is known as cyberbullying.

Cyberbullying refers to the use of digital means, such as internet-connected smart devices, to publish content that harms or embarrasses others. It can have negative effects, including depression, emotional and physical stress, destruction of self-esteem, and social isolation. According to the Cyberbullying Research Center in 2021, 45.5% -of 12-year-old children in the United States become victims of cyberbullying each month [7], with cases often being underreported. This highlights the alarming prevalence and impact of cyberbullying on a global scale. It is not limited to specific regions, as evidenced by incidents around the world. For instance, the city of Kairouan in Tunisia recently witnessed a tragic incident where a 17-year-old girl took her own life after being subjected to relentless cyberbullying. This tragic event serves as a stark reminder of the urgent need to address cyberbullying and its devastating consequences in different societies and languages [6].

Indeed, the issue of cyberbullying has received significant attention in recent times. According to the National Center for Health Statistics (NCHS), the increase in cyberbullying incidents has been linked to youth suicides [4]. Research conducted by the NCHS suggests that individuals under the age of 25 who have been exposed to cyberbullying had at twice the risk compared to others [6,10]. While social media is often associated with cyberbullying, it is important to note that this behavior can occur on various other platforms as well. Online gaming platforms, cell phone services, websites, and other sharing platforms can also be venues for cyberbullying incidents [8]. The consequences of cyberbullying can be severe, particularly for young individuals who may already be vulnerable. It is crucial for individuals, parents, educators, and policymakers to address this issue seriously and take steps to prevent and combat cyberbullying effectively.

While social media, is often associated with cyberbullying, it occurs on various platforms such as online games, mobile services, websites, and sharing platforms. It can take different forms, including text, images, videos, and audio. However, text-based cyberbullying is the most prevalent form. Given the enormous amount, variety, and speed of data generated by users, manual detection and reliance on user reports are not effective or efficient in combatting cyberbullying [7].

Although numerous studies have focused on automatic cyberbullying detection in recent years, Cyberbullying continues to increase. Various tools and techniques have been employed to analyze text content and detect cyberbullying phenomena, with Natural Language Processing (NLP) techniques commonly used to process textual data and extract relevant patterns. Textual data is typically unstructured. Therefore, NLP techniques and algorithms are used to convert textual features into structured features suitable for machine learning algorithms. However, cyberbullying detection faces several challenges, particularly when dealing with the Arabic language. The Arabic language comprises Modern Standard Arabic (MSA), Classical Arabic, and Dialectal Arabic, each used in different contexts within Arab society. For example, Classical Arabic is used for religious content while MSA is used for education, writing, and reporting. Dialectal Arabic, on the other hand, is the language used in daily conversations with family and friends. Most social media and online communication employ the dialectal Arabic variety, and individuals often mix these three types in informal writing and speech. These unique characteristics of the Arabic language make solutions developed for other languages ineffective when applied to Arabic.

Despite the impact of cyberbullying and offensive content on social media in Arab society, limited research has been conducted on cyberbullying detection in Arabic content. Existing work often adopts models designed for other languages, especially English. Additionally, the use of small datasets in building detection models leads to data scarcity issues that further degrade the accuracy of detection. However, collecting massive datasets for Arabic cyberbullying is a challenging task that requires significant effort, time, and costs. Therefore, it is crucial to improve detection accuracy without increasing data size.

This study aims to enhance the efficiency of existing cyberbullying detection models for Arabic content by designing and developing a detection model ensemble. To achieve this goal, a four-phase methodology is adopted. The first phase involves collecting and combining multiple datasets containing instances of cyberbullying. The second phase focuses on data preprocessing, including orthographic normalization, noise cleaning, tokenization, stop word removal, URL and punctuation removal, and corpus construction using NLP techniques with annotation. The third phase is feature extraction and representation, where unstructured text features are converted into structured and numerical word representations. Deep learning algorithms are then trained using the dataset collected from different platforms, and the best set of these trained classifiers is used to construct the proposed ensemble model. The F1-score, a harmonic mean of recall and precision, is used to rank the classifier outputs. These scored outputs are aggregated to make decisions based on consensus, where each classifier contributes to the final decision. Finally, the model makes a final decision to detect cyberbullying or not. The results demonstrate that the proposed model is more effective than the other trained classifiers. Section 2 presents related work, Sect. 3 describes the methodology of this study, Sect. 4 presents the experimental results and discussion, and Sect. 5 concludes the paper and outlines future work.

2   Related Work

Many researchers have worked on detecting cyberbullying with sentiment analysis. One notable observation regarding the conducted research is the focus on analyzing sentiment scores based on a single aspect. Some studies solely analyze sentiment using words, while others concentrate solely on emojis. In general, there have been several studies conducted on the detection and analysis of cyberbullying, especially in the Arabic language.

Farid et al. [5] introduced an Egyptian benchmark dataset to detect cyberbullying and cyberstalking on Twitter. The dataset consisted of over 151,000 comments labeled into balanced classes of positive and negative. Their model utilized LP techniques for feature representation and employed a hybrid and lexicon-based approach for sentiment analysis, focusing on the Egyptian dialect. Data collection involved the Twitter API and specific hashtags, followed by data preparation through the removal of stop words, links, special characters, symbols, and non-Arabic words. The data was then classified using sentiment scores, sessionization to consider user history, ground truth comparison, and the use of hashtags to derive a cyberbullying score. The results showed an accuracy of 73% for negative words and emoticons, while neutral and positive words achieved accuracies exceeding 85%.

Mouheb et al. [9] introduced a model for detecting cyberbullying in Arabic texts using Naive Bayes (NB) techniques. The training and testing dataset was collected from Twitter and Youtube about 26,000 Arabic comments. The reported accuracy is 95%. However, the testing dataset used is relatively small (less than 10% as inferred from the confusion matrix of the testing dataset), and it mainly consists of obvious keywords indicating cyberbullying. However, the system was designed based on a collection of keywords extracted from the dataset and weightage mechanisms. This heuristic approach may result in high false alarms due to the lack of consideration for the semantic expression in the dataset.

Alharbi et al. [3] proposed an automatic method for detecting cyberbullying and cyberharassment in Arabic using sentiment analysis, comprising lexical and machine learning techniques. The lexical methods included Corpus-Based, Dictionary-Based, and Manual Approaches, which involved extracting suitable words from the corpus based on semantic similarity, employing a dictionary with synonyms and antonyms, and manually correcting errors. The research consisted of two main stages: data collection, processing, and classification, followed by lexicon-based evaluation using a test set. The authors applied PMI, Chi-square, and entropy to calculate word weights, and the results indicated PMI achieved the best performance, with an 81% detection rate for cyberbullying.

Albayari et al. [1] developed a method to detect cyberbullying in the Arab world using an Arabic Instagram corpus. They collected 200,000 comments from Instagram, filtered and preprocessed the data, resulting in 198,000 comments. The dataset was labeled into three categories (positive, neutral, and negative) with a focus on identifying toxic and bullying comments. They used SVM as a classifier, which performed better than other algorithms, achieving an 86% accuracy in detecting cyberbullying and negative comments. The study highlights the importance of AI-based approaches in addressing cyberbullying and emphasizes the potential for further improvement and testing in this area.

Alduailaj et al. [2] conducted research on cyberbullying detection using data extracted from Twitter API and YouTube in Arabic. Their methodology involved data collection, preprocessing, feature extraction, and classification using SVM. They evaluated the results based on accuracy, recall, precision, and F1 score. The study compared different scenarios and found the SVM model with TF-IDF vector and Stemmed-no-stopwords scenario performed best. SVM with BoW vector also showed promising results. Additionally, they compared the results with the NB classifier using various parameters and feature extraction. The study suggests exploring deep learning methods for future improvements and reported detection accuracy varying from 70% to 95%.

Shannag et al. [11] conducted a comprehensive study focused on designing, constructing, and evaluating a multi-dialect and annotated corpus called ArCybC for cyberbullying detection in Arabic. The methodology comprised five steps, involving corpus design, data preprocessing, feature engineering, machine learning model creation, and performance evaluation. Social media platforms, especially Twitter, were the main sources of cyberbullying content, which was filtered and normalized. The data was transformed into vectors using techniques like TD/IDF, VSM, and Word2vec, and the performance of five machine learning algorithms was evaluated using various measures. The proposed Arabic cyberbullying detection model achieved an accuracy of 86%.

The related work on cyberbullying detection in Arabic has provided valuable insights, with researchers exploring various techniques, including sentiment analysis, lexicon-based approaches, and machine learning algorithms [1,3,5,9,11]. Benchmark datasets, like the Egyptian benchmark dataset [5], and innovative methods, such as lexicon-based approaches [3], have been introduced. SVM has shown promising results in achieving high accuracy [1]. However, challenges remain, such as small testing datasets and the potential for false alarms [9]. The groundwork laid by these studies emphasizes the importance of AI-driven approaches for combating cyberbullying effectively in the Arabic language [2]. In the next section, we propose a Transfer Learning model for cyberbullying detection in Tunisian social networks, aiming to build upon the existing research and contribute to a safer online environment.

3 Proposed Method

Most current cyberbullying detection models are trained using tools based on textual datasets in the English language. However, there is a lack of proposed cyberbullying detection models for other languages, such as Arabic, which exhibit distinct syntax and semantics compared to other languages. Therefore, further extensive testing and research by scholars are required. The performance of models built using the English language is ineffective when applied to Arabic text due to its linguistic variations, implicit sentiments, and grammatical complexity. Figure 1 shows the proposed classification model of using deep-learning algorithm.

In this study, we propose a method that consists of four phases: data collection, data preprocessing, feature extraction and representation, and model construction. These phases are designed to address the specific challenges and characteristics of Arabic text, ultimately enhancing the effectiveness of cyberbullying detection in this language.

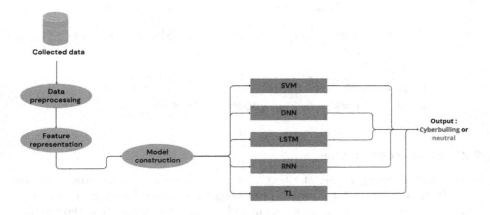

Fig. 1. The proposed method to cyberbulling detection model.

3.1 Data Collection Stage

Due to the lack of available Arabic datasets for cyberbullying detection, a two.
steps approach was employed to acquire suitable data. In the first step, a collection of data in the Tunisian dialect was gathered from various social media
platforms, ensuring a representative sample of online content in that particular
dialect. The collected data spanned a diverse range of sources, including Facebook, Twitter, and YouTube. The corpus used in this study consists of comments
was extracted from the official pages of Tunisian radios and TV channels, specifically Mosaique FM, Jawhra FM, Shemes FM, HiwarElttounsi TV, and Nessma
TV[1]. The data collection period for this corpus spans from January 2023 to April
2023. This initial dataset provided valuable insights into the linguistic nuances
and expressions commonly used in Tunisian dialect cyberbullying instances. The
collected corpus exhibits several distinct characteristics. One prominent charac-
teristic is the frequent use of informal and non-standard vocabulary, including
repeated letters and non-standard abbreviations. Additionally, the corpus contains onomatopoeic expressions (e.g., pff, hhh) and non-linguistic content such
as emoticons. It is worth noting that the dataset includes comments written in
Arabic script, as well as Latin script known as Arabizi, and even a combination of
both. These diverse linguistic elements add complexity to the corpus and require
special considerations for analysis and processing. Therefore, in the second step,
the dataset was subjected to a semi-manual correction process. A translation
code specifically designed for Arabizi data was employed to translate this content into Arabic, ensuring linguistic accuracy and consistency. The resulting
dataset underwent meticulous validation and quality control measures to maintain data integrity. Table 1 provides detailed information about the collected
dataset, including the size of the dataset and the distribution of cyberbullying
instances across different social media platforms.

---

[1] https://exportcomments.com/.

Table 1. List of the used dataset

Platform	Number of samples	Normal Data	Cyberbullying Data
Twitter	2950	–	–
Facebook	4017	–	–
Youtube	6727	–	–
Total	**13694**	**5546**	**8148**

3.2 Preprocessing Stage

In the preprocessing phase, the text undergoes a series of transformations to make it more suitable for effective processing by machine learning algorithms. This phase involves several key steps, including word tokenization, orthographic normalization, and stemming. Tokenization is the process of dividing the text into smaller units called tokens. To produce "clean" text various preprocessing techniques are applied to the collected data. These techniques involve the removal of irrelevant or unnecessary components from the text. Examples of such components include numbers, hyperlinks, special characters, Latin words, symbols, dates, punctuation marks, stop words, sparse terms, and white spaces. These elements are considered noise that can interfere with the classification accuracy. Additionally, stemming is performed on the text to convert words to their original source or base form. Orthographic normalization in NLP refers to the process of transforming and standardizing text data to a common representation or format. It aims to reduce the variation and complexity within the text, making it easier for downstream NLP tasks such as text classification, information retrieval, or machine translation. Our proposed method performs text normalization in several steps. First, it defines correspondence words or phrases to be replaced and their normalized versions. Then, for each pair, it substitutes all occurrences of the key with its corresponding value in the Arabic comments. After all substitutions have been made, normalized text is returned. Table 2 presents an example to highlight the orthographic heterogeneity issue in Tunisian dialect. Normalization makes it possible to take a single word that could be written using several variant spellings in Tunisian script in the context of social networks.

3.3 Feature Representation Stage

In this phase, the textual features of the dataset are transformed into a numerical representation using the CountVectorizer technique. It is a class in the scikit-learn library in Python, that converts a collection of textual documents into a matrix of word occurrence counts within those documents. CountVectorizer builds a vocabulary, which is a list of all unique words present in the document collection. Each unique word is assigned a unique integer identifier. The creation of the vector matrix involves transforming each document into a vector representation. Each document is represented by a vector of a length equal to the

Table 2. Example of Tunisian Dialect Errors

Normalisation Script	Tunisian Script
فماش	فماش
فماش	فمايي
فماش	فمشي

size of the vocabulary. Each dimension of the vector corresponds to a word in the vocabulary, and the value in each dimension indicates the count of occurrences of the corresponding word in the document. By using CountVectorizer, a collection of textual documents can be efficiently transformed into a matrix of counting vectors. This conversion facilitates the utilization of machine learning algorithms for various tasks such as text classification, clustering, and sentiment analysis.

3.4 Model Construction Stage

The dataset is divided into distinct categories: 70% for the training set and the remaining for the testing set. Various machine learning algorithms, including SVM, ANN, LSTM and Transfer Learning (TL), have been investigated and compared in this study. These algorithms are widely recognized and utilized in the field of machine learning for their effectiveness in classification tasks. Our algorithm generates outputs based on accuracy, enabling it to provide very precise results in determining whether a case involves cyberbullying or not. By employing multiple algorithms, a comparative analysis can be conducted to assess their respective performance in terms of cyberbullying detection, which will be the subject of the next section.

4   Performance Analysis

4.1   Experimental Configurations

To address the class imbalance between normal and cyberbullying samples, oversampling techniques were employed to balance the data. by oversampling the cyberbullying samples. The experimental setup involved the use of Python programming language along with libraries such as NLTK for natural language processing, scikit-learn for conventional machine learning classifiers, Imbalanced-learn for resampling imbalanced data, and Keras for deep learning, among other relevant libraries.

These tools were employed for dataset preprocessing, oversampling, feature extraction, representation, model training, and testing. Five machine learning classifiers were applied for comparison with the proposed model, namely: ANN, SVM, DNN, LSTM, RNN and TL. From these classifiers, the six best performing ones were selected to construct the proposed ensemble model. We start with

the implementation of SVM provided by the scikit-learn library. We split our
data into training and test sets using the "train-test-split" function. Next, we
built the SVM model using the "SVC" (Support Vector Classifier) class from
scikit-learn. To start, we used the linear kernel, which is the simplest and most
commonly used. The linear kernel works well when the data is linearly separable.
We adjusted the model parameters, such as margin penalty (C), to optimize performance. Then, we experimented with the RBF (Radial Basis Function) kernel,
which allows to model non-linear decision boundaries. The RBF core works well
when the data is nonlinearly separable. We adjusted the model parameters, such
as kernel coefficient (gamma) and margin penalty (C), to get the best results.
We evaluated the performance of each kernel architecture using metrics such
as accuracy, precision, recall, and F1-score using the "classification-report" from
scikit-learn. In our experiments, we found that both kernel architectures (i.e. linear kernel and RBF kernel) performed well. However, it is important to note that
the choice of kernel architecture may depend on the specific characteristics of
the problem and the data used. It is therefore essential to experiment and adjust
parameters to find the kernel architecture that gives the best results for each
use case. We tested the RNN algorithm using the Python programming language
and the TensorFlow library. Specifically, we used the Keras framework to build
and train an RNN model. The first step was to split the data into train and test
sets using the "train-test-split" function from the scikit-learn library. We chose
to reserve 30% of the data for testing and set the random seed (random-state)
to 1 to ensure the reproducibility of results. Then, we applied the RNN model
using Keras' Sequential class. Our model had three dense layers. The first layer
had 64 neurons with a ReLU activation function, and we added a Dropout regularization layer with a rate of 0.2 to avoid overfitting. The second layer had 32
neurons with a ReLU activation function, and we added another Dropout layer.
Finally, the last layer had a single neuron with a sigmoid activation function
to perform binary classification. After defining the architecture of the model,
we compiled the model specifying the "binary-crossentropy" loss function and
the "adam" optimizer. We also chose to use the "accuracy" metric to assess the
performance of the model. Next comes the model training stage, the number of
epochs set to 280 and the batch size set to 64. Also, we used the validation data
to evaluate the performance of the model during training. In this experiment,
we have chosen these specific values for the number of epochs and the batch size,
but it is important to note that these parameters can be adjusted depending on
the specific characteristics of the problem and the data used. Next, we tested
an RNN model by specifying its LSTM architecture (a combination between the
two algorithms) and choosing different metrics to evaluate its performance. We
then trained the model by adjusting parameters, such as number of epochs and
batch size, and assessed its accuracy on the test set. Thanks to this experience,
we was able to explore the best combinations of parameters to obtain the most
efficient results.

We evaluated the DNN algorithm, using three dense layers. The first layer had
64 neurons with a ReLU activation function. We added a second layer with 32

neurons, also with a ReLU activation function. The last layer had a single neuron with a sigmoid activation function, suitable for our binary classification problem. After defining the architecture of the model, we compiled the model using the "binary-crossentropy" loss function and the "adam" optimizer. To evaluate the performance of the model, we chose to measure several metrics: accuracy, precision, recall and the F1-score. We compiled the model several times, using different metrics for each compilation. During training, we also used the validation data to evaluate the performance of the model. In this experiment, we tried different numbers of epochs and batch sizes to find the best settings. By experimenting with these different parameters, we set the number of epochs to 100 and the batch size to 64.

Moreover, we built the LSTM model using the Sequential class from Keras. Our model had three dense layers. The first layer had 64 neurons with a ReLU activation function. We added a Dropout layer with a rate of 0.2 to avoid overfitting. Then, we added a second layer with 32 neurons and a ReLU activation function. We added another Dropout layer with the same rate of 0.2. The third layer had a single neuron with a sigmoid activation function. We used the "binary-crossentropy" loss function and the "adam" optimizer for compiling the model. We tried different numbers of epochs and batch sizes to find the best settings. By experimenting with different parameters, it is possible to optimize the performance of the model and obtain the best results.

We proceed to tokenize the comments using the AutoTokenizer method of the Transformers library. We use the pre-trained "distilbert-base-uncased" model and specify parameters such as padding, truncation and maximum sequence length. Next, we converted the class labels to category vectors using TensorFlow's to-categorical function. This allows class labels to be represented as binary vectors. We convert the indices from the training and test sets into TensorFlow tensors using Boolean masks and the corresponding indices. Then, we loaded the TFAutoModelForSequenceClassification model, which is the pre-trained DistilBERT model suitable for sequence classification. We compiled and trained the model using the Adam optimizer with a learning rate of 5e-5. The loss function is categorical cross-entropy loss. We set the number of epochs to 30 and the batch size to 16.

4.2 Performance Measures

Four commonly used performance measures in the literature were employed to evaluate the proposed cyberbullying detection model. The first measure is classification accuracy (Acc) (1), which represents the ratio of correctly classified samples to the total number of samples in the dataset. The second measure is precision (pre) (2), which denotes the ratio of correctly classified normal samples to the total number of samples classified as normal. The third measure is recall (Rec) (3), which indicates the ratio of correctly classified normal samples to the total number of actual normal samples. The F1-score (4), the fourth performance measure, can be calculated as the harmonic mean between recall and precision. In this equation, precision represents the ratio of true positive predictions to the total number of predicted positives, and recall represents the ratio of true positive predictions to the total number of actual positives. The F1-score provides a balanced evaluation by considering both precision and recall, making it a useful metric for assessing the overall performance of a classification model. These additional performance measures provide a more comprehensive evaluation of the proposed model, considering various aspects such as true negatives, adjusting the balance between precision and recall, analyzing the classifier's performance across different thresholds, and considering the average precision across multiple query instances.

$$Acc = \frac{Number\ of\ True\ Classified\ Samples}{Total\ Number\ of\ Samples} \tag{1}$$

$$Pre = \frac{Number\ of\ True\ Classified\ Normal\ Samples}{Total\ Number\ of\ Samples\ Classified\ Normal} \tag{2}$$

$$Rec = \frac{Number\ of\ True\ Classified\ Normal\ Samples}{Total\ Number\ of\ Normal\ Samples} \tag{3}$$

$$F1 - score = \frac{2 \times Pre \times Rec}{Pre + Rec} \tag{4}$$

5 Results and Discussion

The performance of our model was compared against various machine learning and deep learning algorithms, and the evaluation was conducted using metrics such as accuracy, precision, recall, and F1 score, as presented in Tables 2 and 3. During the training phase, the combined dataset (Facebook Dataset, Twitter Dataset and Youtube Dataset) was utilized to train the proposed models. Among the tested classifiers, the proposed model demonstrated the highest accuracy, SVM showcasing its superior performance. In particular, the ensemble deep learning-based algorithm, TL classifier, exhibited superior predictions compared to other classifiers. This can be attributed to its comprehensive learning approach and the utilization of a majority voting system for decision-making. The F1 score, which provides a harmonic mean between precision and recall, was deemed suitable for evaluating the classifiers' performance, as it effectively captures the balance between these two metrics. In the SVM experiments, the proposed model showcased the best trade-off between precision and recall, achieving a rate of 73% in comparison to the other classifiers. This outcome can be attributed to the inherent sparsity issue in the Arabic language, where the availability of training data significantly impacts the classifier's performance. TL outperformed the other tested models, especially the deep learning algorithms. TL classifier exhibited the highest accuracy of 83%, surpassing the performance of other tested classifiers. Detailed performance measures presented in Table 4 offer comprehensive insights into the effectiveness of the proposed model, confirming its superior overall performance. Therefore, employing a diverse set of heterogeneous classifiers can address the challenges posed by data scarcity and enhance the accuracy of detecting Arabic language cyberbullying incidents on the internet. This concept can be extended to other languages and domains to improve performance across various contexts. The SVM contains several architectures. In its basic form, SVM performs binary classification using a linear hyperplane. This means that data examples are represented as vectors in a feature space and are separated by a linear hyperplane that maximizes the margin. The data examples that lie on the edges of the margin, known as support vectors, play a crucial role in defining the optimal hyperplane. However, SVMs can also be extended to handle nonlinear classification problems using kernels. Kernels allow for the transformation of the original feature space into a higher-dimensional space where the data can be linearly separable. Commonly used kernel types include the linear kernel, polynomial kernel, and RBF kernel. Training an SVM involves finding the parameters of the hyperplane that optimally separates the classes. This is typically achieved by solving a quadratic optimization problem, where the objective is to minimize a loss function while maximizing the margin.

Table 3. Results of SVM algorithm

SVM architecture	Accuracy	Precision	Recall	F-score
Linear	**75%**	**70%**	**75%**	**68%**
RBF	**76%**	**70%**	**75%**	**70%**
Multi-class	75%	68%	75%	69%
Soft error penalty	75%	71%	75%	67%
Polynomial kernel	**75%**	**56%**	**75%**	**64%**
Hierarchical	75%	71%	75%	67%

Table 3 compares different SVM architectures with varying kernel types. The RBF kernel enables SVM to handle non-linearly separable data by mapping features to a higher-dimensional space and creating non-linear decision boundaries. This flexibility comes at the cost of increased computational complexity and the need to tune the kernel and regularization parameters. Linear SVM, on the other hand, seeks linear decision boundaries and is computationally efficient but may struggle with non-linearly separable data. The table presents accuracy, precision, recall, and F-score values for each architecture. According to the results, the RBF and Multi-class architectures obtain the best accuracy, with a value of 76%. The Linear, Soft Error, Polynomial and Hierarchical architectures all have an accuracy of 75%. This indicates that the RBF and Multi-class architectures can be considered to perform slightly better in terms of correctness compared to the other architectures. However, it is important to consider other performance metrics such as precision, recall, and F-score to get a more complete evaluation of the models.

Table 4 provides a detailed overview of the performance metrics for various deep learning classifiers, including RNN, DNN, LSTM, and TL. Among the

Table 4. Results of deep learning algorithms

Classifier	Accuracy	Precision	Recall	F1-score
RNN	80%	78%	78%	78%
DNN	77%	74%	74%	74%
LSTM	81%	81%	81%	81%
TL	**84%**	**82%**	**82%**	**83%** 4788888889+

classifiers, TL showed an encouraging accuracy of 84%. It consistently demonstrated strong performance across all metrics, indicating its capability to effectively detect instances of cyberbullying. Comparatively, the other classifiers also showcased respectable performance, with RNN achieving an accuracy of 80%, DNN achieving 77%, and LSTM achieving 81%.

According to the related work section, we find that the article by Alduailaj et al and the article by Mouheb et al. gives a high performance result compared to other articles which are respectively 85%, 85%, and 86%. In addition, the results that we have already tested are almost close to the results of the articles, between 77% and 84%.

6 Conclusion and Future Work

In this study, a cyberbullying detection model is proposed to effectively identify and address cyberbullying and offensive speech in the Arabic language. The proposed method consists of essential four key components: text preprocessing, feature extraction and representation, classification, and decision-making. While existing cyberbullying detection models primarily cater to English speakers or languages with similar characteristics, they often fail to capture the unique nuances of the Arabic language. This limitation results in a misrepresentation of cyberbullying instances within Arabic data. To overcome this challenge, the proposed model leverages the power of diversity and incorporates advanced decision-making techniques, leading to improved accuracy in cyberbullying detection. The performance evaluation demonstrates that the TL outperforms other existing models in terms of cyberbullying detection. However, future studies should focus on further exploring and enhancing the techniques used for feature extraction, representation, and selection the model. Additionally, it is important to note that the dataset used in this study comprises translations from other languages into Tunisian Dialect. Given the intricacies of Arabic culture, certain expressions in the Arabic language that may be considered offensive speech while being deemed normal in another language. Therefore, the development of a labeled dataset that accounts for regional variations of cyberbullying in Arabic is crucial to further enhance the performance of future research endeavors.

References

1. ALBayari, R., Abdallah, S.: Instagram-based benchmark dataset for cyberbullying detection in Arabic text. Data **7**(7), 83 (2022)
2. Alduailaj, A.M., Belghith, A.: Detecting Arabic cyberbullying tweets using machine learning. Mach. Learn. Knowl. Extraction **5**(1), 29–42 (2023)
3. AlHarbi, B.Y., AlHarbi, M.S., AlZahrani, N.J., Alsheail, M.M., Alshobaili, J.F., Ibrahim, D.M.: Automatic cyber bullying detection in Arabic social media. Int. J. Eng. Res. Technol. **12**(12), 2330–2335 (2019)
4. Alhashmi, A.A., Darem, A.A.: Consensus-based ensemble model for Arabic cyberbullying detection. Comput. Syst. Sci. Eng. **41**(1) (2022)
5. Farid, D., El-Tazi, N.: Detection of cyberbullying in tweets in Egyptian dialects. Int. J. Comput. Sci. Inf. Secur. (IJCSIS) **18**(7), 34–41 (2020)
6. Guizani, R.: Key, children in Tunisia are victims of violence and hate speech. Alarab (2023)
7. Hinduja, S., Patchin, J.W.: Bullying, cyberbullying, and suicide. Arch. Suicide Res. **14**(3), 206–221 (2010)
8. McInroy, L.B., Mishna, F.: Cyberbullying on online gaming platforms for children and youth. Child Adolesc. Soc. Work J. **34**, 597–607 (2017)
9. Mouheb, D., Abushamleh, M.H., Abushamleh, M.H., Al Aghbari, Z., Kamel, I.: Real-time detection of cyberbullying in Arabic Twitter streams. In: 2019 10th IFIP International Conference on New Technologies, Mobility and Security (NTMS), pp. 1–5. IEEE (2019)
10. Nixon, C.L.: Current perspectives: the impact of cyberbullying on adolescent health. Adolescent Health, Medicine and Therapeutics, pp. 143–158 (2014)
11. Shannag, F., Hammo, B.H., Faris, H.: The design, construction and evaluation of annotated Arabic cyberbullying corpus. Educ. Inf. Technol. **27**(8), 10977–11023 (2022)

Modeling and Data Management

Node2Vec Stability: Preliminary Study to Ensure the Compatibility of Embeddings with Incremental Data Alignment

Oumaima El Haddadi[1,2]([✉]), Max Chevalier[1], Bernard Dousset[1],
Ahmad El Allaoui[2], Anass El Haddadi[2], and Olivier Teste[1]

[1] IRIT, SIG, Université de Toulouse, CNRS, Toulouse, France
{elhaddadi.oumaima,chevalier.max,dousset.bernard,teste.olivier}@irit.fr
[2] LSA, SDIC, ENSAH, Abdelmalek Essaadi University, Tetouan, Morocco
{elhaddadi.oumaima,elallaoui.ahmad,elhaddadi.anass}@uae.ac.ma

Abstract. In dynamic information systems, data alignment addresses challenges like data heterogeneity, integration, and interoperability by connecting diverse datasets. To ensure the stability and effectiveness of these alignments over time, an incremental process may be required, allowing the alignments to be updated as the data evolves. While embedding-based methods are valuable for handling incremental data in the graph learning field, they are underexplored in data alignment. However, before implementing such an approach, it is essential to verify the stability of the embeddings in order to guarantee their reliability and temporal consistency. So, we study the most promising model (i.e. Node2Vec) that exhibits favourable stability in embeddings, particularly with respect to the stability of node embeddings. Despite potential variability in pairwise similarities, the idea of an incremental approach remains reliable, especially with a fixed model. Implementing such an approach can efficiently manage data dynamics in information systems with reduced resource needs. By applying this incremental process to data alignment, it will be possible to efficiently manage heterogeneous data in dynamic information system environments, while minimising resource requirements.

Keywords: Heterogeneous Data · Incremental Data Alignment · Embedding Stability · Dynamic Environment

1 Introduction

In today's dynamic information systems context, data alignment addresses the challenges of integrating diverse data sources coherently [1]. This approach identifies alignments (matches) between different data sources, including schemas and instances, to manage their heterogeneity effectively. Among the various alignment methodologies, embeddings offer a powerful way to represent and compare

M. Mosbah et al. (Eds.): MEDI 2023, CCIS 2071, pp. 79–88, 2024.
https://doi.org/10.1007/978-3-031-55729-3_7

data from diverse sources, revealing underlying similarities and relationships that might be elusive with other methods [2]. The alignment results are used in both requirements-centered storage approaches, such as data integration or schema mapping [3], and non-requirements-centered approaches, such as data lakes [4] or ontologies matching [5].

However, dynamics in data sources requires maintaining and updating alignments as sources evolve, incurring high computational costs. To optimize resource use and ensure long-term alignment efficiency, we aim to propose an illustrative solution for incremental data alignment based on embeddings. This approach enables alignment updates as sources evolve. It can serve as a solution for managing dynamic data, eliminating the necessity of totally recalculating alignments. This incremental process should support a wide range of data changes, including data additions, modifications, and deletions.

Prior to apply incremental embedding approach to achieve incremental data alignment, it's crucial to assess the stability of obtained embeddings to ensure alignment reliability and temporal consistency. The study of embedding stability involves evaluating their sensitivity to data and learning condition variations, ensuring robust alignment maintenance over time. In this paper, our focus is solely on the learning conditions. This assessment determines the reliability of incremental data alignment in dynamic information systems, eliminating the need for recalculating alignments from scratch. To achieve this, we address in our research two research questions: 'How can we study embedding stability?' and 'What is the impact of unstable embeddings on the incremental alignment process?'

In this article, we focus on embedding stability in the following structure: Sect. 2 defines embedding stability. Section 3 provides a review. Section 4 studies the stability of the most promising embedding model for data-alignment: Node2Vec.

2   Definition of Embedding Stability

According to [7], stability in this context is observed when the embedding method consistently manages to generate similar representations for the same data across multiple runs. Furthermore, within the scope of this research, [8] aims to pinpoint the key factors responsible for the instability of the embedding method, drawing from training data. By merging these two objectives, the study of embedding stability can generally be defined as the exploration of the coherence and robustness of numerical vector representations of data over time, in response to data variations and learning conditions.

3   How is Embedding Stability Studied in the Literature?

To examine the compatibility and stability of the embedding method within the context of incremental data alignment, it is crucial to consider the concept of stability of embeddings. Several studies have explored the stability of embedding methods in various domains. For example, [7] investigated the sensitivity of embeddings obtained from corpora (documents) in relation to classification. The study found that distances between nearest neighbors are highly sensitive to minor changes in the corpus, particularly for smaller corpora. As a recommendation, they suggest employing multiple embedding methods and averaging the distances for corpus classification (it is unclear whether this method is computationally expensive in terms of volume and processing time). Similarly, [6] examined the stability of word embedding methods (specifically Word2Vec, fast-Text, and GloVe) for clustering. The results indicated that fastText exhibited greater stability compared to the other two methods. However, it was observed that the stability of Word2Vec improved with multiple executions.

As highlighted in the article by [8], it is important to note that for each execution approach, if reapplied, the constructed embeddings differ even for the same initial data. However, after a series of executions, the model stabilizes. In the context of a dynamic graph, aligning the embeddings between new and previous executions becomes essential. Therefore, considering the insights from these studies, it is necessary to investigate the stability and sensitivity of the chosen embedding method in the context of incremental data alignment. This will help determine the appropriate alignment approach and ensure reliable and consistent results when dealing with evolving data sources.

Nonetheless, it is crucial to underline that the stability of the Node2Vec method (a graph embedding technique we intend to support our incremental alignment approach) has not been extensively explored in prior studies. Furthermore, these studies exclusively relied on cosine similarity to compute the likeness between vector representations. In our specific case study, executing the full Node2Vec-based method may not be imperative. However, a thorough stability analysis of this method remains indispensable to assess any potential risks when deploying it in the context of evolving data sources. By carrying out a stability analysis, we can glean valuable insights into the robustness and reliability of the Node2Vec method itself, as well as its effectiveness when processing dynamic data sources. This contribute to a deeper comprehension of the constraints and potential challenges associated with using the model on evolving datasets. Aligned with the provided definition, we are confronted with two research objectives:

- Examine the stability of the method regarding the condition learning, for example, the selection of hyperparameters (see Sect. 4.1 for details).
- Investigate the stability of the method when data changes.

Note that this paper only focuses on the first objective. In the following section we introduce our experiments.

4 Experiments: Studying Embedding Stability of Node2Vec Model

In the context of incremental data alignment, we have opted for the incremental embedding approach [9]. The main objective of this approach is to learn representations from temporal graphs. It involves generating embeddings for the new nodes using the embedding matrix computed for the initial graph and updating the embeddings of influenced nodes (usually neighbors nodes). The method follows these steps:

- Compute the embedding matrix for the existing graph using a standard graph embedding technique (Node2Vec, as proposed by [10]).
- When new nodes are added, generate embeddings for these nodes and update the unfluenced nodes using Algorithm 1 and Algorithm 2 introduced by [9].

At present, the selected approach only takes into account data additions and modifications. We are actively looking for methods to update alignments in the case of data deletions. Before delving into further development, our first step is to study the stability of Node2Vec, as outlined in the following description section.

4.1 Description and Setup of Our Experiments

Node2vec is unsupervised learning method aims to learn node representations in graphs. It aims to capture the structural and contextual similarity between graph nodes by assigning dense vectors in a reduced-dimensional space. The technique is based on Word2Vec techniques, which is commonly used for word embedding, but adapted to the graph domain.

To investigate the stability of Node2Vec, we construct a graph using the methodology proposed by [2]. The graph is generated from two distinct sources defined by [11]: Authors 1 (with attributes: Authors, Title, DOI, Year, EID, Source Title, and Cited By) and Authors 2 (including attributes: EID, Authors, Cited By, Country, Document Type, City, Access Type, and Aggregation Type). By merging data from these sources, we create a graph that encompasses both instances and schema elements. The resulting graph (Fig. 1) comprises 219 nodes and 870 edges, illustrating relationships between different elements.

Node embeddings are generated using the Node2Vec method, implemented in the Python library [12]. The model is executed 10 times on the graph, employing the following parameters:

DIMENSION $= 100$, WALK_LENGTH $= 30$, NUM_WALKS $= 10$, WINDOW $= 10$

In both datasets, we identified three true alignments of schema elements: EID *(Authors1.EID–Authors2.EID)*, Authors *(Authors1.Authors–Authors2.Authors)*, and Cited By *(Authors1.Cited By–Authors2.Cited By)*. To assess the model's performance, we computed the Root Mean Square Error (RMSE) metric for the 10 scores alignments obtained. According to Table 1, the RMSE values are quite low, indicating that the predictions are close to the actual values.

To address the first research question on how to study stability, we define two scenarios: one focusing on the dynamics of random walks and the other involving stable random walks.

- **Scenario 1:** we perform random walks independently for each of the 10 runs.

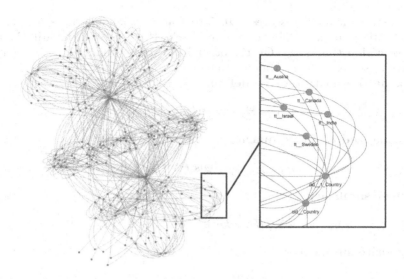

Fig. 1. The left image shows the entire graph obtained. The right image shows a zoomed-in view

- **Scenario 2:** we keep the same walks generated during the initial run for the subsequent 9 runs.

These two scenarios allow us to study the stability of Node2Vec independently from different perspectives, without considering the source changes.

Table 1. Model performance

	EID	Authors	Cited by
RMSE	0.055	0.063	0.052

To examine the stability of the embeddings in the both scenarios, we defined two strategies. Firstly, we compute the similarity of each node to the centroid of the embedding obtained from the 10 runs for the same node. Secondly, we compute the pairwise similarity between nodes within each run and compare these similarities. These strategies enable us to assess the consistency and stability of the embeddings in different contexts.

To compute similarity, we use the following metrics. Unlike some other researchers, we do not solely rely on cosine similarity (Eq. 1), which yields results ranging from -1 to 1. Instead, we employ three other metrics that produce similarity scores within the range of 0 to 1. To achieve this, we normalize the cosine similarity as shown in Eq. 2. Additionally, we have defined two other metrics (Eqs. 3 and 4). According to Fig. 2 (the figure presents three similarity metrics within the range [0, 1]), the normalized cosine curve remains relatively flat between strong similarity scores of 0.95 to 1 and weak similarity scores of 0 to 0.5, indicating minimal differences. Conversely, the opposite similarity is more sensitive within this range. On the other hand, the normalized cosine is more sensitive to scores ranging from 0.5 to 0.95.

Cosine similarity (cosine defined by [13]):

$$cos(\Theta) = u \cdot v / \|u\| * \|v\| \tag{1}$$

Normalized cosine similarity in the range [0:1]:

$$S_{cos_{norm}} = (cos(\Theta) + 1)/2 \tag{2}$$

Linear similarity:

$$S_{lin} = 1 - \Theta/\Pi \; ; \; where : \quad \Theta = arcos(cos_{norm}) \tag{3}$$

Opposite similarity:

$$S_{opp} = 2 * S_{lin} - S_{cos_{norm}} \tag{4}$$

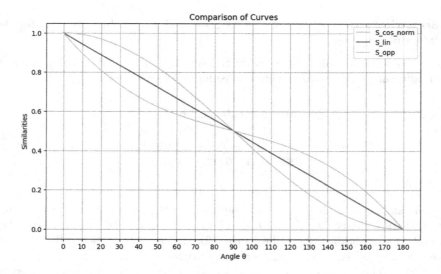

Fig. 2. The figure reveals that cosine similarity (blue curve) tends to be more optimistic than linear similarity (red curve). In contrast, opposite similarity (green curve) demonstrates the opposite effect of cosine similarity compared to linear similarity. (Color figure online)

To compare the variation in the obtained results, we compute the dispersion value. Dispersion refers to the distribution of values within a dataset, measuring the degree of separation between values. In the context of embeddings or similarity scores, dispersion can provide insights into the diversity or similarity of node pairs in a particular graph. In our case, dispersion is the average of the standard deviations obtained for all node embeddings across the 10 runs.

$$Dispersion = 1/n \sum_{i=1}^{n} std_i \; ; \qquad (5)$$

where:

- *n is the total number of node embeddings*
- std_i is the standard deviation of similarity scores for the i_{th} node embeddings across the 10 runs

4.2 Results and Discussion

We obtained the following results after evaluating the different scenarios:

- **Scenario 1 (random walk):** We conducted 10 runs of the model, generating 10 embedding matrices (each 219×100). For each node, we computed similarity to the centroid of the 10 embeddings for that node and the similarity between pairs of nodes in each matrix, resulting in a 23762×10 pairwise similarity matrix. The dispersion for both cases using four similarity metrics is shown in Table 2. The dispersion of similarity values between nodes and the centroid is relatively small (0.004 to 0.008), indicating stable embeddings. However, normalized cosine similarity between pairs of nodes is less stable (0.0013).

  To gain a deeper understanding, we conducted another experiment. We focused on pairs with normalized cosine similarity values greater than 0.95, aiming to ensure a higher level of similarity between the nodes. The results revealed that only a very low percentage of such pairs 0.63% of such pairs (out of 23762) met the criteria in the first run (Fig. 3). According to the figure, we observe a slight difference between the different results of each execution. When we display the alignment results obtained during the 10 executions and compare them with the three true alignments, we consistently obtain the three expected alignments.

- **Scenario 2 (walk fixed):** In this scenario, we also executed the model 10 times, resulting in 10 embedding matrices of size (219×100). Similar to Scenario 1, we calculated the similarity between each node and the centroid of each embedding node.

  Throughout our observations, we consistently found that the similarity between each node's embedding and the centroid, as well as the similarity between pairs of nodes, remained consistently perfect, with a dispersion value of 0.0. This indicates that the embeddings remain stable when using the same walks generated in the first run for subsequent runs. The high consistency in similarity values demonstrates the reliability and robustness of the embeddings in capturing the underlying patterns and relationships in the data across multiple runs.

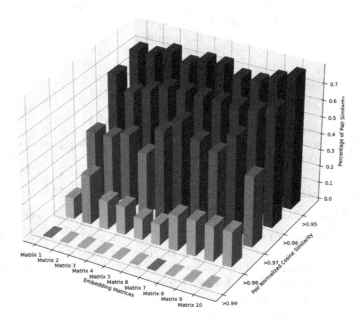

Fig. 3. Bar Plot of the Percentage of pairwise normalized cosine Similarities greater than [0.95, 0.96, 0.97, 0.98, 0.99]

To resume, the embeddings obtained in this study demonstrate desirable stability in capturing node embedding stability and pairwise similarities. The analysis of dispersion of node-to-centroid similarities showed relatively small values, indicating that the embeddings remained stable across the 10 runs. However, pairwise similarities exhibited slightly higher dispersion values, suggesting some variability in pairwise relationships. Despite this, the embeddings remained consistently perfect in both cases, with a dispersion value of 0.0, emphasizing their reliability when using the same walks for subsequent runs. Additionally, the experiment focusing on pairs with high similarity values further reinforced the embeddings' stability. Furthermore, the study highlights the importance of considering the efficiency of fixing the walks in the Node2Vec model.

These findings highlight the importance of verifying the stability of embeddings before implementing any approach to ensure their reliability and temporal consistency, especially in dynamic information systems. Striking a balance between stability and efficiency is crucial in developing an optimal data alignment solution for dynamic information systems. Further research and experimentation are necessary to determine the most effective configuration and parameters for the Node2Vec model to ensure both stability and computational efficiency in the incremental data alignment process.

Table 2. Minimum, Maximum and dispersion of embeddings in both scenarios

			Cosine Similarity Dispersion	Cosine Normalized Dispersion	Lin Similarity Dispersion	Opposite Similarity Dispersion
Random Walk	Centroid	min	0.004	0.002	0.002	0.003
		max	0.016	0.008	0.010	0.012
		dis	**0.008**	**0.004**	0.006	**0.008**
	Pairwise	min	0.004	0.002	0.001	0.0
		max	0.055	0.027	0.014	0.011
		dis	0.026	**0.013**	0.005	0.002

5 Conclusion and Outlook

Incremental alignment methods can play a crucial role in resource optimization within dynamic information systems, reducing computational costs associated with recalculating alignments as data sources evolve. In line with this, our study focuses on examining the stability of Node2Vec, a graph embedding model that we intend to use in the context of incremental data alignment. Evaluation results reveal a favorable embedding stability, especially with fixed generated walks. Despite this result, the existing embeddings were still effective in supporting incremental data alignment without the need for frequent recomputations. However, if frequent recomputations were necessary, it could impact the incremental alignment process as the embeddings might become unstable with other data sources, thus affecting the alignment quality. To improve Node2Vec's stability in dynamic data scenarios, future research and method refinement, such as exploring alternative models like fastText as demonstrated by [6], could improve performance.

In light of these promising results, it is imperative to direct our focus towards advancing the incremental alignment process itself. For future work, it is important to study the stability according to the second research objective (data dynamism), as well as to consider the quality of the base model and the scalability of the process in handling larger datasets and real-world scenarios. This entails evaluating the computational efficiency and memory requirements when dealing with substantial data sources, while also addressing potential challenges related to scalability. By addressing these crucial aspects, the incremental data alignment process can be further optimized, offering a robust and efficient solution for managing evolving information systems with diverse and extensive datasets.

References

1. Sutanta, E., Wardoyo, R., Mustofa, K., Winarko, E.: Survey: models and prototypes of schema matching. IJECE **6**(3), 1011 (2016). https://doi.org/10.11591/ijece.v6i3.9789

2. Cappuzzo, R., Papotti, P., Thirumuruganathan, S.: Local embeddings for relational data integration. In: Proceedings of the 2020 ACM SIGMOD International Conference on Management of Data, pp. 1335–1349 (2020). https://doi.org/10.1145/3318464.3389742

3. Miller, R.J., Haas, L.M., Hernandez, M.A.: Schema mapping as query discovery. In: Very Large DataBase Conference (VLDB), pp. 77–88 (2000)

4. Alserafi, A., Abelló, A., Romero, O., Calders, T.: Keeping the data lake in form: proximity mining for pre-filtering schema matching. ACM Trans. Inf. Syst. 2(38), 3 (2020)

5. Aumueller, D., Do, H.-H., Massmann, S., Rahm, E.: Schema and ontology matching with COMA++. In: ACM International Conference on Management of Data (SIGMOD 2005), pp. 906–908. Association for Computing Machinery, New York (2005)

6. Borah, A., Barman, M.P., Awekar, A.: Are word embedding methods stable and should we care about it? In: Proceedings of the 32st ACM Conference on Hypertext and Social Media, Virtual Event, USA, pp. 45–55. ACM (2021). https://doi.org/10.1145/3465336.3475098

7. Antoniak, M., Mimno, D.: Evaluating the stability of embedding-based word similarities. TACL 6, 107–119 (2018). https://doi.org/10.1162/tacl_a_00008

8. Tagowski, K., Bielak, P., Kajdanowicz, T.: Embedding alignment methods in dynamic networks. In: Paszynski, M., Kranzlmüller, D., Krzhizhanovskaya, V.V., Dongarra, J.J., Sloot, P.M.A. (eds.) ICCS 2021. LNCS, vol. 12742, pp. 599–613. Springer, Cham (2021). https://doi.org/10.1007/978-3-030-77961-0_48

9. Liu, X., Hsieh, P.-C., Duffield, N., Chen, R., Xie, M., Wen, X.: Real-time streaming graph embedding through local actions. In: Companion Proceedings of the 2019 World Wide Web Conference, San Francisco, USA, pp. 285–293. ACM (2019). https://doi.org/10.1145/3308560.3316585

10. StreamNode2Vec. https://github.com/husterzxh/StreamNode2Vec. Accessed 31 June 2023

11. Koutras, C., et al.: Valentine: evaluating matching techniques for dataset discovery. In: IEEE 37th International Conference on Data Engineering (ICDE) (2021)

12. Node2vec python. https://github.com/eliorc/node2vec. Accessed 10 July 2023

13. Cosine.   https://scikit-learn.org/stable/modules/generated/sklearn.metrics.pairwise.cosine_similarity.html. Accessed 18 July 2023

Towards Enabling Domain-Specific Modeling Language Exchange Between Modeling Tools

Rohit Gupta[1]($\boxtimes$), Christoph Binder[2], Nico Jansen[3], Ambra Calà[1],
Jan Vollmar[1], Nikolaus Regnat[1], David Schmalzing[3], and Bernhard Rumpe[3]

[1] Siemens Technology, Munich, Germany
{rg.gupta,ambra.cala,jan.vollmar,nikolaus.regnat}@siemens.com
[2] FH Salzburg, Salzburg, Austria
christoph.binder@fh-salzburg.ac.at
[3] RWTH Aachen University, Aachen, Germany
{jansen,schmalzing,rumpe}@se-rwth.de

Abstract. Domain-specific modeling languages (DSMLs) enable various stakeholders in solving complex modeling problems that are related to their domains. However, as challenges in domain-specific modeling grow in complexity, consistent exchange of domain-specific information between various stakeholders across projects becomes a challenge, as such stakeholders often use a variety of modeling tools suited for their needs. Stakeholders often live within specific modeling tools relevant for developing and using their DSMLs, therefore there is little consideration for generalizing these domain-specific concepts across modeling tools. Further, there also exists a certain lack of exchanging domain-specific constructs effectively for such tools. To solve this challenge, we propose a bi-directional exchange mechanism between Enterprise Architect (EA) and MagicDraw, two commercially established modeling, that allows exchanging individually created DSMLs and their constructs, essential in promoting tool interoperability. As DSMLs represent domain-specific peculiarities within a single area, the proposed exchange mechanism evaluates with a simple illustrative example the applicability of DSML information exchange by extracting and translating these peculiarities across modeling tools. The approach is demonstrated by developing individual extensions to the mentioned tools that support the seamless exchange of domain-specific constructs. Ultimately, the paper presents a first step towards enabling DSML exchange between all the concerned stakeholders and fosters the engineering of DSMLs across modeling tools.

Keywords: Domain-Specific Modeling Language (DSML) · Modeling Tools · Language Exchange

1 Introduction

Model-driven engineering introduces a system model as a unique source of truth including several viewpoints that address all involved stakeholders and their

M. Mosbah et al. (Eds.): MEDI 2023, CCIS 2071, pp. 89–103, 2024.
https://doi.org/10.1007/978-3-031-55729-3_8

cross-cutting concerns. While one model can effectively describe the entire system, it is often broken down into smaller sub-systems that help detail every aspect of the complete system. Stakeholders therefore need to consider the entire product lifecycle to cope with growing complexities in multi-disciplinary modeling projects. To this end, different modeling tools and framework, such as MagicDraw [28], Rational Rhapsody [25], MetaEdit [36], and Enterprise Architect (EA) [16], are used to create various parts of a model within these individual projects [32]. While such tools generally consider and allow the modeling of language constructs, their application in a domain-specific scenario is often challenging in terms of reusability and interoperability. Exchanging artifacts of Domain-Specific Modeling Languages (DSMLs) between proprietary modeling tools is still challenging. While there are studies that detail tool interoperability and model synchronizations between modeling tools [8], applicability of such studies in a real world context is still missing. Consideration for all kinds of stakeholders at all stages of modeling using a DSML is often lost in translation, as DSML projects are often time-bound and only exist in a single modeling environment. Little consideration is made for developing and reusing metamodels with the idea of a language isomorphism across different modeling environments in mind (Sect. 2). In this paper, we share our experiences in establishing a bi-directional exchange mechanism between two established commercial modeling frameworks, MagicDraw and EA, in an industrial context. These tools have been chosen as they are established within the systems engineering community and the need for exchanging artifacts has appeared in actual industrial projects [8]. Further, these tools are primarily based on Unified Modeling Language (UML) standards and can be extended to include domain-specific aspects for a variety of domains. The introduced exchange mechanism enables the synchronization of DSMLs across modeling environments by exchanging the respective modeling language artifacts, where the language definition in an individual tool is extracted and translated to a format reusable by the other tool. An advantage of this technique is that stakeholders can benefit from such an interchange of the DSML across modeling tools, projects, and organizations. The use of such a mechanism allows language engineers to effectively exchange similar concepts of a DSML across multiple tool and do not need to develop DSMLs always from scratch. However, in contrast to other promising model transformation approaches like ATLAS Transformation Language (ATL) [26], our approach does not mainly target exchanging of finished models but rather transforming its meta-information, such as the UML Profile, which can be used for jointly creating those models across a variety of tools. We realize the implementation of the mechanism using custom plugins written in Java that enhance and extend the functionalities of the respective tools. While the proposed approach targets the mentioned modeling frameworks and represents a proof-of-concept (PoC) for introducing such a mechanism, it is generally applicable to similar modeling tools that support language development and where the exchange of a DSML is required. The concepts described in this study takes a first step in ensuring tool interoperability and consistent DSML development views between language engineers across multi-disciplinary modeling projects and modeling environments. The main contributions of the paper, given our expertise in language engineering in the industry and the academia as well as with our experience in developing DSMLs with multiple modeling tools and language workbenches, are as follows:

- We detail a concept for a bidirectional exchange mechanism (Sect. 4) for enabling tool interoperability for the exchange of DSML constructs using the modeling tools MagicDraw and EA (Sect. 5).
- We discuss the extension mechanisms of the modeling tools MagicDraw and EA (Sect. 3) that form the underlying basis of the implementation of the exchange mechanism, along with related approaches (Sect. 8).
- We discuss using a simple example of use cases, actors, and their tasks (Sect. 6), how the concepts of the described exchange mechanisms can be generally transferred to other modeling tools (Sect. 7), and finally conclude the paper in Sect. 9.

2   Background

To easily manage and evolve complex systems across business units and organizations, it is important to build modular reusable DSML elements that can be easily interchanged between modeling tools. Often large organizations have multiple business units that use different modeling tools to realize and solve similar challenges in their domains. On the other hand, small and medium enterprises are limited to using a single modeling tool in a single modeling environment, requiring extensive engineering efforts in developing conceptually similar DSMLs. While efforts have been made to enable the globalization of Domain-Specific Languages (DSLs) using model-based engineering approaches [10], the engineering of DSMLs is still challenging in organizations that require support for development and usage of DSMLs in multiple modeling environments. The exchange of models and language constructs between various model-driven software and systems development tools and workbenches require a large effort [34]. Generally, language engineers and modelers operate within the ecosystem of their modeling environments and do not specifically consider the aspect of reusability of a DSML and its constructs beyond the boundaries of the respective technological spaces. However, more recently the Object Management Group (OMG) has come up with ways to address challenges of exchanging models in a more standard way, such as by using XML Metadata Interchange (XMI) file formats [3]. While this is beneficial in environments that use a more vanilla form of UML, considerations for exchanging models between DSML environments is still lacking. Modeling tools do not particularly generate a standard form of exporting and importing domain-specific constructs for similar models, often leading to issues determining the model elements' semantics in such exchange formats. As an example, if we model UML stereotypes with the tool MagicDraw and export it to an XMI format, it generates elements configured with a metaclass *uml:Stereotype*, while the same model generates a plain UML metaclass *uml:Class* when exported from EA. Such inconsistencies in the underlying stored format of a DSML hinders the reuse of constructs between modeling environments and delays the successful deployment of DSMLs across organizations. It is important to align the metamodels in different modeling tools such that the mapping of DSML constructs is beneficial in easily interchanging and reusing domain concepts across modeling environments.

3   DSML Specification in Modeling Tools

3.1   MagicDraw

MagicDraw is primarily based on UML and supports customization possibilities to enhance the modeling experience of DSML users [21] through modular reusable building blocks of DSMLs [22]. These building blocks consist of reusable language components, that define the language wholly or in part [34]. The customization capabilities of MagicDraw can be leveraged to create a language profile consisting of language component artifacts. An example of such an artifact is a language element, referred to as a *stereotype* in MagicDraw. For each *stereotype*, a set of *customizations* can be configured that are, in essence, rules to define where model elements can be created and which specific properties of the model elements can be displayed to users. MagicDraw supports Java Open API that allows language engineers to integrate automation and creation of custom functionalities that are not supported by default. Model templates allows for the creation of a predefined model that is automatically instantiated during design time. Perspectives in MagicDraw help display various tool and DSML functionalities that users require based on their skill level, novice or advanced. The language profile of the DSML is exported as an Extensible Markup Language (XML) file which allows for a language definition to be reused across other projects and be translated to other modeling tools. The final archived plugin file consists of an additional descriptor XML file that references all the language artifacts and loads the source files into memory so that the DSML is ready available to modelers on tool start-up. In various modeling projects such as in [7], we naturally encountered challenges in translating language profiles [35] across modeling tools with heterogeneous domain concepts as well as in bridging the gap between textual and graphical modeling.

3.2   Enterprise Architect

Within EA, a DSML is implemented in the form of a model-driven generation (MDG) technology [30] file. This term is the EA-specific representation of an individual modeling notation. Thereby, the core concept of the DSML is the UML metamodel, which represents the conceptual architecture and the interconnection of the domain-specific elements. By doing so, the metamodel inherits all elements needed to describe the intended application domain and shows the dependencies with the real world. The MDG allows the extension of EA's modeling capabilities, similar to the customizations in MagicDraw, and consists of three main parts: (1)

UML Profile: the UML Profile consists of all domain-specific elements including their UML metaclass and relationships or restrictions; (2) *Diagram Profile*: the Diagram Profile selects the corresponding UML diagram on which the DSML is built and maps a toolbox to this diagram. Each diagram only allows modeling with a particular set of elements; and (3) *Toolbox Profile*: within the Toolbox Profile, all UML elements are classified within groups according to a modeling context. A natural distinction is separating elements and relationships. Apart from these parts, additional information could be stored in the MDG-file. This information could consist of alternative representations of model elements by selecting suitable images or additional attributes for those elements. As those are not part of the UML Profile, they are additionally exported and stored in an XML file. Ultimately, the file is stored within the MDG Technologies folder of the EA instance. Within this folder, any other DSMLs, such as those implementing the Zachman framework [37], that have been developed and introduced, are stored for provisioning. However, when storing the created MDG into this folder, its information is loaded directly with the start-up of EA and hence no additional setup needs to be performed. Diagrams including the mapped model elements are directly added via the context menu and used for modeling domain-specific system architectures.

4   Concept for a DSML Exchange Mechanism

The capabilities of both tools set the precedent for deriving a generic concept for the transformation of DSMLs between modeling tools as described in Fig. 1. The general concept of exchanging DSML constructs is through: (1) a modeling tool extension that imports and exports DSML constructs and their information through; (2) a standard file format and; (3) by identifying the appropriate metaclasses. Here, the concept details both the export and import processes from one modeling tool to another.

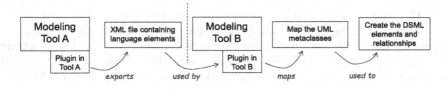

Fig. 1. A general concept for interchanging DSML elements between modeling tools.

Certain customizations are possible in modeling tools that extend their functionalities. This can be achieved through adding a custom code in any General Purpose Language (GPL) in the form of tool plugins or add-ins. Here, modeling tool *A*'s plugin extracts language elements and their properties, such as symbols and relations into an XML formatted file. This is done through Application

Programming Interfaces (APIs) exposed by the modeling tools. Modeling tool B's plugin then imports the XML file and provides capabilities to parse, map, and create the DSML elements. The exported XML file is parsed by B's plugin. This XML file consists of both UML and DSML constructs that convey the necessary information about the various elements of a DSML. In this way, semantic properties of a construct can also be defined as part of the exchange. Next, B's plugin parses the XML file from A and maps the individual elements to its appropriate UML metaclass. This mapping ensures that metadata information is not lost during the exchange process. Finally, the mapped data is translated into DSML elements through a UML profile. B's plugin creates elements and their properties on the profile through APIs so that the DSML consists of the language profiles, elements, and their relationships exported from A to B.

5 Implementation

5.1 Plugin for MagicDraw

While XMI allows defining a common format for standard UML models, it has limitations in encoding accompaniment information for domain-specific constructs, making the interchange of DSML information in modeling tools challenging. Domain-specific XMI models exported from EA contain XML attributes and EA-specific data that is incomprehensible to default MagicDraw import mechanisms. As discussed in Sect. 3, custom functionalities can be added in the form of additional plugins bundled within the final DSML profile in MagicDraw. To this end, we develop a plugin, using MagicDraw's API, to enable importing a language profile and its constructs from EA. The plugin adds an additional context menu item to MagicDraw's default import mechanism for selecting an EA exported XMI file to extract information from it. Once this information is extracted and translated, the respective stereotypes and their customizations are configured and created on a MagicDraw profile. The *referentPath* is the attribute exported from MagicDraw and used for import into EA.

The plugin in MagicDraw imports the EA-XMI file that is constructed in a way that the elements of the language are configured under the XML nodes *uml:Model* and *packagedElement*. An example of a EA-XMI file is shown in Listing 1.1, where the identifiers (*xmi:id*) for each node is modified to illustrate the relations to the respective language elements. The elements from the XMI nodes are stored in custom objects. Next, MagicDraw's OpenAPI is used to create a DSML project, a language profile, and a UML profile diagram, for setting the stereotypes, their customizations and metaclasses. To correctly configure the stereotypes, the extracted information must be translated for the domain-specific classifiers. As there is a possibility for XMI conflicts such as with domain-specific classifiers, special cases must be handled by the plugin, such as identifying the correct metaclasses for a specific *xmi:type* attribute. For example, a *uml:Task* type is translated to a *Class* metaclass, as in a domain-specific context we consider tasks as activities in a UML activity diagram to be the most general UML metaclass. On the other hand, a *uml:Association* type is directly extracted and

Listing 1.1. An example of an (incomplete) XML file generated in EA detailing a DSML with use cases, actors, tasks, and their relations.

```
<uml:Model xmi:type="uml:Model" name="EA_Model">
<packagedElement xmi:type="uml:Package" xmi:id="pkg_ID" name="Package">
<packagedElement xmi:type="uml:Actor" xmi:id="actor_ID" name="Actor"/>
<packagedElement xmi:type="uml:UseCase" xmi:id="uc_ID" name="UseCase"/>
<packagedElement xmi:type="uml:Association" xmi:id="assoc_ID" name="Performs">
<memberEnd xmi:idref="dst_ID"/>
<ownedEnd xmi:type="uml:Property" xmi:id="dst_ID" association="assoc_ID"/>
<memberEnd xmi:idref="src_ID"/>
<ownedEnd xmi:type="uml:Property" xmi:id="src_ID" association="assoc_ID"/>
</packagedElement>
<packagedElement xmi:type="uml:Task" xmi:id="task_ID" name="Task"/>
</packagedElement>
</uml:Model>
```

used, since MagicDraw also uses the same classifier for an association connector. For an association, there must also be restrictions set on the configured stereotypes that allows associations to be created only between certain stereotypes. In this case, the *ownedEnd* nodes of a *packagedElement* in the XMI is first extracted and then the identifiers that specify the source and destination ends of the association are looked up. These identifiers are used to set the *typesForSource* and *typesForTarget* customization properties in MagicDraw that help restrict the use of a connector between specific model elements. A limitation of this import process is that icons for the model elements cannot be stored directly within the XMI file, but have to be transmitted and processed individually outside of the XMI extraction process. Then the stereotypes are created within the language profile. Once all the artifacts are generated, they are stored in a *.mdzip* file, an archive file storing all the information related to the DSML, including any additional plugins. This also includes icons, as scalable vector graphic images, and any model templates that can be provided to modelers for quickly creating models. This DSML profile is now installed in the modelers' MagicDraw environment. Language engineers can, therefore, configure a family of similar DSML profiles across both MagicDraw and EA. MagicDraw provides functionality to export the entire language profile as XMI, which we now use to showcase the import process from MagicDraw to EA.

5.2   Add-In for Enterprise Architect

To enable export and import of DSML information, an Add-In for EA, the so-called RAMI Toolbox [6], is expanded in functionality. More specifically, the RAMI Toolbox allows the engineering of complex production systems for various industrial domains. The toolbox is used for exporting and importing such elements making it ideal to be applied in the context of this paper. Exporting domain-specific information from EA is straightforward, as the MDG file is exported in XML format. This is done as the XML stores the needed information within a single file that requires extraction. However, importing domain-specific elements into EA via the RAMI Toolbox is more complex, as information needs to be extracted from the MagicDraw XMI file that contains the modeled elements. Those elements must then be properly integrated within an MDG file

that can be interpreted by EA. We extract the information out of the Magic-
Draw XMI file to find all domain-specific elements. These are embedded in the
packagedElement XML nodes. The RAMI Toolbox deals with iterating through
the file and storing all such elements for further processing. In general, we consider the elements classified as *uml:Stereotype* to represent a domain-specific
element. Within such a stereotype, the name could be easily extracted via its
same-called attribute. However, the underlying UML class is of major importance, as this attribute defines the underlying foundation of each element. This
means, the third attribute deals as a standardized exchange format between
both frameworks, MagicDraw as well as EA, since DSMLs in either of them
is based on UML standard types. Apart from those attributes, relationships
between the elements also need to be exported from the MagicDraw XMI. To do
so, the attribute *DSL_Customization* is parsed within the file. This node also
contains three attributes, the type of relationship, the source element, and the
target element. Within the relationship type, the *customizationTarget* indicates
the relationship used between the DSML elements. Next, the *typesForSource*
and *typesForTarget* specify the source and target element. When parsing this
information, only the specified relationship is used to interconnect the DSML
elements within the model. Finally, after exporting this information, it needs
to be embedded within an EA-MDG file. More specifically, the parsed DSML
elements including their UML related aspects are stored within the UML Profile
of the MDG, where the Diagram Profile is adjusted and the toolbox is finally
linked for utilization.

6   Application

We illustrate the applicability of our research with an illustrative example involving actors, tasks, and use cases. The goal is to model individual use cases, actors,
tasks, and their relationships independently in both EA and MagicDraw using
the bi-directional exchange mechanism described in Sect. 5. A use case language
is used to model the high-level functionality of a system. An actor language can
be used to model actors, their tasks, and the relations between their tasks. In this
example, we combine both the use case language and the actor language into a
single language, to demonstrate the how the DSML constructs for this language
can be translated from EA to MagicDraw. The MagicDraw plugin allows users
to import an exported XMI file from EA. This XMI file consists of a language
definition with use cases similar to UML use cases, actuators, and their tasks and
an example of this XMI file was listed in Listing 1.1. Generally, use cases, actors,
and associations are directly translated into their respective UML metaclasses.
The plugin extracts the domain-specific constructs from the EA XMI file and
creates the respective stereotypes and their customizations in MagicDraw on a
UML profile diagram. Figure 2 shows the constituents of this profile diagram
consisting of the various stereotypes for the use case, task, actor, association,
and their configured properties that have been imported from EA.

   While the use case, actor, and association elements have been assigned their
respective stereotypes, the domain-specific task element from EA is assigned the

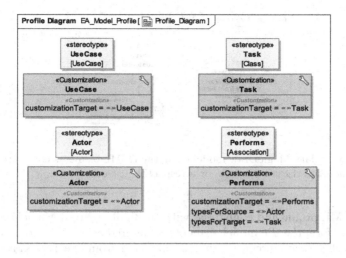

Fig. 2. A MagicDraw UML Profile Diagram for the extracted EA DSML elements.

class metaclass. With a standard XMI file, either the domain-specific constructs or some of their properties cannot be directly interchanged from EA to MagicDraw. To solve this challenge, the plugin is configured to identify constructs that are domain-specific and performs the necessary translation for import into MagicDraw. While the constraints are mainly embedded into properties within MagicDraw elements, EA uses so-called metarelationships or metaconstraints to restrict the misuse of the modeling elements. Thus, the performs relationship directly specifies source and target elements, which is stored into the metaconstraint. To only allow this connector to be used for the actor and task elements, this information is placed within the metarelationship. In order to ensure interoperability between EA and MagicDraw, the plugin deals with translating each other's information and transforms the properties into connectors and vice versa. The plugin is also responsible for calculating the references between the elements based on the XMI file and configures those references, such as setting the source and target elements for a relationship. In doing so, EA can also generate further information specific to an element, and that would be parsed and utilized by the MagicDraw plugin. Similarly, the XMI file exported from MagicDraw, containing the DSML definition, can be imported into EA. On successful import, the DSML elements are embedded into the EA-MDG file and the required information is stored within the UML profile in EA.

6.1 Model Example

Figure 3 shows an example model created in MagicDraw using the DSML constructs that are imported from EA. Here, the model elements are created individually and the respective stereotypes are assigned to each of these elements. This can be done automatically with a model template, that is created for the

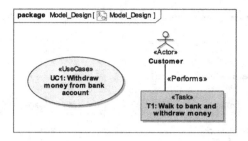

Fig. 3. An exemplary MagicDraw model using the DSML elements configured in Fig. 2 showing an actor performing a task for a respective use case.

imported UML profile and configured with the final archived MagicDraw DSML plugin. Therefore, the *T1* model element, configured as a UML *Class* metaclass, is assigned the *Task* stereotype that is imported from the EA XMI file. Similarly, the *Customer* model element is configured as a UML *Actor* metaclass and receives the stereotype *Actor*. An association between *Customer* and *T1* is assigned the *Performs* stereotype, which is a UML *Association* with the configured source and target stereotypes. Finally, the *UC1* model element is configured with the UML *UseCase* stereotype. The illustrated model can also be replicated in EA using the same DSML exported from MagicDraw as an XML file.

7   Discussion

The approach presented in this paper to solve the challenges of DSML interoperability between modeling tools was conducted with a group of practitioners and researchers. The challenge to enable the exchange of DSML and its constructs was identified as a key research topic in improving the overall DSML engineering process across different research units. While exchanging standard UML constructs across different modeling environments is possible via XMI file formats, achieving the same in a domain-specific environment is currently lacking. Therefore, the presented methodology brings a first perspective using two popular commercial modeling tools, EA and MagicDraw. Previously, language engineers had to build DSMLs that represent similar domain concepts from scratch as concepts that detail the reuse DSML of constructs were lacking in the literature. Although the OMG tried to solve this challenge by creating a common file interchange mechanism, with XMI, it did not consider domain-specific aspects which are crucial to effectively realize Model-based Systems Engineering (MBSE) methodologies. Further, different modeling tools often generate such XMI file formats that are unusable in another modeling environment. Extending the existing modeling tools creates the opportunities for language engineers to design DSMLs in a way that their constructs are now reusable. We developed two Java plugin extensions in each of the modeling tools to showcase the bidirectional interchange of DSML constructs using an example of use cases, actors, tasks, and their relations. The solution enables both standard and domain-specific constructs to be translated across business lines that work on different tools and fosters the reusability of DSML constructs without losing domain-specific information. The presented approach in this paper separates the concerns of collecting DSML constructs in an XML file, parsing those XML files using GPL code, and finally using the tool capabilities to create the language. This separation allows language engineers to easily adopt this solution to their modeling environments as it considers standard file formats that are frequently used [4]. Although our study is conducted in a vendor-locked scenario which introduces a threat to the study, the implementation is described in a way it is seamlessly transferable to other modeling tools that support language development. The use of an XML format and Java code to extend a modeling tool's functionalities makes the solution independent of a modeling tool. This is based on the assumption that a modeling tool exposes APIs, e.g., Java OpenAPI in our case, that allows DSML information such as language elements, models, and their properties to be accessed using an independent GPL code. Although maintaining the plugins require additional effort, we deem this effort low, as modifications to the plugins depend primarily on updates to the API specifications of the involved modeling tools. The applicability of the research using a simple illustrative example demonstrates the capability of the solution to exchange both UML and domain-specific constructs, and can be extended to other modeling tools, or even to other modeling languages such as with SysML. We are currently working to further validate our research in other modeling environments, such as Rational Rhapsody. Therefore, we believe the concepts presented in this paper will encourage language engineers to develop extensions that enable an easy interchange of a DSML and its constructs between various modeling environments that eventually reduces the effort needed in modeling a family or variants of DSMLs across complex modeling environments.

8 Related Work

One technique of interchanging constructs of a modeling language is using standard file formats such as XMI or XML [1,2]. However, with every MBSE approach [10], it is often very challenging to engineer [11], exchange [24], and reuse standard file formats to model domain-specific elements in a variety of domains and across various modeling tools or language workbenches [15,23]. There still exist several challenges on model interchange between model-driven software and systems development tools [34], as the methods and concepts are often only described for a specific purpose and do not consider aspects for generalization. Modeling tools often use different file formats and data structures to store their language concepts such as UML or the Systems Modeling Language (SysML) [13]. The OMG has introduced XMI file formats [3] to exchange models in a more standard way and foster model-to-model transformations such as by using query/view/transformation (QVT) techniques. However, not all tools generate a standard format for exporting domain-specific elements for similar models [38], meaning semantics of the exchange formats are not clearly specified [19,29]. This means that the MBSE tools often lack of conformance to OMG standards and are strictly designed to consider only plain UML concepts. Existing work on bridging the gap between different technological spaces focuses on translating languages between different technological spaces [9,12], improving modeling language variability [20], and the interoperability of models and language elements [5,14,15]. Additionally, techniques for extending DSLs, which are embedded in a predefined tool, via tagging languages [18], tool integration frameworks [31], or through model federation [17] exist. However, realizing a seamless exchange of DSML constructs between different model-driven development tools in a real-world context is still challenging as it requires domain-specific knowledge across multiple modeling environments that involves a large number of stakeholders. Even though tools such as EA and MagicDraw are powerful for exchanging UML constructs [27,33], truly achieving interoperability, exchange of models, and DSML constructs across different modeling tools needs special consideration. This paper therefore describes how we aimed to reduce this gap and show how we enable DSML exchange between two commercial modeling tools, with the basis that the implementation can be extended to other modeling tools.

9 Conclusion

As systems grow more complex and heterogeneous, so does challenges in the interchange of domain-specific constructs between modeling tools that support DSML development. Standard file interchange formats such as XMI have emerged to solve challenges to exchange metadata of UML models. However, different modeling tools generate different XMI file formats for the concerned domain-specific constructs preventing a seamless language exchange between modeling environments. To solve this challenge, we build an exchange mechanism between two commercial modeling tools, Enterprise Architect and MagicDraw, that allows standard UML and DSML constructs to be interchanged. We create Java-based plugins in the modeling tools that extracts domain-specific information and creates language definitions in the respective tools. This allows language and model elements to be exchanged across different modeling environments without losing domain-specific information. Cross-functional teams across different organizations can therefore reuse language definitions for a single domain. Although this paper constitutes a first step towards DSML exchange between modeling tools, further work is ongoing to validate the exchange mechanism in other modeling tools. Ultimately, such a DSML exchange mechanism allows for the interoperability of DSML constructs in complex modeling environments.

References

1. Extensible Markup Language (XML) (2023). https://www.w3.org/XML/
2. Model Interchange Wiki (2023). https://www.omgwiki.org/model-interchange/doku.php

3. XML Metadata Interchange (XMI) (2023). https://www.omg.org/spec/XMI/
4. Bézivin, J.: Model driven engineering: an emerging technical space. In: Generative and Transformational Techniques in Software Engineering: International Summer School, GTTSE 2005, Braga, Portugal, 4–8 July 2005, pp. 36–64 (2006)
5. Bézivin, J., Brunelière, H., Cabot, J., Doux, G., Jouault, F., Sottet, J.S.: Model driven tool interoperability in practice. In: 3rd Workshop on Model-Driven Tool & Process Integration (co-located with ECMFA 2010), pp. 62–72 (2010)
6. Binder, C., Neureiter, C., Lüder, A.: Towards a domain-specific approach enabling tool-supported model-based systems engineering of complex industrial internet-of-things applications. Systems 9(2) (2021)
7. Böhm, W., Broy, M., Klein, C., Pohl, K., Rumpe, B., Schröck, S. (eds.): Model-Based Engineering of Collaborative Embedded Systems. Springer, Cham (2021)
8. Brunelière, H., Cabot, J., Clasen, C., Jouault, F., Bézivin, J.: Towards model driven tool interoperability: bridging eclipse and Microsoft modeling tools. In: Kühne, T., Selic, B., Gervais, M.-P., Terrier, F. (eds.) ECMFA 2010. LNCS, vol. 6138, pp. 32–47. Springer, Heidelberg (2010). https://doi.org/10.1007/978-3-642-13595-8_5
9. Butting, A., Jansen, N., Rumpe, B., Wortmann, A.: Translating grammars to accurate metamodels. In: International Conference on Software Language Engineering (SLE 2018), pp. 174–186. ACM (2018)
10. Cheng, B.H.C., Combemale, B., France, R.B., Jézéquel, J.-M., Rumpe, B.: On the globalization of domain-specific languages. In: Cheng, B.H.C., Combemale, B., France, R.B., Jézéquel, J.-M., Rumpe, B. (eds.) Globalizing Domain-Specific Languages. LNCS, vol. 9400, pp. 1–6. Springer, Cham (2015). https://doi.org/10.1007/978-3-319-26172-0_1
11. Clark, T., van den Brand, M., Combemale, B., Rumpe, B.: Conceptual model of the globalization for domain-specific languages. In: Cheng, B.H.C., Combemale, B., France, R.B., Jézéquel, J.-M., Rumpe, B. (eds.) Globalizing Domain-Specific Languages. LNCS, vol. 9400, pp. 7–20. Springer, Cham (2015). https://doi.org/10.1007/978-3-319-26172-0_2
12. Dalibor, M., et al.: Mind the gap: lessons learned from translating grammars between MontiCore and Xtext. In: International Workshop on Domain-Specific Modeling (DSM 2019), pp. 40–49. ACM (2019)
13. Dalibor, M., Jansen, N., Michael, J., Rumpe, B., Wortmann, A.: Towards sustainable systems engineering-integrating tools via component and connector architectures. In: Jacobs, G., Marheineke, J. (eds.) Antriebstechnisches Kolloquium 2019: Tagungsband zur Konferenz, pp. 121–133. Books on Demand (2019)
14. Diallo, P.I., Champeau, J., Lagadec, L.: A model-driven approach to enhance tool interoperability using the theory of models of computation. In: Erwig, M., Paige, R.F., Van Wyk, E. (eds.) SLE 2013. LNCS, vol. 8225, pp. 218–237. Springer, Cham (2013). https://doi.org/10.1007/978-3-319-02654-1_12
15. Drux, F., Jansen, N., Rumpe, B., Schmalzing, D.: Embedding textual languages in MagicDraw. In: Modellierung 2022 Satellite Events, pp. 32–43. Gesellschaft für Informatik e.V. (2022)
16. Enterprise Architect (2023). https://sparxsystems.com/
17. Golra, F.R., Beugnard, A., Dagnat, F., Guerin, S., Guychard, C.: Using free modeling as an agile method for developing domain specific modeling languages. In: Proceedings of the ACM/IEEE 19th International Conference on Model Driven Engineering Languages and Systems, pp. 24–34 (2016)
18. Greifenberg, T., Look, M., Roidl, S., Rumpe, B.: Engineering tagging languages for DSLs. In: Conference on Model Driven Engineering Languages and Systems (MODELS 2015), pp. 34–43. ACM/IEEE (2015)

19. Grönniger, H., Ringert, J.O., Rumpe, B.: System model-based definition of modeling language semantics. In: Lee, D., Lopes, A., Poetzsch-Heffter, A. (eds.) FMOODS/FORTE -2009. LNCS, vol. 5522, pp. 152–166. Springer, Heidelberg (2009). https://doi.org/10.1007/978-3-642-02138-1_10

20. Grönniger, H., Rumpe, B.: Modeling language variability. In: Calinescu, R., Jackson, E. (eds.) Monterey Workshop 2010. LNCS, vol. 6662, pp. 17–32. Springer, Heidelberg (2011). https://doi.org/10.1007/978-3-642-21292-5_2

21. Gupta, R., Jansen, N., Regnat, N., Rumpe, B.: Design guidelines for improving user experience in industrial domain-specific modelling languages. In: Proceedings of the 25th International Conference on Model Driven Engineering Languages and Systems: Companion Proceedings. ACM (2022)

22. Gupta, R., Kranz, S., Regnat, N., Rumpe, B., Wortmann, A.: Towards a systematic engineering of industrial domain-specific languages. In: 2021 IEEE/ACM 8th International Workshop on Software Engineering Research and Industrial Practice (SE&IP), pp. 49–56. IEEE (2021)

23. Hölldobler, K., Rumpe, B.: MontiCore 5 Language Workbench Edition 2017. Aachener Informatik-Berichte, Software Engineering, Band 32, Shaker Verlag (2017)

24. Hölldobler, K., Rumpe, B., Wortmann, A.: Software language engineering in the large: towards composing and deriving languages. Comput. Lang. Syst. Struct. **54**, 386–405 (2018)

25. IBM Rhapsody (2023). https://www.ibm.com/products/systems-design-rhapsody/

26. Jouault, F., Allilaire, F., Bézivin, J., Kurtev, I., Valduriez, P.: ATL: a QVT-like transformation language. In: Companion to the 21st ACM SIGPLAN Symposium on Object-Oriented Programming Systems, Languages, and Applications, pp. 719–720 (2006)

27. Kern, H.: Study of interoperability between meta-modeling tools. In: 2014 Federated Conference on Computer Science and Information Systems, pp. 1629–1637. IEEE (2014)

28. MagicDraw Enterprise (2023). https://www.3ds.com/products-services/catia/products/no-magic/magicdraw/

29. Maoz, S., Ringert, J.O., Rumpe, B.: Semantically configurable consistency analysis for class and object diagrams. In: Whittle, J., Clark, T., Kühne, T. (eds.) MODELS 2011. LNCS, vol. 6981, pp. 153–167. Springer, Heidelberg (2011). https://doi.org/10.1007/978-3-642-24485-8_12

30. MDG Technologies (2023). https://sparxsystems.com/resources/mdg_tech/

31. Mustafiz, S., Denil, J., Lúcio, L., Vangheluwe, H.: The FTG+PM framework for multi-paradigm modelling: an automotive case study. In: Proceedings of the 6th International Workshop on Multi-paradigm Modeling, pp. 13–18 (2012)

32. Odukoya, K.A., Whitfield, R.I., Hay, L., Harrison, N., Robb, M.: An architectural description for the application of MBSE in complex systems. In: 2021 IEEE International Symposium on Systems Engineering (ISSE), pp. 1–8. IEEE (2021)

33. Ozkaya, M.: Are the UML modelling tools powerful enough for practitioners? A literature review. IET Softw. **13**(5), 338–354 (2019)

34. Rumpe, B.: Modeling with UML: Language. Concepts, Methods, Springer, Cham (2016)

35. Gupta, R., Jansen, N., Regnat, N., Rumpe, B.: Implementation of the SpesML workbench in MagicDraw. In: Modellierung 2022 Satellite Events, pp. 61–76. Gesellschaft für Informatik (2022)

36. Tolvanen, J.P.: MetaEdit+ integrated modeling and metamodeling environment for domain-specific languages. In: Companion to the 21st ACM SIGPLAN Symposium on Object-Oriented Programming Systems, Languages, and Applications (2006)
37. Zachman, J.A.: The Zachman framework for enterprise architecture. Primer for Enterprise Engineering and Manufacturing.[si]: Zachman International (2003)
38. Zusane, U.I., Nikiforova, O., Gusarovs, K.: Several issues on the model interchange between model-driven software development tools (2015)

Healthcare Applications

The Power of Prognosis: Cox Model Prediction of Disease-Free Survival in Colon Cancer

Oussama Belhouichet[1(✉)], Aymen Yahyaoui[1,2(✉)], Wadii Boulila[3,4], Aref Zribi[5], and Rabah Attia[1]

[1] SERCOM Lab, Polytechnic School of Tunisia, University of Carthage, Carthage, Tunisia
oussama.oussema@hotmail.fr
[2] Military Academy of Fondouk Jedid, Nabeul, Tunisia
aymen.yahyaoui@ept.rnu.tn
[3] Robotics and Internet-of-Things Laboratory, Prince Sultan University, Riyadh, Saudi Arabia
[4] RIADI Laboratory, National School of Computer Sciences, University of Manouba, Manouba, Tunisia
[5] Department of Medical Oncology, Military Hospital of Instruction of Tunis, Tunis, Tunisia

Abstract. Colon cancer requires a lot of continuous monitoring either before the first discovery of the disease or even after the cure since, at any time, the patient can suffer a recurrence. Adequate treatments for colon cancer patients need to be determined using modern techniques. Indeed, artificial intelligence offers advanced techniques and methods to analyze the disease-free survival of patients with different types of treatment. The appropriate treatment choice, especially for chemotherapy, is very difficult and needs careful monitoring and analysis by doctors. In this work, an innovative method based on statistical algorithms, namely the Cox model, is proposed to help oncology doctors make the right treatment decision by allowing them to discover the different results and consequences of the different possible treatments following disease-free survival prediction. This work was tested and validated by medical staff at the military hospital of instruction in Tunisia.

Keywords: Statistical Algorithms · Colon cancer · Survival Analysis · CoxPH

1 Introduction

Colon cancer, also known as colorectal cancer, is a type of cancer that affects the colon (the large intestine) and the rectum [3]. It develops when abnormal cells in the colon or rectum grow and divide uncontrollably, forming a tumor. Over time, these tumors can grow and invade nearby tissue, eventually spreading to

M. Mosbah et al. (Eds.): MEDI 2023, CCIS 2071, pp. 107–120, 2024.
https://doi.org/10.1007/978-3-031-55729-3_9

other parts of the body. Colon cancer may manifest through signs such as weight loss, a change in bowel movements, abdominal pain, and blood in the feces [9]. Several risk factors for colon cancer exist, including age, a family history of the disease, and particular lifestyle habits such as smoking, obesity, and a diet that includes high amounts of red or processed meats [20]. Colon cancer has four stages, requiring surgical intervention to remove the tumor. Afterward, patients with early-stage colon cancer only need to be followed up. However, patients in the third and fourth stages need to receive chemotherapy. The problem then occurs for second-stage patients who can either be monitored only or undergo chemotherapy [8].

In this paper, an innovative approach is proposed to help medical staff identify the disease-free survival of the second stage of colon cancer. A predictive system for colon cancer is presented which is dedicated to the Tunisian population that differs in several aspects from other populations in terms of lifestyle, including diet, gastronomy, environment, and race. Oncologists are provided with a handy tool to predict disease-free survival for second-stage colon cancer in the Tunisian population, accounting for unique lifestyle factors [17]. The tool offers benefits such as early detection, targeted screening, reduced costs, personalized treatment, and enhanced disease understanding.

This paper is structured as follows. First, Sect. 1 introduces the research topic and outlines the research questions and objectives. Section 2 provides the background of the study, explaining the context and importance of the research topic. In Sect. 3, previous research relevant to the study is reviewed, and the existing knowledge is linked to the new discoveries presented in this paper. Section 4 details the proposed approach, outlining the methodology and data analysis techniques used in the study. The results of the study are presented in Sect. 5, followed by a detailed discussion of the findings and their implications in Sect. 6. Finally, Sect. 7 provides a conclusion that summarizes the main points of the paper, highlights the contributions of the study, and suggests avenues for future research.

2 Background

Colorectal cancer is the second most common cancer in terms of mortality, causing nearly 17,000 new deaths per year. The 5-year relative (cancer-related) survival is 57% for all stages combined. More than 90% of colon and rectal cancers are sporadicheir incidence regularly increases with age. We present, in the following, some information about its stages, treatments, prognosis, and survival analysis.

2.1 Colon Cancer Stages

According to [14], Colon cancer progresses through four stages. The first stage involves cancer confined to the colon lining, while the second sees growth through the lining and possible lymph node involvement. In stage 3, cancer spreads to nearby organs or nodes, and in stage 4, it metastasizes to distant organs. Detecting cancer earlier enhances treatment options, influenced by invasion depth, lymph node presence, and distant metastasis. The prognosis worsens as the cancer advances. Treatment options include surgery, radiation, and therapies like chemotherapy, immunotherapy, and targeted therapy, aiming to manage the disease and symptoms. The cancer's stage is a vital prognostic factor, influencing predictions of disease-free survival. Figure 1 shows the different stages of colon cancer, which present one of the most important prognostic factors that will later be used in the prediction of disease-free survival of the patient.

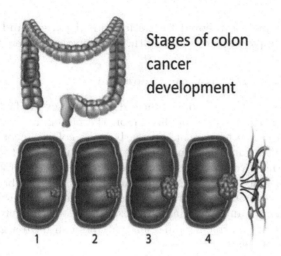

Fig. 1. Tumor evolution according to stage [4]

2.2 Colon Cancer Treatment

Although surgery is the primary treatment for colon cancer, chemotherapy and targeted therapies [21] are often given alone or in combination. The treatment of colon cancer typically depends on the stage of cancer, as well as the patient's overall health and personal preferences. The most common treatments for colon cancer include [7]:

– **Surgery:** It is typically the primary treatment for colon cancer, and the goal is to remove the cancerous tumor along with a margin of healthy tissue. Depending on the cancer stage, the surgeon may remove only a portion of the colon or the entire colon.
– **Chemotherapy:** It is a treatment that uses drugs to kill cancer cells. It can be used before or after surgery to shrink the tumor or to kill any remaining cancer cells after surgery.

- **Radiation therapy:** It uses high-energy rays to kill cancer cells. It can be used before or after surgery, and it is often used in combination with chemotherapy.
- **Targeted therapy:** It uses drugs that target specific molecules in cancer cells to stop them from growing and spreading. These drugs can be used alone or in combination with chemotherapy.
- **Immunotherapy:** It is a treatment that helps the immune system fight cancer. It can be used alone or in combination with chemotherapy.
- **Clinical trials:** Patients with colon cancer may be eligible for clinical trials, which are research studies that test new treatments or new combinations of treatments.

The treatment plan is tailored to the individual patient and considers the stage of cancer, the patient's overall health, and personal preferences.

2.3   Prognosis and Survival for Colon Cancer

The prognosis and survival for colon cancer depend on several factors, including the stage of cancer, the location of the tumor, the patient's overall health, and the patient's response to treatment. For early-stage colon cancer (stages 1 and 2), the 5-year survival rate is around 90%. If cancer has spread to nearby lymph nodes (stage 3), the 5-year survival rate drops to about 70–80%. For patients with distant metastasis (stage 4), the 5-year survival rate is about 10–15%. It is important to note that these survival rates are general estimates and cannot predict the outcome for an individual patient. Some people can have a recurrence even years after their treatment, and some patients can have a good prognosis despite the cancer stage.

Early detection of colon cancer can improve survival rates [11,13]. Regular screening colonoscopies, starting at age 50 or earlier if there is a family history of colon cancer, can detect colon cancer early when it is most treatable.

The survival rate also varies depending on the location of the tumor. The survival rate is higher for colon cancer located in the proximal colon (right side of the colon) than for cancer located in the distal colon (left side of the colon) and rectum.

The following are some prognostic or predictive factors for colorectal cancer:

- **Stage:** At the point of diagnosis, cancer can be categorized and identified according to its location and the degree to which it has spread throughout the body. This process is referred to as staging and serves to classify cancer based on these factors.
- **Surgical margins:** Surgical margin refers to the presence of cancerous tissue in contact with the inked boundaries of the resection area1. Surgical margin analysis helps to establish a reliable prognosis for the future course of cancer and the risk of recurrence.
- **Carcinoembryonic antigen level:** it is a glycoprotein involved in cell adhesion. Normally, CEAs are produced in gastrointestinal tissues during fetal

development and cease production before birth. As a result, CEAs are present only at low levels (about 2–4 ng/mL) in the blood of healthy adults. However, serum CEA levels increase in some types of cancer and heavy smokers.
– **Grade:** describes the appearance of the cancerous cells.

2.4 Survival Analysis

Survival analysis is a statistical method crucial for estimating the probability of survival in patients facing specific diseases, like colon cancer. It assesses treatment effectiveness and identifies influential factors. Types of survival analysis include Kaplan-Meier, useful for comparing treatment outcomes [6], the Cox proportional hazards model, evaluating factors' impact on death risk, and the Fine and Gray model, addressing competing risks. This technique analyzes time until events like death or recurrence. For colon cancer, it gauges survival likelihood, revealing key factors like tumor attributes and patient characteristics. This data aids treatment decisions and prognostication, facilitating disease management and research. In essence, survival analysis empowers clinicians, enhancing colon cancer treatment choices and patient well-being.

3 Related Work

This section will review and compare important related works that predicted colon cancer in several populations. Then, we will present a review summary in Table 1.

3.1 Prediction Using Random Forest on a US Population

The prediction model for colon cancer in the US population was constructed using a 2-class decision forest architecture based on the random forest method [10]. The variables examined were categorized into four groups: patient, facility, tumor, and treatment characteristics.

Patient: This group included age, sex, race/ethnicity, and comorbid diseases, as well as insurance status, education level, median household income, rural or urban residence, and distance from the hospital.

Facility: Hospital characteristics such as community, academic, integrated network cancer program, or others were considered.

Tumor: The T, N, and M scores and stage group, both clinically and pathologically, were evaluated. Other tumor variables, such as tumor grade, extracapsular spread, and perineural invasion, were also analyzed. To avoid redundancy, information on metastatic disease was merged into a new variable.

Treatment: Primary course information was limited to surgical or radiotherapy treatment modalities.

The study yielded a 5-year overall survival prediction. However, there were some limitations, including missing data in over 50% of cases for certain variables, such as lymphovascular invasion and human papillomavirus status, which could hinder survival prediction. The model obtained an accuracy equals to 71%.

3.2 Prediction Using coxPH on a US Population

The method used in this study was a nomogram that estimated the likelihood of cancer recurrence after curative surgery [22]. Prognostic factors were evaluated using multivariable analysis through Cox regression, and nonlinear continuous variables were represented using cubic splines.

The research gathered clinicopathologic factors that could potentially predict tumor recurrence. Several elements were taken into account, such as the patient's age, gender, the site of the tumor, levels of carcinoembryonic antigen before surgery, tumor differentiation, the number of lymph nodes that tested positive or negative, the presence of lymphovascular and perineural invasion, and how deeply the tumor penetrated the colon wall (known as T stage).

If any pathologic factors were missing from the original reports, a pathologist reviewed the specimens again. The institutional review board approved the study before it began.

Cox proportional hazards regression was utilized for multivariate analysis. To enable non-linear relationships, restricted cubic splines were used to model continuous variables. The grouping of categorical variables was decided before modeling, and the proportional hazards assumption was confirmed through tests of correlations with time and residual plot analysis.

The c-indexes of the nomograms for cancer-specific survival (CSS) and overall survival (OS) were 0.816 and 0.777, respectively.

3.3 Prediction Using Competing Risk Model on a Japanese Population

The aim of the study conducted by [16] is to develop a predictive model for organ-specific recurrence after colon cancer resection. It involved 1720 patients treated at a Tokyo hospital from 1997 to 2015. Retrospective data collection produced a risk score via a competing risk model. The model was validated with two patient groups: 973 from 1997–2009 and 747 from 2010–2015. Multiple factors, including age, sex, tumor attributes, and treatment details, were analyzed. Specific factors were chosen for liver and lung metastasis prediction models. External validation showed promising results with AUCs of 0.78 for liver metastasis and 0.72 for lung metastasis at 60 months.

Table 1. Related Works

Population	Variables	Model	Result
USA [10]	Grouped into the patient, facility, tumor, and treatment	Decision Forest	71% Accuracy
USA [22]	age, sex, location, antigen level, differentiation, positive and negative nodes, stage, peri- neural invasion, lymphovascular invasion	Cox Regression	0.816 c-index for CSS 0.777 c-index for OS
Japanese [16]	age, sex, site og primary tumor, size, differentiation, histology, T, perioperative blood transfusion, anastomotic leakage, CT, N, type of surgery	Competing Risk Model	0.78 Liver(AUC) 0.72 Lung(AUC)

4   Cox-Based Approach

The proposed system is described in Fig. 2. It has three main steps: data collection and cleaning, data transformation, and survival algorithm execution and evaluation.

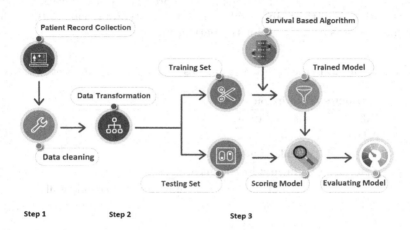

Fig. 2. The design of the proposed system.

4.1   Data Collection and Selection

Patient Records Collection: The effectiveness of the model hinges on data quality [1,5,12]. While exploring existing public datasets, it became evident that a dataset meeting the specific needs for predicting prognostic factors in Tunisian colon cancer patients was unavailable. Consequently, we undertook the task of gathering patient records from a military hospital in Tunis, Tunisia. Over two months, with the aid of a Medical oncologist due to handwritten and complex records, we meticulously compiled a dedicated dataset for Tunisia's colon cancer patients.

Data Selection: We selected the medical records of the patients of the oncology department who had already spent 5 years of follow-up in this department from the year 2012 to 2016, and we have chosen all the records that do not lack any feature. We went through all the medical records found in this period and then extracted the prognostic factors determined by the Oncologist. We ended up with a dataset of 100 patients described by prognostic factors recommended by our oncologist.

4.2 Data Preparation and Transformation

Prognostic factors recommended by our oncologist are shown and described in Table 2. For instance, the differentiation (Diff) feature can have 3 values: poor, moderate, and good. We represented the poor value with 1, the moderate value with 2, and the good value with 3. The Tumour location (T_loc) feature can have three values: left, right, or Transversal. We represent the left location with 1, the right with 2, and the transversal with 3. Chemotherapy feature (CT) takes two values: 1 if was considered for the patient and 0 otherwise.

Table 2. Representation of prognostic factors in the dataset

Attributes	Description
Diff	Differentiation
Adeno	Adenocarcinoma
Ev	Vascular Emboli
Epn	Perineural Envelopment
T	Depth of tumour penetration into the colonic wall
Occ	Occlusion
Ace	Carcinoembryonic Antigen
T_loc	Tumor Location
Op_u	Emergency surgery
CT	Chemotherapy
N	Infected nodes

4.3 Cox Survival Algorithm

Survival analysis is a statistical technique that seeks to forecast when an event will occur, such as death, the identification of a disease, or the breakdown of a mechanical component. The most popular method for analyzing censored data (any data for which we do not know the exact event time) is the Cox proportional hazards model. Although this method does not scale well to large dimensions datasets, it is efficient for small datasets [18]. Algorithm 1 describes in details the Cox Proportional Hazards Algorithm. The input of the algorithms is a set of observations, each with a time-to-event variable (line 1) (e.g. time until patient recurrence). In the initialization phase (line 3), covariates (e.g. occlusion, differentiation, etc.) are set. The hazard of an event (e.g. recidivism) at time t, $h(t|x)$ for an individual with covariate values x is given in line 5, where $h0(t)$ is the baseline hazard function, and beta is a vector of coefficients to be estimated. A loop (lines 6 to 13) is entered until all coefficients converge. Beta coefficients are estimated by maximizing the partial likelihood function shown in line 11 where T is the maximum time in the dataset, $h(ti|xi, beta)$ is the hazard function for individual i at time t_i, $S(ti|xi, beta)$ is the survival function for individual i at time t_i, and $d(i)$ is an indicator variable that is 1 if individual i experienced an event and 0 if they did not. Estimated coefficients are used to make predictions about the hazard or survival for new individuals with different covariate values. The model can be extended to handle more complex situations, such as time-dependent covariates and competing risks.

Algorithm 1. Cox Proportional Hazards Model

1: **Input:** Data set with time-to-event variable and covariates
2: **Output:** Estimated coefficients of the model
3: Initialize the coefficients β to some starting values
4: Assume hazard function
5: $h(t|x) = h_0(t) \exp(\beta^T x)$
6: **while** coefficients have not converged **do**
7:     **for** i = 1 to n **do**
8:         Calculate the hazard function $h(t_i|x_i, \beta)$
9:         Calculate the survival function $S(t_i|x_i, \beta) = \exp(-\int_0^{t_i} h(t|x_i, \beta)dt)$
10:     Calculate the partial likelihood function
11: $L(\beta) = \prod_{i:t_i<T}(h(t_i|x_i,\beta))^{d_i} \prod_{i:t_i\geq T}(S(t_i|x_i,\beta))^{1-d_i}$
12:     Update the coefficients β by taking the derivative of $L(\beta)$ and setting it to zero (taking a step in the negative gradient direction: $beta = beta - step * \frac{\partial L}{\partial beta}$)
13:     Check convergence criteria (e.g. change in beta is below a threshold)
14: **Return** β

---

5   Experimentation and Results

In this section, we present the different steps done in order to create the model that meets our needs. In order to use a survival model, we need to add a "Date" column for the observed time (the length of time over which we have a complete view of the patient's situation). The Date feature takes values from 1 (end of the first semester) to 10 (end of 5 years). We added also our target feature "RCD" in which we have indicated the event studied: a patient who does not suffer a relapse. The RCD feature takes two values: 1 if cancer reappeared for the patient and 0 otherwise. We noticed that the prognostic factor "Adenocarcinoma" (Adeno) was present in all the medical records we processed, so we decided to drop this factor.

Figure 3 in the study displays how the predictors influence the DFS (disease-free survival). A predictor that has a hazard ratio close to 1 does not have a significant impact on survival. If the hazard ratio is less than 1, the predictor is considered protective, meaning it is associated with better survival. On the other hand, if the hazard ratio is greater than 1, the predictor is associated with increased risk or reduced survival. The two most predictive factors that badly affect a patient's condition are Op_rug (if they are operated on emergency) followed by the number of positive nodes (N). On the other hand, the factors that affect the patient's condition are chemotherapy (CT) and differentiation (Diff).

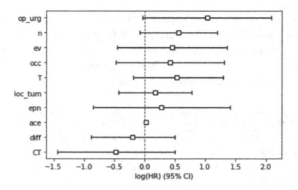

Fig. 3. Predictors impact on survival

5.1   Model Creation

We divided our dataset into two parts: Train Set (80%) and Test Set (20%). We assigned the prognostic factor columns (Diff, Epn, Rv, T,...) to the dataframes we created from the Train and Test sets. X_Train contains the prognostic factors for the training and, X_Test contains the prognostic factors for the test. The column RCD is also assigned to the event indicator E where it is specified whether the event has occurred or not. The Date column is assigned to the observed time T during which we have information on the status of the event (has occurred or not).

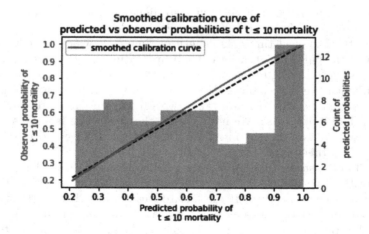

Fig. 4. Calibration curve

In Fig. 4, we present a calibration curve for our Cox regression model, showcasing the alignment between predicted and observed probabilities of survival over time. Notably, this calibration curve closely follows the ideal diagonal line, signifying the overall reliability of our model's predictions. Towards the end of the curve, a slight deviation is observed, with predicted probabilities marginally surpassing the diagonal. This indicates that our model tends to be slightly optimistic in estimating survival probabilities in the later stages of the analysis. However, the near-diagonal alignment for the majority of the curve underscores the model's strong performance and its ability to provide trustworthy survival probability estimates.

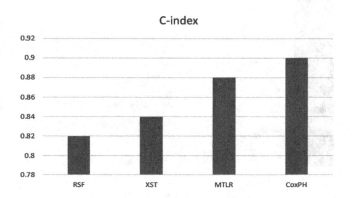

Fig. 5. C-index comparison for different models

5.2   Metrics and Model Choice

The concordance index (C-index) [19] was considered as an evaluation metric. It is a form of generalization of the area under the ROC curve that can handle censored data. It is the overall assessment of the discriminatory ability of the model. It evaluates the capacity of the model to correctly provide a reliable ranking of survival times according to individual hazard scores. Figure 5 shows the C-index for different models. RSF and XFT have the lowest scores with 0.82 and 0.84, respectively. On the other hand, MTLR and CoxPH have 0.88 and 0.9, respectively. Therefore, Cox which has the highest score was considered in the study.

5.3   Comparison with Other Tools

There is a Web tool accredited by oncology services worldwide made by MSKCC, the cancer treatment and research institution in New York City. This tool is very powerful for DFS prediction, but it sometimes becomes unavailable because of technical problems and it does not consider the prognostic factors elected by the medical staff of the military hospital in Tunisia. It is not adapted to the Tunisian population which is neither a Caucasian population nor a Chinese population. Each population has its own characteristics from a genetic point of view, diet, rhythm of life, etc. So it is quite normal that they are not similar. By comparing the results of our research with MSKCC, we can note a quite resemblance in terms of efficient prediction. However, since the prognostic factors are different, each tool is constructed to deal with a specific population and our tool is adapted to the Tunisian population. We have integrated our model into a Web application so that HMPIT doctors can use it easily to predict Disease-free survival.

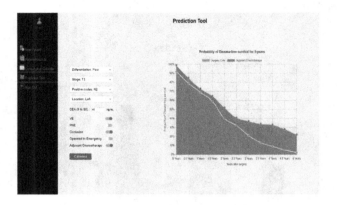

Fig. 6. DFS prediction

Figure 6 shows our tool DFS curves for five years according to prognostic factors (differentiation, stage, location...). The blue curve corresponds to surgery only and the red curve corresponds to adjuvant chemotherapy. From the two curves, we can determine chemotherapy benefits which is very helpful to make doctors decide to give the treatment or not.

6 Discussion

Survival models are important tools in predicting disease-free survival for cancer patients. In the case of colon cancer, the recurrence of the disease is the event of interest. Survival models can incorporate multiple variables, including demographic information, medical history, and treatment history, to predict the risk of an event occurring. One of the most commonly used survival models is the Cox proportional hazards regression model. This model estimates the effect of each predictor on the hazard function, which represents the instantaneous risk of the event of interest occurring at a given time. The model can then be used to make predictions for new patients by inputting their medical and treatment information. In conclusion, survival models are useful tools for predicting disease-free survival for cancer patients. The Cox proportional hazards regression model is one of the most commonly used models. However, survival models have limitations and should be used alongside other factors when making treatment decisions. To improve the accuracy of the model's predictions, it is important to use a large and diverse dataset, to validate the model using cross-validation techniques, and to consider additional predictors that may be relevant to disease-free survival.

7 Conclusion

This paper introduces a decision-support and management tool for colon cancer patients, utilizing a survival analysis approach. The primary contribution of this work is the development of a model for predicting colon cancer DFS tailored to the Tunisian population, taking into account its unique characteristics. Our study emphasizes the importance of continuous monitoring and treatment for cancer patients and highlights the predictive value of the recurrence rate for patient outcomes. The model we have developed has the potential to assist healthcare professionals in identifying the best treatment options for their patients. Future research directions for this study include integrating diverse data sources such as genomics, imaging, and electronic health records into survival models for enhanced accuracy. Leveraging deep learning algorithms can further advance precise survival predictions for colon cancer patients [2, 15, 17]. An essential expansion involves applying personalized medicine and customizing treatments based on individual genomic and relevant data. Combining personalized medicine with survival models enables more tailored predictions and treatment suggestions.

References

1. Al-Sarem, M., Saeed, F., Alsaeedi, A., Boulila, W., Al-Hadhrami, T.: Ensemble methods for instance-based Arabic language authorship attribution. IEEE Access **8**, 17331–17345 (2020)
2. Ben Atitallah, S., Driss, M., Boulila, W., Ben Ghezala, H.: Randomly initialized convolutional neural network for the recognition of Covid-19 using X-ray images. Int. J. Imaging Syst. Technol. **32**(1), 55–73 (2022)
3. Burkitt, D.P.: Epidemiology of cancer of the colon and rectum. Cancer **28**(1), 3–13 (1971)
4. Cruz, K.D.: Cytecare. https://cytecare.com/media/stages-of-colon-cancer-what-does-it-mean/
5. Driss, K., Boulila, W., Batool, A., Ahmad, J.: A novel approach for classifying diabetes' patients based on imputation and machine learning. In: 2020 International Conference on UK-China Emerging Technologies (UCET), pp. 1–4. IEEE (2020)
6. Durczak, K., Selech, J., Ekielski, A., Żelaziński, T., Waleński, M., Witaszek, K.: Using the Kaplan-Meier estimator to assess the reliability of agricultural machinery. Agronomy **12**(6), 1364 (2022)
7. Eslami, M., et al.: Importance of probiotics in the prevention and treatment of colorectal cancer. J. Cell. Physiol. **234**(10), 17127–17143 (2019)
8. Haghi, M., Hashemi Doulabi, H., Contreras, I., Bhuiyan, N.: Integrated consultation and chemotherapy scheduling with stochastic treatment times. J. Oper. Res. Soc. 1–16 (2022)

9. John, S., George, S., Primrose, J., Fozard, J.: Symptoms and signs in patients with colorectal cancer. Colorectal Dis. **13**(1), 17–25 (2011)
10. Karadaghy, O.A., Shew, M., New, J., Bur, A.M.: Development and assessment of a machine learning model to help predict survival among patients with oral squamous cell carcinoma. JAMA Otolaryngol.-Head Neck Surg. **145**(12), 1115–1120 (2019)
11. Koppad, S., Basava, A., Nash, K., Gkoutos, G.V., Acharjee, A.: Machine learning-based identification of colon cancer candidate diagnostics genes. Biology **11**(3), 365 (2022)
12. Kumar, A., Kaur, A., Singh, P., Driss, M., Boulila, W.: Efficient multiclass classification using feature selection in high-dimensional datasets. Electronics **12**(10), 2290 (2023)
13. Masud, M., Sikder, N., Nahid, A.A., Bairagi, A.K., AlZain, M.A.: A machine learning approach to diagnosing lung and colon cancer using a deep learning-based classification framework. Sensors **21**(3), 748 (2021)
14. Mukund, K., Syulyukina, N., Ramamoorthy, S., Subramaniam, S.: Right and left-sided colon cancers-specificity of molecular mechanisms in tumorigenesis and progression. BMC Cancer **20**(1), 1–15 (2020)
15. Murugesan, M., Arieth, R.M., Balraj, S., Nirmala, R.: Colon cancer stage detection in colonoscopy images using YOLOv3 MSF deep learning architecture. Biomed. Signal Process. Control **80**, 104283 (2023)
16. Nagata, H., et al.: Development and validation of a prediction model for organ-specific recurrences after curative resection of colon cancer. Diseases Colon Rectum **62**(9), 1043–1054 (2019)
17. Pacal, I., Karaboga, D., Basturk, A., Akay, B., Nalbantoglu, U.: A comprehensive review of deep learning in colon cancer. Comput. Biol. Med. **126**, 104003 (2020)
18. Spooner, A., et al.: A comparison of machine learning methods for survival analysis of high-dimensional clinical data for dementia prediction. Sci. Rep. **10**(1), 1–10 (2020)
19. Su, W., He, B., Zhang, Y.D., Yin, G.: C-index regression for recurrent event data. Contemp. Clin. Trials **118**, 106787 (2022)
20. Thompson, C.A., Begi, T., Parada, H., Jr.: Alarming recent rises in early-onset colorectal cancer (2022)
21. Xie, Y.H., Chen, Y.X., Fang, J.Y.: Comprehensive review of targeted therapy for colorectal cancer. Signal Transduct. Target. Ther. **5**(1), 22 (2020)
22. Zhang, Z., Luo, Q., Yin, X., Dai, Z., Basnet, S., Ge, H.: Nomograms to predict survival after colorectal cancer resection without preoperative therapy. BMC Cancer **16**, 1–21 (2016)

Transfer Learning in Segmenting Myocardium Perfusion Images

Yasmin E. Younis[1]([✉]), Sahar Fawzi[1,2], and Mustafa Elattar[1]

[1] Medical Imaging and Image Processing Group Center for Informatics Science, Nile University, Giza 12588, Egypt
{ya.emad,sfawzi,melattar}@nu.edu.eg
[2] Faculty of Engineering, Cairo University, Giza, Egypt

Abstract. Cardiac magnetic resonance perfusion (CMRP) images are used to assess the local function and permeability of the heart muscle. The perfusion analysis requires the segmentation of cardiac inner and outer walls of the left ventricle (LV). However, the available perfusion datasets are limited or have no annotations. A fair dataset was annotated to employ the latest and most effective Deep Learning (DL) methodologies. In this paper, we employ similar cardiac imaging protocols in terms of cardiac geometry by initially training using CINE images and performing domain adaptation to CMRP images using Unet architectures with different backbones (VGG16, ResNet50, and ResNet152). We also experimented transfer learning (TL) with ImageNet weights by using these architectures separately. Surprisingly, the results were considerable; using CINE images' weights with ResNet50 as a backbone encoder had better results than other models. This experiment's validation results of dice coefficient, recall, precision, and dice loss results are 0.85, 0.776, 0.94, and 0.148, respectively. The complexity of the data was investigated by finding the intra-observer error using the dice coefficient; the mean result of the intra-observer was 0.796. This study showed how valuable finding TL may help in studying the CMRP images and if the insufficiency of data could be overcome to develop more models to assist in diagnosing heart diseases.

Keywords: Deep Learning · Cardiac Magnetic Resonance Perfusion · CINE · Cardiovascular Diseases · Myocardium · MRI · Stochastic Processes · Coronary Artery Diseases · Medical Imaging

1 Introduction

Recently, cardiovascular diseases have been the most common disease globally. About 17.9 million people died from cardiovascular diseases in 2019 especially coronary heart diseases (CAD), representing 32\% of all global deaths according to WHO [1]. CAD can be diagnosed using different modalities. These modalities have some limitations, such as exposure to radiation, while difficult acoustic windows in certain patients limit echo-cardiograph.

M. Mosbah et al. (Eds.): MEDI 2023, CCIS 2071, pp. 121–129, 2024.
https://doi.org/10.1007/978-3-031-55729-3_10

Consequently, CMRP imaging is now considered the gold standard for its non-invasive assessment [2], non-radiation exposure, and its rapid growth and improvement in signal-to-noise ratio and the spatial and temporal spaces significantly.

Moreover, Breath-holding becomes a significant issue in CMRP imaging during pharmacological stress (Adenosine) imaging especially. The problem is handling the inter-frame motion artifact caused by respiration. Therefore, segmentation of the heart's walls is first required to correct the breathing motion in the CMRP images. Our primary target is to enhance the diagnostic process leading to early medical therapy, and helping doctors in evaluating CAD.

DL needs a vast dataset to work on, which is not the case with CMRP images. The only available online dataset for CMRP is the motion correction data offered by Cardiac Atlas Project [3], which is used in image registration processes. The need for more data is overcome using annotating the available images and TL. The TL was made by CINE Images as they are included in the CMRP acquisition process [4]. Moreover, CINE data had some close features that make it reliable to use in the learning process of CMRP as displayed in Fig. 1, While ImageNet is a huge dataset, its weights can have many features that may help in the learning process.

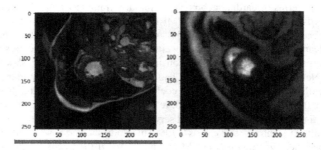

Fig. 1. CINE Image (Right) and CMRP Image (Left) Examples

The steps of our proposed solution are: (1) Annotation has been made manually to increase the data as much as it can. (2) The CMRP and the CINE datasets were pre-processed. (3) CINE dataset was trained using Unet architectures with different backbones (VGG16, ResNet50, and ResNet152) to obtain CINE weights. (4) TL using CINE weights and ImageNet weights separately with the same architectures to experiment with the effect of the shallow and deep networks. (5) The data was annotated by a different observer to calculate the intra-observer error.

2   Literature Review

Nadalur's [5] meta-analysis demonstrated that in an intermediate to high-risk patient (>40% probability of CAD), when the stress CMR is positive, it increases the probability of CAD to approximately 80%. This study hints at how critical the assessment of CAD is in diagnosing CMRP. Although many studies have tried to help diagnosing CAD, few studies were made using CMRP images. The main objective of the availability of CMRP data online was to apply non-rigid registration techniques as mentioned in its benchmark article in cardiac atlas to correct the heart's motion due to short breath during MRI examination, long breath, heart deformation, and heart dislocation.

The proposed model used U-Net architecture which is widely used in medical imaging by many researchers with CMRP and was designed by Ronneberger [6] for its high speed [7] and using small datasets to work [8] (see Fig. 2).

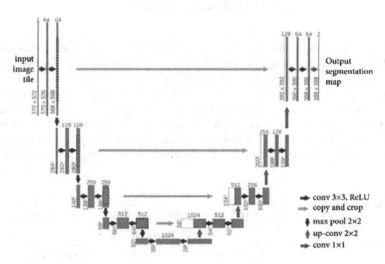

Fig. 2. The Unet Architecture

Different Backbones for Unet architecture have been used; VGG16 [9], ResNet50, and ResNet152 [10]. The choice of these architectures is for their popularity in the field of medical imaging [11].

In the learning process, VGG with Unet architecture is made of two parts: an encoder part and a decoder part as shown in. The encoder part uses five down-sampling blocks based on the VGG16 structure to capture context [12]. The decoder part is based on U-Net. It comprises five up-sampling blocks and uses a symmetric expanding path for precise localization. While ResNet [10] is a deep neural network. Despite the fact that building deeper neural networks is needed, training them is quite challenging as the error rates increased due to the vanishing gradient problem. ResNet unravels this problem by adding skip connections as in Fig. 3.

These connections skip several layers and connects directly to the output. In this way, the vanishing gradient problem is solved. For ResNet50 with Unet, the encoder part is changed to ResNet50 instead of VGG16 and the same for ResNet152. ResNet152 is much deeper than ResNet50 (up to 152 layers).

The segmentation metrics used in many studies are the dice coefficient, dice loss, recall and precision. Moreover, All the proposed models used them as their metrics. Dice coefficient [13] is a metric which is used to calculate the accuracy of the spatial overlap

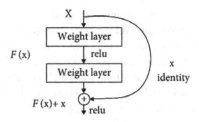

Fig. 3. Residual Block of ResNet Network

between the two corresponding images. It reflects size and localization agreement [14], more in line with perceptual quality compared to pixel-wise accuracy. According to the Eq. (1), It ranges between zero and one, where a value of 0 indicates no overlap of the sets of two compared segmentation masks and a value of 1 indicates a perfect agreement between the two sets. However, dice loss [15] as in Eq. (2), it only addresses the imbalance problem between foreground and background yet overlooks another imbalance between easy and hard examples that also severely affects the training process of a learning model. That's why dice coefficient was indeed a good option to validate the segmentation process.

$$Dice\ coefficient = \frac{2 \times TruePositive}{2 \times TruePositive + false\ Positive + False\ Negative} \tag{1}$$

$$Dice\ Loss = 1 - \frac{2 \times TruePositive}{2 \times TruePositive + false\ Positive + False\ Negative} \tag{2}$$

The precision is the proportion of true positive to the total number of positive predictions (either correct or incorrect predictions). The precision csompute the model's accuracy in classifying samples as positive. The precision concerns to correctly classify all positive class and avoid declassifying negative samples as positive. It was used to detect how many pixels were segmented as depicted in Eq. (3).

$$Precision = \frac{TruePositive}{TruePositive + False\ Positive} \tag{3}$$

While the recall was classified how many pixels were actually segmented correctly as depicted in Eq. (4). The recall determines the model's capability to classify positive samples [16]. In contrast to precision, the recall considers how accurately determining all positive samples, but it does not consider if a negative sample is incorrectly labeled.

$$Recall = \frac{TruePositive}{TruePositive + FalseNegative} \tag{4}$$

Moreover, there was a DL pipeline made by [17]. This pipeline worked on a different dataset given privately to the author. The dataset was 175 (350 CMRP scans; 1050 image series) clinical patients under both rest and stress conditions. An automated pipeline was made including a segmentation with an accuracy (0.8) using Unet architecture.

In agreement with [18], A convolutional neural network model (CNN) was trained on their CMRP dataset, which contains 1825 perfusion time series from 1034 patients for validation and training sets; while testing, 200 scans from 105 patients were used. Their main target was to segment the left ventricular cavity, myocardium, and right ventricle. The mean Dice ratio of automatic and manual segmentation was 0.93 ± 0.04. That study had a huge data as the time series will be divided into images for DL.

Another DL approach [19] was proposed to segment the heart pool and LV myocardium by using Unet and self-attention module. That approach was applied on 96 cases with suspected or confirmed CAD. That approach was validated by modified Hausdorff distance (MHD), dice ratio (DR), and 3D MHD. Their approach improved the average DR from the traditional Unet by 0.905 ± 0.0193 to 0.9202 ± 0.0164, and decreased the average of the 3D MHD from 0.4611 ± 0.0349 to 0.4304 ± 0.0339. The average relative error of LV volume between proposed method and ground truth is $1.09 \pm 3.66\%$. According to that study, the results of that study were worthwhile and adding attention had improved the results. However, the dataset was considerably big and attached with physiological data to clinically guarantee their results which wasn't the case with our study.

3 Materials and Methods

3.1 Datasets

The datasets used in this approach are CMRP, CINE and ImageNet. CMRP dataset consists of ten cases from two centers: The University of Utah and The University of Auckland. For each case, a single short axis slice time series at both stress and rest is provided. The Utah datasets were acquired as described in [20] and Four of their subjects are considered having coronary artery disease. However, None of the Auckland cases have overt coronary disease. Expert-drawn contours only at a reference frame about ten annotations, chosen when contrast is present in both ventricles for both datasets. The CINE images are obtained from Automated Cardiac Diagnosis Challenge (ACDC) images [21] which was created from real clinical exams acquired at the University Hospital of Dijon in France. The cases are all from different patients, 100 cases for training, and 50 cases for testing. While ImageNet dataset contains about 14 million annotated images. The accuracy of VGG16, ResNet50, and ResNet152 with ImageNet are 90.1%, 92.1%, and 93.1%, respectively. The weights of these models are available online for research studies.

3.2 Annotation and Data Preprocessing

The annotation increased the number of the CMRP images, as mentioned previously. The number of annotated images was only 20, which needed to be increased to build a DL model. Therefore, a manual annotation was made to increase the number of the dataset to be 349. The personnel who made the annotation was trained and mentored by expert medical staff to check that the images were annotated correctly. The manual segmenting was made using label-me package [22]. The segmentation was made in two steps as that segmenting tool could not segment hollow objects. First, Applying segmentation to the LV walls with the heart pool for each patient. Second, the heart pool of the LV was segmented alone. Afterward, a bit-wise XOR operation was made between the two segmented images to get the LV's heart wall. Over and above the training images, about 50 images were annotated by the same personnel to study the intra-observation error and to compare the best-automated analysis and the manual one.

The preprocessing steps made for CMRP and CINE datasets: (a) local-normalizing, (b) shuffling, (c) resizing to 256 × 256 for width and height of each image, and (d) train-test split (70% for training and 30% validation). After preprocessing, the CMRP images needed an additional step to be pre-trained using ImageNet. A modification was made to each medical image by equalizing red, green, and blue components to the gray one of the original medical images. The programming language was Python as it offers image processing packages, and it is easy to build DL models.

3.3 The Proposed Pipeline

The DL models will be named in this paper in order to prevent any potential misunderstandings. CMRP trained with Unet and VGG (CMRP, Unet, and VGG16) as a decoder will be referred to as Model 1 (M1). (CMRP, Unet, and ResNet50) will be named Model 2 (M2). (CMRP, Unet, and ResNet152) will be named Model 3 (M3). CMRP transfer learned with CINE weights by Unet with VGG16 (CMRP, CINE, Unet, and VGG16) will be named Model 4 (M4). (CMR, CINE, Unet, and ResNet50) will be named Model 5 (M5). (CMRP, CINE, Unet, and ResNet152) will be named Model 6 (M6). CMRP transfer learned with ImageNet weights by Unet with VGG16 (CMRP, ImageNet, Unet, and VGG16) will be named Model 7 (M7). (CMRP, ImageNet, Unet, and ResNet50) will be named model 8 (M8). (CMRP, ImageNet, Unet, and ResNet152) will be named model 9 (M9). An analysis and comparison were made between these different models. The DL framework for this study is shown in Fig. 4.

The metrics which were used in all the models (3 CINE models and 9 CMRP models) are dice coefficient as accuracy and loss, recall and precision. Dice coefficient is a metric which is used to calculate the accuracy of the spatial overlap between the two corresponding images. However, dice loss only addresses the imbalance problem between foreground and background. Precision is the number of correct results (true positives) relative to the number of all results. Recall is the number of correct results relative to the number of expected results Both precision and recall were considered as good choices for examining the performance of the models.

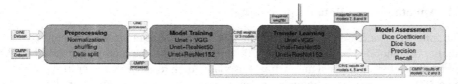

Fig. 4. The DL pipeline for CMRP segmentation

All the DL models had the same epochs numbers (50), the same learning rate 10^{-3} with Adam as an optimizer and batch size of four. These parameters were chosen by experiments and by previous studies made on small datasets as CMRP. The packages used to perform the learning processes were Keras [23] and TensorFlow [24].

4 Results

The measured values were dice coefficient, precision, dice loss and recall. The results for CINE and Unet with ResNet50 based model, the results of that model were 0.112 for dice coefficient loss, 0.846 for recall, 0.938 for precision and dice coefficient accuracy was 0.887. Then for ResNet152 based model, the results of dice coefficient loss, recall, precision and dice coefficient accuracy were 0.153, 0.757, 0.9458 and 0.846 respectively. Subsequently, these models' weights were taken to transfer-learn the CMRP dataset.

The predicted results of the different models for the validation data with different backbone encoders had reached promising values as follows in Table 1. The results may vary from each other in decimal numbers, however, improving the performance metrics have been one of the main concerns in the medical imaging studies. While the average results of predictions of each model are 0.825, 0.844, 0.837, 0.843, 0.848, 0.845, 0.840, 0.838, and 0.836 for M1, M2, M3, M4, M5, M6, M7, M8, and M9, respectively. Therefore, the best model is Model 5 using ResNet50 on CINE dataset with CMRP data.

Table 1. Validation Results

Models	M1	M2	M3	M4	M5	M6	M7	M8	M9
Dice Coeff	0.831	0.843	0.841	0.845	**0.851**	0.846	0.844	0.843	0.842
Recall	0.746	0.773	0.765	**0.791**	0.776	0.757	0.763	0.740	0.787
Precision	0.938	0.939	0.938	0.932	0.940	0.945	**0.941**	**0.951**	0.927
Dice Loss	0.168	0.151	0.158	0.154	**0.148**	0.153	0.155	0.156	0.158

The results of these models were close to each other. The best model was M5, which was by using CINE data with ResNet50 [25] as a backbone encoder. That model was not as shallow as the VGG16 model or as deep as ResNet152. Taking into consideration that using VGG16 with small data may not give the best results. However, ResNet152 needs big data to perform better. Having these values indicates how much these data can be reliable on TL. In addition, the results of CINE depending models are almost better than the values of the other models that makes CINE dataset a good candidate to study the perfusion images using them.

As shown in Fig. 5, A box plot is used to compare between the DL models. M5 gave better results than its competitors a. It has the most compact box and the least number of outliers. That was because the model was not as deep as others due to ResNet50 and the weights of CINE that offered most of all the features of CMRP and auto-tuned by CMRP images afterwards. The complexity of the problem was investigated. The mean results of the inter-observer error were 0.796 which is much lower than M5 (0.848). This indicates that the problem is hard to be solved.

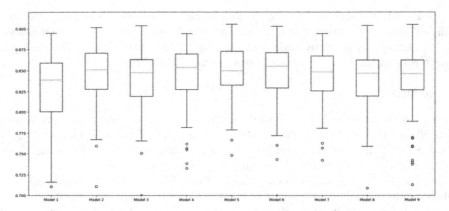

Fig. 5. A Box plot to compare between the learning models

5 Conclusion

In conclusion, the study of CMRP images is difficult because of heart motion which is caused by short breath during MRI examination. There is a need to be more than the available data online to build the DL models, which directed the researchers to use TL. The proposed work discussed how much DL could depend on TL to study CMRP images. It studied the comparison between different models to give the best results without increasing the dataset's size and the effect of the deepness of the DL models.

This approach can be considered scalable because the data is from different sources (CMRP dataset are from two different universities and CINE dataset from hospitals) and can be applied on other CMRP datasets to calculate the cardiac wall parameters. Finally, the results of CMRP were promising after using the CINE dataset, the limitations of this study are the data size which affects the accuracy deeply. The data provided has no more heart radiomics that can help in further full DL automated studies.

References

1. Cardiovascular diseases (cvds) key facts (2021). https://www.who.int/en/newsroom/fact-she ets/detail/cardiovascular-diseases-(cvds). Accessed May 2021
2. Moya, A., Buytaert, D., Penicka, M., Bartunek, J., Van-derheyden, M.: State-of-the-art: noninvasive assessment of left ventricular function through myocardial work. J. Am. Soc. Echocardiogr. **36**(10), 1027–1042 (2023)
3. Pontre, B., et al.: An open benchmark challenge for motion correction of myocardial perfusion MRI. IEEE J. Biomed. Health Inform. **21**(5), 1315–1326 (2017)
4. Zhou, W., et al.: Qualitative and quantitative stress perfusion cardiac magnetic resonance in clinical practice: a comprehensive review. Diagnostics **13**(3), 524 (2023)
5. Choudri, A.F., Nandalur, K.R., Dwamena, B.A.: Diagnostic performance of stress cardiac magnetic resonance imaging in the detection of coronary artery disease: a meta-analysis. J. Am. College Cardiol. **50**, 1343–1353 (2007)

6. Ronneberger, O., Fischer, P., Brox, T.: U-Net: convolutional networks for biomedical image segmentation. In: Navab, N., Hornegger, J., Wells, W.M., Frangi, A.F. (eds.) MICCAI 2015. LNCS, vol. 9351, pp. 234–241. Springer, Cham (2015). https://doi.org/10.1007/978-3-319-24574-4_28

7. Liu, X., Song, L., Liu, S., Zhang, Y.: A review of deep-learning-based medical image segmentation methods. Sustainability **13**(3), 1224 (2021)

8. Yin, X.-X., Suna, L., Fu, Y., Lu, R., Zhang, Y.: U-net-based medical image segmentation. J. Healthcare Eng. **2022**, 16 (2022)

9. Simonyan, K., Zisserman, A.: Very deep convolutional networks for large-scale image recognition (2014)

10. He, K., Zhang, X., Ren, S., Sun, J.: Deep residual learning for image recognition (2015)

11. Lu, H., et al.: Research progress of machine learning and deep learning in intelligent diagnosis of the coronary atherosclerotic heart disease. Comput. Math. Methods Med. **2022**, 14 (2022)

12. Shi, J., et al.: Improvement of damage segmentation based on pixel-level data balance using VGG-Unet. Appl. Sci. **11**(2), 518 (2021)

13. Hanbury, A., Taha, A.A.: Metrics for evaluating 3D medical image segmentation: analysis, selection, and tool. BMC Med. Imaging **15**, 1–28 (2015)

14. Bertels, J., et al.: Optimizing the dice score and jaccard index for medical image segmentation: theory and practice. In: Shen, D., et al. (eds.) Medical Image Computing and Computer Assisted Intervention – MICCAI 2019: 22nd International Conference, Shenzhen, China, October 13–17, 2019, Proceedings, Part II, pp. 92–100. Springer, Cham (2019). https://doi.org/10.1007/978-3-030-32245-8_11

15. Zhao, R., et al.: Rethinking dice loss for medical image segmentation. In: 2020 IEEE International Conference on Data Mining (ICDM), pp. 851–860 (2020)

16. Aljuaid, A., Anwar, M.: Survey of supervised learning for medical image processing. SN Comput. Sci. **3**, 292 (2022)

17. Scannell, C.M., et al.: Deep-learning-based preprocessing for quantitative myocardial perfusion MRI. J. Magn. Reson. Imaging **51**(6), 1689–1696 (2020)

18. Xue, H., et al.: Automated inline analysis of myocardial perfusion MRI with deep learning. Radiol. Artif. Intell. **2**(6), e200009 (2020). PMID: 33330849

19. Zhang, Y., et al.: An automatic segmentation method with self-attention mechanism on left ventricle in gated pet/ct myocardial perfusion imaging. Comput. Methods Programs Biomed. **229**, 107267 (2023)

20. Dibella, E., et al.: The effect of obesity on regadenoson-induced myocardial hyperemia: a quantitative magnetic resonance imaging study. Int. J. Cardiovasc. Imaging **28**, 1435–1444 (2011). https://doi.org/10.1007/s10554-011-9949-4

21. Bernard, O., Lalande, A., Zotti, C., Cervenansky, F., et al.: Deep learning techniques for automatic MRI cardiac multi-structures segmentation and diagnosis: Is the problem solved? IEEE Trans. Med. Imaging **37**(11), 2514–2525 (2018)

22. Wada, K.: Labelme: image polygonal annotation with python. GitHub Repository (2018)

23. Chollet, F., et al.: Keras (2015). https://github.com/fchollet/keras

24. Abadi, M., et al.: TensorFlow: large-scale machine learning on heterogeneous systems. Software available from tensorflow.org (2015)

25. Shafiq, M., Gu, Z.: Deep residual learning for image recognition: a survey. Appl. Sci. **12**(18), 8972 (2022)

Smart Saliency Detection for Prosthetic Vision

Nermin Khalifa[1]([✉])(iD), Walid Al-Atabany[1,2](iD), and Sahar Selim[1,2](iD)

[1] School of Information Technology and Computer Science, Nile University,
Giza 12677, Egypt
n.khalifa@nu.edu.eg
[2] Medical Imaging and Image Processing Research Group, Center for Informatics
Science, Nile University, Giza 12677, Egypt

Abstract. People with visual impairments often have difficulty locating misplaced objects. This can be a major barrier to their independence and quality of life. Retinal prostheses can restore some vision to people with severe vision loss. We introduce a novel real-time system for locating any misplaced objects for people with visual impairments using retinal prostheses. The system combines One For All (OFA) for Visual Grounding and Google Speech Recognition to identify the object to be located. It then uses an image processing technique called grabCut to extract the object from the background to emphasize the located object and incorporate it with the background frame to send it to the retinal implant for stimulation. The system was evaluated on a set of images containing misplaced objects and was able to locate the objects in real-time successfully. We believe that this system could be used to improve the independence and quality of life of people with visual impairments. The system is still in the early stages of development, but we are working to improve its performance.

Keywords: prosthetic vision · visual grounding · vision language models · simulated prosthetic vision · vision augmentation

1 Introduction

Retinal degenerative diseases, such as retinitis pigmentosa and age-related macular degeneration, are the leading causes of blindness worldwide. These diseases cause the progressive death of photoreceptor cells in the retina, which convert light into electrical signals sent to the brain. As a result, people with retinal degenerative diseases experience a gradual loss of vision, which can eventually lead to blindness. Most visual prosthesis designs consist of three main components: a camera, a video processing unit (VPU), and an electrode array [12]. The camera captures images of the scene and sends them to the video processing unit. The video processing unit converts the images into electrical signals that are sent to the electrode array implanted into the eye or brain and are used to artificially stimulate surviving cells in the visual pathway to restore vision to people with retinal degenerative diseases.

The electrical stimulation prosthetic visual devices can restore some vision to people who are blind. This stimulation can produce the sensation of a point of light, called a (phosphene) or precept. Researchers are working to develop devices that can stimulate the visual cortex or optic nerve to produce more complex visual perceptions [17] and other techniques such as developing optogenetic methods for visual prosthesis.

The researchers are working to improve the design and performance of these devices so that they can provide a more natural and useful vision to people who need them, despite some companies dissolved in the past few years for many reasons such as financial challenges after Covid-19 [16] and frustration as in Retina Implant AG (maker of the AlphaIMS/AMS subretinal implants) as they mentioned that their device not leading to "the concrete benefit in everyday life of those affected" [5]. However, a proposal to move away from the (largely academic) discussion of what constitutes proper restoration of sight and instead design experiments that probe an implant's potential to support functional vision in real-world tasks was presented in the work referenced as [5]. Most blind people spend a considerable amount of time indoors, they almost depend on the routine and organized environment around them which makes them always in isolation and need special treatments, they also face challenges in various daily activities like locating kitchen appliances, and ingredients while cooking, or locating dirty spots on cloth while cleaning and other activities [18].

Hence, in this research paper, we address The task of locating an object instance that we call a salient object from an image referred to by a query sentence taken by voice instruction. Querying an object from an image scene is called Visual grounding in Artificial intelligence, and we believe this smart salient detection approach presented in this paper has the potential to significantly advance the field of image simplification in the prosthetic vision field for people who are blind due to retinal degenerative diseases. The proposed methods and techniques could improve the quality of life, independence, and confidence for a lot of blind people around the world by allowing them to interact with the world around them in more natural ways, making it easier for them to stay connected with the world around them.

2   Related Work

Since the discovery of electrical stimulation of human tissues in 1799, humanity could say there have been visual prostheses. Foerster a German neurosurgeon who is considered one of the pioneers of modern neurosurgery first showed in 1929 how electrical stimulation of the visual cortex may cause a participant to perceive a light spot (Phosphene) [2]. By Working on the concepts of Foerster there have been significant advances in the field of retinal prosthesis research in recent years, even though restoring perfect vision with a retinal prosthesis is unlikely to be possible in the near future it is possible that we will see even more progress in the years to come.

The retinal prosthesis of today can offer some restricted visual functions, such as the ability to distinguish between light and dark or to identify basic shapes. These technologies cannot offer the same level of visual acuity as natural eyesight because of their still-very-low resolution. In the future, These devices may eventually be able to provide patients with useful visual functions, such as the ability to read, drive, or recognize faces. However, the main goal is to restore scene recognition to the patients, in other words, to help them understand their surroundings and identify objects from visual information to interact with the world around them. Therefore, some form of reduction for the visual information should be applied before transferring images to the retinal implants. Many papers in the literature focused on the Non-trivial image processing approaches to address the low-resolution issue of these prosthetic devices in order to make the best use of the few stimulation points that are available, one paper transferred important objects segmented using mixed visible-infra-red imaging. With this segmentation approach, complex objects are still distinguishable even with low effective resolution this also reduced the power and saved the batteries of the processing devices for a longer time [1], another study processed the stimuli by four different scene simplification strategies, adapted from state-of-the-art computer vision algorithms, the study showed that object segmentation may better support scene understanding than models based on visual saliency and monocular depth estimation [11].

Another study introduced an automated approach to reduce the difficulty in recognizing objects in a scene in visual prostheses. This was achieved by first using YOLO deep neural network to detect and recognize the objects in a scene. The corresponding simplified clip art representation is then obtained and displayed to the virtual patients after some pre-processing performed prior to phosphene simulation [10]. Likewise, [9] used a clip art representation in place of the actual object as a scene simplification method, in addition to utilizing edge and corner enhancement techniques as well as sharpening for better detail preservation. and finally, A dropout handling technique was used to compensate for malfunctioning electrodes.

Recently, [5] proposed that research on visual prostheses should focus on creating practical and useful artificial vision that can help people with blindness perform everyday tasks, rather than trying to restore natural vision. The authors pointed out that visual question answering models are an unexplored application domain with the potential for this purpose. For example, a patient could verbally instruct a Smart Bionic Eye to retrieve misplaced items. The prosthesis could then use artificial intelligence to understand the scene while the user is looking around the room and provide him with the location.

In summary, previous research has commonly worked on segmenting and simplifying the content of images and testing these approaches on virtual patients. However, recent papers are directed toward the practical use of the available phosphenes to support visual perception and behavior. Thus, in this paper, we developed a system that uses AI-based scene understanding combined with a smart object-extraction technique for salient objects, which represents a significant step toward realizing this potential. This system could be used to help people with visual impairments interact in their environment. We will describe the system in the next sections.

3 Methodology

The smart saliency detection system architecture typically consists of an Input preparation module, a Transformer based Multimodal neural network, an Image processing module, and Phosphenes computation module. The first module is responsible for acquiring the input from the user and environment, while the multimodal receives the data and locates the target object based on them. The image processing module extracts the object from the scene and performs certain operations that highlight the region on which people's eyes should focus first, and finally, the Phosphenes Computing module which predicts the elicited visual percepts (phosphenes). We put forward a proposal for integrating this system with visual prostheses as a temporary mode as the patient may need it in his daily life in certain moments when he needs to find and grasp a certain object. In this paper, we refer to this mode as a "Finding mode". The proposed system is shown in Fig. 1. In this section, we will introduce each module in detail.

Input Preparation. In many life activities sighted people are more comfortable using speech as a mode of input for various machines. For example, it is easier to say "Turn on the lights" than to type "Turn on the lights" or to physically turn the lights on, due to the fact speech is a more natural and efficient way to communicate. An ideal Automatic Speech Recognition (ASR) system should be able to perceive the given input by capturing the audio signal from the user's voice and converting it into a digital signal. It should then recognize the spoken words by breaking down the digital signal into individual words and identifying their corresponding meanings. Then, the recognized words can be used as input to another system so that some action can be performed based on them [13]. Therefore, Speech recognition is a powerful tool that can be used to improve the independence and productivity of people with visual impairment by acquiring their voice as input to the system. As a proof of concept, we used the SpeechRecognition library [22] with the help of an external microphone to record the patient's query. The library supports a variety of speech recognition APIs, including Snowboy Hotword Detection, Tensorflow, Vosk API, OpenAI whisper, Google Speech Recognition, and Google Cloud Speech API. Some of these APIs can be used online or offline. We exploit a generic key for testing Google Web Speech API, the API allows applications running in the browser to incorporate speech input. This API Leverages Google's most advanced deep-learning neural network algorithms for automatic speech recognition to transcribe speech into text. Furthermore, we display the top-ranked transcription, which ensures that the user is getting the most accurate transcription possible. The free service also supports multiple languages including English, Spanish, and Chinese.

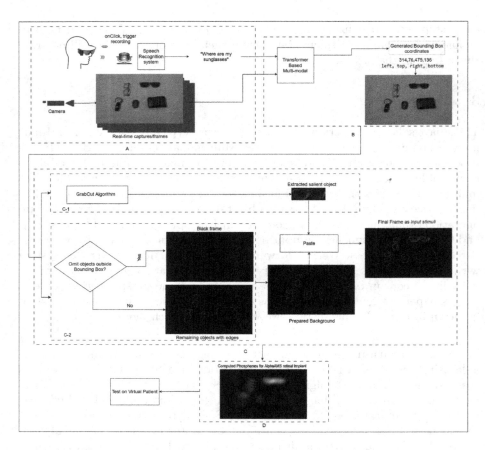

Fig. 1. Proposed system, the system is divided into four main modules, A: Input preparation module, B: Transformer based multimodal neural network module C: Image Processing module, C-1 block: shows extracting the object inside the bounding box, and C-2 block: demonstrates the two approaches to prepare the background of the output frame, C-1 and C-2 are concurrent blocks that use the bounding box and frame as input, and D: Phosphenes computation module

In the proposed design, A button shall be pressed to activate the "Finding mode" which will automatically start to record the user's speech which is the detailed description of the object, then the speech recognition system will transcript the recorded description into a text as a substitution for typing. From there on, the camera will start working to capture the environment in real-time, these captured frames will be sent to the multi-modal network frame by frame alongside the generated text as shown in Fig. 1.

(a) the input query "cloth ironing" on Image contains home appliances   (b) the input query "blood stain on t-shirt" on Image contains white T-shirt

Fig. 2. visual grounding task

A Transformer Based Multimodal Neural Network. The problem of finding a specific object in a scene based on transcribing verbal input to text can be mapped to the visual grounding task. The verbal input provides the name of the object that is being searched for, and the image provides the context in which the object is located. By combining these two pieces of information, a visual grounding system can find the object in the scene. Visual grounding is a challenging task that requires computers to understand the meaning of language and the content of images. This task is complex because language is often ambiguous, and images can be complex and contain many objects and relations [8]. However, even if objects are partially occluded or difficult to see, models can be trained to locate them. Visual grounding can be very helpful in various home activities, for example, finding a lost remote control, locating a specific food item in the refrigerator, finding home appliances, or stains on clothes as shown in Fig. 2

We utilized a multi-modal framework Called OFA [19] "One For All", which achieves the objectives of unifying architectures, tasks, and modalities. It is a transformer-based model that is trained on a massive dataset of text and images. it uses a unified instruction-based task representation to represent a wide range of tasks. It is task-agnostic and modality-agnostic that supports Task Comprehensiveness, meaning that it can be used for a wide range of tasks, without having to be specifically trained for each task, and with any type of data such as text, images, and audio also, it can transfer to unseen tasks with new task instructions and achieves competitive performance in zero-shot learning. In a series of vision & language downstream tasks, including image captioning, visual question answering, and referring expression comprehension OFA achieves state-of-the-art performances. and is also comparable to State-Of-The-Art (SOTA) pretrained models in language or vision on unimodal tasks. Based on that, we decided to adopt OFA for the visual grounding task.

The generated output sequence of the visual grounding task are location tokens specifying the region position ⟨x1, y1, x2, y2⟩ based on the input of the image xi and the instruction "Which region does the text xt describe?" where xt refers to the region caption and x1, y1 points to the upper left corner of the rectangle and x2, y2 refers to the bottom right. The green bounding box shown in the Fig. 2 and Fig. 1B is drawn according to the location tokens.

Image Processing. By locating the bounding box and identifying the target object, a few processing steps were applied to the image in order to emphasize the object.

(a) original colored frame contains four objects pink gloves, hand watch, sunglasses, and toy gun

(b) approach one: frame shows only the target object on a black background

(c) approach two: frame shows combining both the target object and the remaining objects after processing

Fig. 3. Image shows the result of two processing approaches, the First approach (b) shows only the target object on a black background. the Second approach (c) combines both the target object and the remaining objects as edges after processing. The bounding box is generated based on input queries "Where are the sunglasses" and "pink gloves", respectively, on the original colored frame shown on (a). (Color figure online)

First, we make the object noticeable from its background by applying a grab-cut algorithm [14] on the frame which is one of several state-of-the-art interactive approaches for segmentation. The grabCut algorithm obtains a hard segmentation in which each pixel is assigned a single label, either foreground or background using iterative graph cut [6], which is a powerful optimization technique that can be used to achieve robust segmentation even in camouflage. the graph cut algorithm involves constructing a graph where each pixel is a node, and the edges represent the similarity between neighboring pixels. Then it finds the minimum energy labeling of the graph, which corresponds to the hard segmentation of the image. What makes the grabCut better than the graph cuts mechanism is that the grabCut puts a light load on the user, whose interaction consists simply of dragging a rectangle around the desired object, which in our case is already known. Secondly, we work on the remaining frame e.g. objects outside the bounding box, here we developed two approaches as shown in Fig. 1C.2. In the first approach, we paste the extracted object on a black frame Fig. 3b, this could help patients to perceive and grasp the object faster without any disturbance of the surrounding objects specifically with low-resolution implants. Although this approach can be harmful as the patient should be aware of the surrounding objects especially, if the objects can cause harm such as heated cups or sharp gadgets, etc., the "Finding mode" can be integrated with the visual prosthesis in a temporary mode which can be only activated once the patient is looking for something and only then, the patient should see the conventional scene. However, this is a questionable method that should be tested, and this is why we also processed the image to show some fine details of the objects with lower intensity levels as shown in Fig. 3c.

To show the fine details of the remaining objects in the image, we used morphological operations to detect objects' edges. First, we used Otsu's method to threshold the image, which converted it to a binary image with black pixels representing low-intensity values and white pixels representing high-intensity values. Next, we used a median filter with a 3×3 kernel to remove any unwanted noise from the image. This helped to smooth out the image and make the edges more pronounced.

Then, we used an eroded version of the image to extract the edges. An eroded image is created by shrinking the noise-canceled image by a certain amount. In this case, we used a 3×3 structuring element to erode the image, which helped to remove any small details that were not part of the edges, then we subtracted the eroded image from the noise-canceled image. after that, we replaced all of the 255 values in the image with 100, this made the edges less bright than the salient object. As a last step, we used bitwise-And operation between the image and a black and white mask where the black region is located at the bounding box coordinates. The output of this process is shown in Fig. 3c.

Finally, the salient object is pasted on the prepared background frame at the same bounding box location to constitute the final image which will be used as input stimuli as shown in Fig. 1C and D.

Phosphenes Computation. A computational model that can generate realistic predictions of what the virtual patients would see, allowing them to grasp the located object and complete tasks accurately called Pulse2precept [3] is adopted, the output of this model can be shown in Fig. 1D. In a right-eye setup, we utilized four implant designs ArgusII, 16×16 Implant, 32×32 Implant, and 40×40 Implant, the four implants are ordered based on the number of electrodes. the design of each implant can be shown in Fig. 4. ArgusII implant is an epiretinal retinal prosthesis that contains 60 electrodes. The electrodes are arranged in a 6×10 grid with a center-to-center separation of $575 \, \mu m$ (um). The implant's electrodes have a diameter of $225 \, \mu m$. [21]. A 16×16 implant is configured to the same electrode dimensions as ArgusII with a bigger number of electrodes. An Implant with 32×32 electrodes has an electrode radius of $30 \, \mu m$ with $280 \, \mu m$ spacing between them. Lastly, the 40×40 Implant mimics the AlphaAMS configurations, the implant consisting of 1600 electrodes $30 \, \mu m$ in diameter, arranged on a rectangular grid with 70 um pixel pitch [15]. The aim of working with those

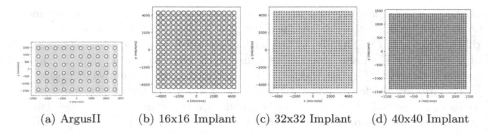

| (a) ArgusII | (b) 16x16 Implant | (c) 32x32 Implant | (d) 40x40 Implant |

Fig. 4. Illustrates the different implants designs

different implants is to explore the effect of changing the number of electrodes on the predicted percepts.

For computation, a scoreboardSpatial model was used which is a computational model to predict visual precepts resulting from electrical stimulation described in [4], the model proposes that all precepts are Gaussian blobs. Moreover, we adjusted the model's parameters in the right eye to accommodate all phosphenes in the grid for each implant. This included adjusting the range of x and y values to simulate in degrees of visual angle, as well as the xystep parameter. The xystep parameter controls the step size for the range of (x,y) values to simulate on the grid, and negative x values correspond to the temporal retina, and positive x values to the nasal retina, while negative y values correspond to the superior retina, and positive y values to the inferior retina. Another configuration is the Visual field map aka Retinotopy which is used to describe the spatial organization of the neuronal responses to visual stimuli, we set it to watson2014 map [20] which provides a more exact transformation than [Curcio1990] [7] who assumes that one degree of visual angle is equal to 280 μm on the retina.

4   Results and Discussion

We implemented a novel real-time system for locating any misplaced objects for people with visual impairments, specifically those using retinal prostheses. The system combined a speech recognition module and a vision language model for visual grounding and used an image processing technique called grabCut to emphasize the located object and incorporate it with the background frame. The system was implemented in a Google Colab notebook which is a cloud-based environment with direct access to the user's webcam and microphone. However, fitting this AI system on a low-power, portable device, such as a VPU, is challenging because AI systems are generally very computationally expensive and require a lot of memory. One potential solution is to use a serverless cloud service when deploying the system [5].

The camera that was used has a maximum resolution of 720p/30fps, which means that it can capture images at 720 pixels per line and 30 frames per second. It also has an auto-light correction feature, which automatically adjusts the brightness and contrast of the image to compensate for changes in lighting conditions.

In our implementation, the size of the frame is set to 640 × 480, which means that each image captured by the camera is 480 pixels height and 640 pixels width. This is a smaller resolution than the maximum resolution of the camera, but it is sufficient for the purposes of the system.

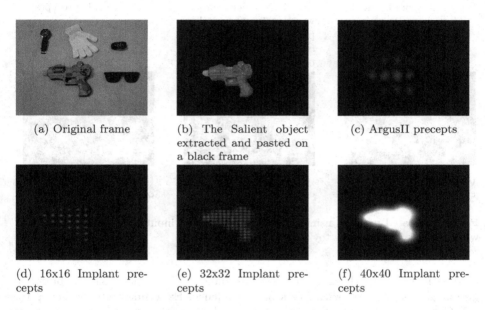

(a) Original frame

(b) The Salient object extracted and pasted on a black frame

(c) ArgusII precepts

(d) 16x16 Implant precepts

(e) 32x32 Implant precepts

(f) 40x40 Implant precepts

Fig. 5. generated precepts using different implants, the inputs are the original frame with the text "where is my toy"

The precepts output was resized to the exact size of the original input frame to simulate what the patients would see when they activate what we call the "finding mode.". Figure 5 and Fig. 6 show the output of phosphenes predictions using different implants on a toy object with clear boundaries. The toy object was extracted from the bounding box that was generated based on the original image and the transcribed text "Where is my toy" that were passed to the vision language model OFA. The difference between the two figures is the background. Figure 5 has a black frame background, while Fig. 6 has a background of processed objects.

We evaluated the system on a variety of commonly misplaced objects in daily life, such as keys, watches, eyeglasses, sunglasses, toys, and utensils. These objects were of different sizes and shapes and were placed in different rooms inside a home. As we experimented with the system more, we were able to choose carefully the appropriate steps in the system flow. For Instance, we modified the output of the OFA model to send back the average score of the generated

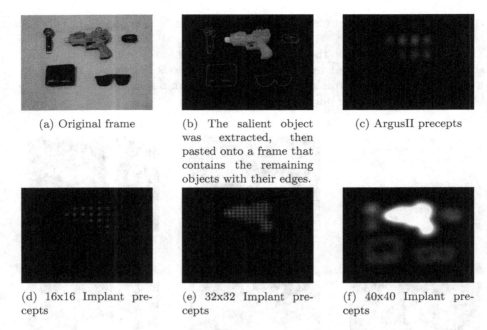

(a) Original frame

(b) The salient object was extracted, then pasted onto a frame that contains the remaining objects with their edges.

(c) ArgusII precepts

(d) 16x16 Implant precepts

(e) 32x32 Implant precepts

(f) 40x40 Implant precepts

Fig. 6. generated precepts using different implants, the inputs are the original frame with the text "where is my toy"

tokens, in order to check it against Threshold "T" as the model is built to ground an object even with low score confidence. Experimentally, we set T to 0.7. Consequently, in the case of finding an object with a low score, the system shows a black frame indicating that the object is not found.

Moreover, while attempting to generate output results, we observed that the generated bounding box coordinates can be influenced by a number of factors, including the exposure to light while capturing, the complexity of the scene, the similarity of objects, and the ambiguity of the language. If the image is too dark or too bright, the model may not be able to accurately identify the objects in the scene. A complex scene with many objects can be more difficult to ground than a simple scene with few objects. If two objects are very similar, the model may have difficulty distinguishing between them. For example, if there is a bottle of perfume and a bottle of water in a scene, the model may not be able to distinguish between the two bottles. If the language used to describe the scene is ambiguous, the model may not be able to understand the query correctly. For instance, if the scene contains multiple gloves, and the user asks "Where are my gloves", the query does not specify which gloves the user is referring to. This problem can be mitigated by providing the model with more information about the query and the scene, such as describing the gloves in more detail. These points are generic or non-specific to the OFA model, but they should be spotlighted as wrong detection can lead to other consequences. For example, we

(a) bounding box contains the gloves and the hand watch
(b) result of grabCut algorithm initialized with bounding box contains the gloves and the hand watch
(c) bounding box contains the gloves only
(d) result of grabCut algorithm initialized with bounding box contains the gloves only

Fig. 7. Image shows how much the grabCut algorithm is sensitive to the quality of the initial bounding box, the bounding box generated is based on input query "where are the gloves" on an original frame containing multiple objects including gloves and a hand watch. The figure shows four images. The first and third images, (a) and (c), depict the bounding boxes that were generated by the multimodal. The second and fourth images, (b) and (d), illustrate the grabcut outputs.

observed that the grabCut algorithm is sensitive to the quality of the initial bounding box, as shown in Fig. 7.

One important issue that we needed to address was the removal of edges that were extracted at the area of the bounding box while preparing the background frame using approach two (shown in Fig. 3). This was necessary to prevent unwanted edges from appearing around the object in the final image, as this could add noise around the segmented object. In our initial design of this approach, we tried to remove the bounding box area using a black mask before generating the edges, but this resulted in a clear rectangle border.

The experiments showed that adding more electrodes to the implant made the edges of objects in the phosphenes output clearer. This is shown in Fig. 6f. This finding answers our previous questionable method which showed that a lower-resolution implant may not be able to show fine details of the surrounding objects, However, a higher-resolution implant with more pixels would be able to show these fine details. This means that showing other objects with a lower-resolution implant would not be beneficial, as they would not appear. However, it would make sense to show these objects with a higher-resolution implant, as the fine details would be visible.

5   Conclusion

Overall, the results showed that the system was able to successfully locate objects from verbal instructions and visual inputs. The processing steps also showed the salient object in a clear manner on a processed or black background frame, so that the final output could be used as stimuli input for phosphenes generation. The generated phosphenes answered the questions that we had. This suggests that the system is ready to be tested with human subjects and has the potential to revolutionize the way that blind people interact with their environment.

This proof-of-concept study suggests that the proposed approach could be used to improve prosthetic vision systems and enable patients to locate any misplaced objects in their homes. We are currently working on designing a real-time experiment to test the approach in a variety of situations. We believe that this experiment will provide valuable insights into the effectiveness of the approach and help to advance the field of smart bionic vision.

References

1. Al-Atabany, W., Degenaar, P.: Efficient scene preparation and downscaling prior to stimulation in retinal prosthesis. In: 2013 IEEE Biomedical Circuits and Systems Conference (BioCAS), pp. 182–185. IEEE (2013)
2. Banarji, A., Gurunadh, V., Patyal, S., Ahluwalia, T., Vats, D., Bhadauria, M.: Visual prosthesis: artificial vision. Med. J. Armed Forces India **65**(4), 348–352 (2009)
3. Beyeler, M., Boynton, G.M., Fine, I., Rokem, A.: pulse2percept: a python-based simulation framework for bionic vision. BioRxiv, 148015 (2017)
4. Beyeler, M., Nanduri, D., Weiland, J.D., Rokem, A., Boynton, G.M., Fine, I.: A model of ganglion axon pathways accounts for percepts elicited by retinal implants. Sci. Rep. **9**(1), 1–16 (2019)
5. Beyeler, M., Sanchez-Garcia, M.: Towards a smart bionic eye: Ai-powered artificial vision for the treatment of incurable blindness. J. Neural Eng. **19**(6), 063001 (2022)
6. Boykov, Y.Y., Jolly, M.P.: Interactive graph cuts for optimal boundary & region segmentation of objects in nd images. In: Proceedings eighth IEEE International Conference on Computer Vision. ICCV 2001, vol. 1, pp. 105–112. IEEE (2001)
7. Curcio, C.A., Sloan, K.R., Kalina, R.E., Hendrickson, A.E.: Human photoreceptor topography. J. Comp. Neurol. **292**(4), 497–523 (1990)
8. Du, Y., Fu, Z., Liu, Q., Wang, Y.: Visual grounding with transformers. In: 2022 IEEE International Conference on Multimedia and Expo (ICME), pp. 1–6. IEEE (2022)
9. Elnabawy, R.H., Abdennadher, S., Hellwich, O., Eldawlatly, S.: Object recognition and localization enhancement in visual prostheses: a real-time mixed reality simulation. Biomed. Eng. Online **21**(1), 91 (2022)
10. Elnabawy, R.H., Abdennadher, S., Hellwich, O., Eldawlatly, S.: A yolo-based object simplification approach for visual prostheses. In: 2022 IEEE 35th International Symposium on Computer-Based Medical Systems (CBMS), pp. 183–186. IEEE (2022)
11. Han, N., Srivastava, S., Xu, A., Klein, D., Beyeler, M.: Deep learning-based scene simplification for bionic vision. In: Augmented Humans Conference 2021, pp. 45–54 (2021)
12. Lin, T.C., et al.: Retinal prostheses in degenerative retinal diseases. J. Chin. Med. Assoc. **78**(9), 501–505 (2015)
13. Malik, M., Malik, M.K., Mehmood, K., Makhdoom, I.: Automatic speech recognition: a survey. Multimedia Tools Appl. **80**, 9411–9457 (2021)
14. Rother, C., Kolmogorov, V., Blake, A.: "grabcut" interactive foreground extraction using iterated graph cuts. ACM Trans. Graph. (TOG) **23**(3), 309–314 (2004)

15. Stingl, K., et al.: Interim results of a multicenter trial with the new electronic subretinal implant alpha AMS in 15 patients blind from inherited retinal degenerations. Front. Neurosci. **11**, 445 (2017)

16. Strickland, E., Harris, M.: What happens when a bionic body part becomes obsolete?: blind people with second sight's retinal implants found out. IEEE Spectr. **59**(3), 24–31 (2022). https://doi.org/10.1109/MSPEC.2022.9729945

17. Thompson, R.W., Barnett, G.D., Humayun, M.S., Dagnelie, G.: Facial recognition using simulated prosthetic pixelized vision. Investigative Ophthalmol. Vis. Sci. **44**(11), 5035–5042 (2003)

18. Turkstra, L.M., Van Os, A., Bhatia, T., Beyeler, M.: Information needs and technology use for daily living activities at home by people who are blind. arXiv preprint arXiv:2305.03019 (2023)

19. Wang, P., et al.: Ofa: unifying architectures, tasks, and modalities through a simple sequence-to-sequence learning framework. In: International Conference on Machine Learning, pp. 23318–23340. PMLR (2022)

20. Watson, A.B.: A formula for human retinal ganglion cell receptive field density as a function of visual field location. J. Vis. **14**(7), 15–15 (2014)

21. Yue, L., Wuyyuru, V., Gonzalez-Calle, A., Dorn, J.D., Humayun, M.S.: Retina-electrode interface properties and vision restoration by two generations of retinal prostheses in one patient-one in each eye. J. Neural Eng. **17**(2), 026020 (2020)

22. Zhang, A.: speech_recognition: Speech recognition module for python, supporting several engines and APIs, online and offline

Automatic Detection of Multiple Sclerosis Using Genomic Expression

Abdullah DH. Ahmed$^{(\boxtimes)}$ ⓘ, Marwa M. A. Hadhoud ⓘ, and Vidan F. Ghoneim ⓘ

Biomedical Engineering Department, Faculty of Engineering, Helwan University, Cairo, Egypt
Abeddhafer23@gmail.com, {Marwa_hadhoud,
vidanfathighoneim}@h-eng.helwan.edu.eg

Abstract. This study leverages microarray data together with statistical and machine learning techniques to investigate the best set of biomarkers in diagnosing multiple sclerosis (MS). In this work to build an automated system to detect MS two phases are approached. The first phase which is of emphasis is to reduce the dimension of features space and select the most discriminative set of features; biomarkers for MS diagnosis. Principal Component Analysis (PCA) was used as a dimension reduction method. Meanwhile, various feature selection methods were used (Fisher score, chi-square, relief, and MRMR). The second phase of this work is the classification phase, where the output of the first phase were assessed. This phase comprises three different classifiers: LDA, SVM, and KNN. Relief feature selection method achieved 100% accuracy with KNN, using 38 differentially expressed genes (DEGs). Out of this set of these DEGs, Key biomarker genes were identified by studying the gene annotation for all. The genes MIF, PTGES3, CYLD, and JAK1 are realized to be associated with immune and neurological functions. Which is of great relevance to MS.

Keywords: Microarray Technology · Statistical techniques · Machine Learning · Dimension Reduction

1 Introduction

Multiple sclerosis (MS) is a chronic neurodegenerative disease affecting mainly young adults, characterized by CNS plaque formation and myelin sheath demyelination, leading to diverse neurological symptoms [1]. Its prevalence varies globally, with higher rates in North America and Europe, affecting approximately 2.8 million people worldwide in 2020 [2]. MS is more common in women, typically worsening between ages 20 and 40 [3].

The exact cause remains unclear, but genetic susceptibility and environmental factors like viral infections and low vitamin D levels are considered contributors [4]. Diagnosis involves patient history, MRI, electrophysiological evaluation, and cerebrospinal fluid analysis [5]. Gene expression analysis using microarrays has been employed in MS research to understand disease mechanisms [6].

M. Mosbah et al. (Eds.): MEDI 2023, CCIS 2071, pp. 144–155, 2024.
https://doi.org/10.1007/978-3-031-55729-3_12

MS manifests in four main forms: Primary progressive MS (PPMS), Secondary progressive MS (SPMS), relapsing-remitting MS (RRMS), and clinically isolated syndrome (CIS) [7].

Previous MS research has utilized statistical and machine learning techniques to identify disease-related biomarkers.

In [8], the authors have identified microRNAs that are up or downregulated in patients with relapsing-remitting MS (RRMS) compared to healthy controls, which can serve as biomarkers for the disease by using machine learning techniques, including support vector machines. The best single miRNA marker achieved an accuracy of 89.7%, and a set of 48 miRNAs achieved 96.3% accuracy in discriminating MS from controls.

Calcagno et al. [9], used Machine learning-based approaches (multilayer perceptron neural network) to predict responsiveness to interferon therapy in MS patients by testing genes in the interferon signaling pathway for single nucleotide polymorphisms (SNPs). They assessed SNPs' connection with interferon therapy response using automatic relevance determination and backwards elimination. This study achieved 70% accuracy in predicting responder and non-responder patients.

In [10], authors studied the peripheral blood mononuclear cells (PBMCs) gene expression of the MS subgroups and the healthy control, and they found that the difference in gene expression can be noticed between the MS and Healthy control, but the difference in gene expression is not significant between the MS subtypes.

In [11], authors developed reliable diagnostic signatures of RRMS by using gene expression data. They used logistic regression with elastic net regression to identify RRMS samples from controls. They tested classifier performance using two feature extraction strategies: one utilizing genes and another using gene pathway data. The two different strategies produced little differences in performance when comparing the 10-fold cross-validation of the training data and prediction on the test data. This study achieved a low classification error ranging from 0.079 to 0.092.

Guo et al. [12], presented a classification model for gene selection by using PBMC gene expression data of MS and control. Recursive Feature Elimination (RFE), ROC analysis, and the Boruta algorithm were used to accomplish this. These techniques were used to identify potential genes for the MS; They found an overlapped collection of 8 genes that showed differential expression between MS and control groups. This study achieved an accuracy of 86% with SVM.

DeMarshall et al. [13], used the human protein microarray to identify autoantibody biomarkers that can be used to diagnose MS. Random Forest examined these biomarkers. The study investigated sera from RRMS, SPMS, PD disease, breast cancer, and healthy controls to determine if biomarkers could distinguish MS patients from normal controls and breast cancer patients. Autoantibody biomarkers achieved an overall accuracy of 95.0% and 100% in distinguishing MS subjects from normal and breast cancer controls respectively. But These biomarkers didn't distinguish MS from Parkinson's.

In [14], authors developed a deep learning model based on an artificial neural network with single hidden layer that reduce the model complexity and prevents overfitting for diagnosing multiple sclerosis disease. This study achieved high accuracy and lower loss compared to traditional methods.

The aim of this study is to explore the biomarkers responsible of MS to improve the classification model for diagnosing MS disease. This objective was achieved using statistical and machine learning techniques. Two phases are adopted in this work. The first phase comprises the identification of biomarkers. In this phase, Principal Component Analysis (PCA) was used for dimensionality reduction, and different Feature selection techniques were used to identify the best set of differentially expressed genes; biomarkers. The second phase representing an assessment step to evaluate the resulting features from the first phase. In this phase different classification models were developed using supervised learning techniques. Also, the resultant biomarkers were assessed by studying their gene annotations to recognize the function of each and its relevance to MS disease.

2   Methodology

The proposed study consisted of two phases. In the first phase, Principal Component Analysis (PCA) was employed for dimension reduction. Moreover, different feature selection techniques were employed to identify the biomarker genes for MS detection. Four feature selection filter methods (Chi Square [15], MRMR [16], Fisher Score [17], and relief algorithm [18]) were investigated.

The second phase comprises the use of three well-known classifiers (SVM [19], LDA [20], and KNN [21]) to evaluate the output of the first phase and complete the process of MS detection. Different kernel functions were used in this phase of microarray data classification.

The proposed analysis is conducted on a dataset of Affymetrix Human Exon 1.0 ST Array presenting 120 samples (comparing 60 patients with MS and 60 control without MS) and each one has 18725 probe sets id (features).

The general scheme for detection of MS using microarray data is illustrated in Fig. 1.

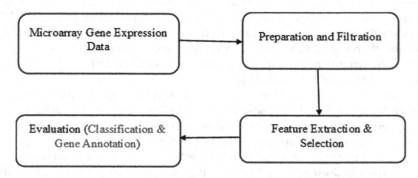

Fig. 1. The proposed Computer-Aided Diagnosis System.

2.1   Data Collection

Gene expression profiles for a total of 120 subjects were obtained from the NCBI Database (https://www.ncbi.nlm.nih.gov/geo/) under the accession number GSE41850

Accordingly, global gene expression in whole blood tissue samples was assessed in 60 multiple sclerosis patients and 60 for control at the time of enrollment (baseline). The specifications of the data can be seen in Table 1.

Table 1. Dataset Specification

Geo dataset	Sample type	Platform	Controls	MS	Visit	Tissue
GSE41850	RNA	GPL16209	60	60	Baseline	Whole blood

2.2 Preprocessing and Filtration

Microarray data was processed to different filters that assists in reducing noise, enhance the quality of the data, and concentrating the research on genes that are more likely to be biologically significant. This stage of preprocessing of the microarray data was done by using MATLAB program. Genes are filtered using small profile variance (***genevarfilter*** function). Then removing genes with low entropy expression values and low absolute values (***geneentropyfilter***, and ***genelowvalfilter*** functions). Each one of these filters used a specific threshold that cleans the data at a certain rate.

Also, Microarray data was processed using the R package "aroma. Affymetrix". The data was background corrected (RMAbackgroundCorrection) and quantum normalized [22]. The summarization step was performed by converting the probe set identifier into a gene official. If the probe corresponds to values of multiple sequences, the average value was calculated. Moreover, removing probes without gene names if present. Figure 2 summarizes the preprocessing and filtration steps.

2.3 Feature Extraction and Feature Selection

This step represents the first phase of this work giving emphasis to identify MS biomarkers. In this phase, Principal Component Analysis (PCA) was used for dimensionality reduction, and different feature selection techniques were used to identify the best set of differentially expressed genes; biomarkers.

2.3.1 Feature Extraction

The main goal of this step is to apply dimensionality reduction technique to explore patterns in the data. From all the possible scenarios, a specific supervised setting is selected. Methods like Principal Component Analysis (PCA), Linear Discriminant Analysis (LDA), and Multidimensional Scaling are utilized to transform the original features into a new feature space, aiming to reveal more meaningful insights. In this study, Principal Component Analysis (PCA) was employed for dimensionality reduction.

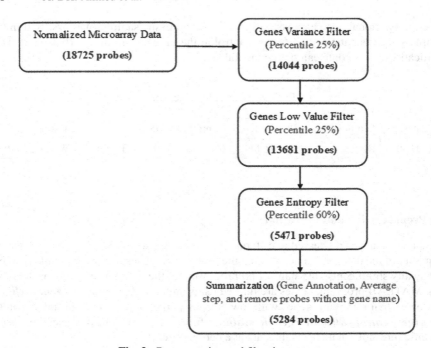

Fig. 2. Preprocessing and filtration steps.

2.3.2 Feature Selection

Feature selection is a crucial process that involves selecting the most relevant and informative features from the initial feature set based on specific criteria. The advantages of feature selection include gaining a deeper understanding of features, reducing computational requirements, and improving classifier performance. There are various ways to categorize feature selection techniques, with filters, wrappers, embedded, and hybrids. In this step, we focus on four feature selection filter methods: Chi Square, Minimum Redundancy and Maximum Relevance (MRMR), Fisher score, and Relief Algorithm.

2.4 Evaluation Phase

This phase representing an assessment step to evaluate the resulting features from the first phase. In this phase different classification models were developed using supervised learning techniques. Also, the assessment is undertaken by studying succinct information regarding the function of each gene, its participation in distinct pathways, and its significance in diverse physiological settings.

2.4.1 Classification

The results of the first phase including feature extraction and feature selection were combined with the classification phase for MS detection. This phase also acts as an evaluation phase for evaluating the out biomarkers of feature selection methods. This phase comprises three classifiers, namely; Linear Discriminant Analysis (LDA), Support Vector Machine (SVM), and K-Nearest Neighbors (KNN) for classification.

2.4.2   Gene Function Annotation

In order to understand functional annotation and interaction of resultant genes in this work, the online STRING database (https://string-db.org/) was used. The retrieved information from the STRING database was analyzed to annotate the functions of the genes. Protein-protein interactions, co-expression patterns, shared pathways, and predicted functional partners were considered for functional annotation.

3   Results and Discussion

This study was conducted through two phases using microarray data from MS patients and healthy individuals. In the first phase, Principal Component Analysis (PCA) was applied for dimension reduction. Along with four feature selection algorithms (chi-square, Fisher score, MRMR, and relief algorithm) for biomarkers detection. In the second phase, the biomarkers are assessed via measuring its predictive power using different classification models as well as investigating the genes' annotations.

3.1   Classification Results

The results of the first phase were combined with three classifiers Linear Discriminant Analysis (LDA), Support Vector Machine (SVM), and K-Nearest Neighbors (KNN) for classification.

The training data was 80 percent of the input dataset, and 20 percent of the input dataset was used for testing the proposed models. For the first experiment that used PCA for dimension reduction, fourteen different experiment scenarios are conducted, and the accuracies are measured for the three types of classifiers LDA, SVM and KNN. The fourteen scenarios are chosen using explained variance threshold. The fourteen thresholds are 50%, 82%, 91%, 94%, 95.7%, 96.7%, 96.9%, 97.4%, 98%, 98.4%, 98.6%, 98.9%, 99%, and 100%. It means first scenario would pick a minimum number of components which satisfies variance kept $\geq 50\%$, and so on. After the PCA conducted, the results are put into three type of classifiers that optimized with different kernel. For evaluating the performance of the different models, four evaluation measures were calculated based on the confusion matrix output by each classifier using testing dataset (i.e., Sensitivity, Specificity, Accuracy, and F1 score). LDA classifier trained with different kernel, linear, quadratic. SVM classifier trained with linear, polynomial, Gaussian and radial basis function. KNN trained with different types of distances and different number of k nearest neighbors. From these attempts, the best accuracy of the LDA obtained by using Linear kernel when the number of components chosen is 26 which keep 96.9% variance during PCA process. From SVM, the best accuracy is obtained by using radial basis function (RBF) when the number of components is 50 which keep 98.8% variance during PCA process. From KNN, best accuracy is obtained by using correlation distance with k = 11when the number of components is 45 which keep 98.9% variance during

PCA process. Finally, the best accuracy of 95.83% was achieved with linear LDA using 26 components.

Table 2 shows the outcomes of applying PCA as a dimension reduction method, together with LDA, SVM, and KNN classifiers. Increasing the number of components retained more relevant information, generally improving classification accuracy. However, accuracy could peak and slightly decline with too many components, indicating the need for a balanced approach to prevent overfitting. Overall, LDA demonstrated higher accuracy compared to SVM and KNN, emphasizing the importance of selecting an appropriate number of components for efficient dimensionality reduction without compromising classification accuracy for different classifiers. Figure 3 presents the outcomes of applying Principal Component Analysis (PCA) as a feature reduction method to the dataset.

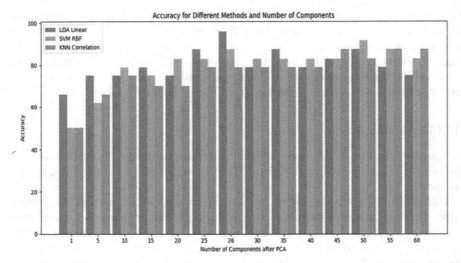

Fig. 3. Result of applying Principal Component Analysis (PCA) as a feature reduction method using the LDA, SVM and KNN classifier

Table 2. Classification results for PCA experiment using multiple sclerosis dataset.

Algorithms	PCA no	Accuracy	Precision	sensitivity	Specificity	F-Score
LDA	**26**	**95.83**	**100**	**91.67**	**100**	**95.65**
SVM	50	91.67	91.67	91.67	91.67	91.67
KNN	45	87.5	84.6	91.67	83.3	88

In the feature selection experiment, four methods were explored: Fisher score, chi-square, relief, and MRMR. Each method exhibited varying accuracies and number of selected features for SVM, KNN and LDA classifiers. Moreover, LDA classifier trained with different kernels (i.e., linear, and quadratic). SVM classifier trained with linear, polynomial, Gaussian, and radial basis function. Different values for K (i.e., the number of neighbors) with KNN classifier were also varying with each feature selection method. After analyzing the performance of different classifiers with the four types of feature selection methods, the KNN classifier (i.e., with correlation distance, and K = 11) considered as the best model for samples prediction with Relief feature selection method with (i.e., k = 5 for Relief), having a predictive accuracy of around 100%.as illustrated in Table 3.

Table 3. Comparison of classification accuracy on MS data set. The number of features used to achieve the maximum is shown inside parenthesis.

Feature Selection Methods	Support Vector Machine	k-Nearest Neighbor	LDA
Fisher score	79 (35)	**79(20)**	91.6(135)
Chi square	87.5(47)	**87.5(7)**	79(45)
Relief	**87.5(30)**	**100(38)**	**87.5(17)**
MRMR	83(80)	**75(27)**	87.5(75)

Fisher score, with a selected subset of 135 features favored LDA with higher accuracy but required more features. Chi-square excelled in accuracy for KNN with fewer features (i.e., just 7 selected features). Relief achieved with best accuracy 100% with KNN and with a moderate number of features (i.e., 38 selected features). MRMR, with 75 selected features, improved LDA accuracy but necessitated more features. These results stress the importance of method choice, as it significantly impacts model performance based on the dataset and classifier used. Further analysis and comparison of these methods can aid in better feature selection decisions. Figure 4 presents the outcomes of applying the different feature selection methods to the dataset.

Figure 5 presents the outcomes of employing the Relief feature selection method in conjunction with the K-nearest neighbor (KNN) classifier, using different numbers of selected features. It displays accuracy percentages for various feature subsets, ranging from 1 to 60 features. The results reveal that as the number of selected features increases, the accuracy of the KNN classifier generally improves until reaching a peak at 38 to 44 features, with accuracy values of 100%. After this peak, including more features leads to a slight decline in accuracy, suggesting that some features may not contribute relevant information or could introduce noise. Moreover, the accuracy drops significantly when using 50 or 60 features, indicating potential overfitting. These findings underscore the importance of feature selection in enhancing the performance of machine learning models, highlighting the significance of striking a balance between the number of features selected and the classifier's performance to avoid overfitting and achieve optimal accuracy on unseen data.

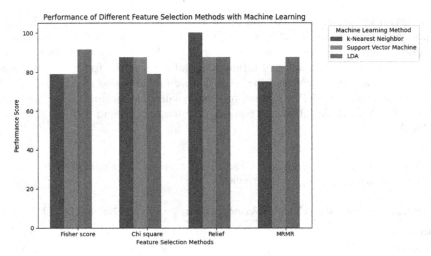

Fig. 4. Result of applying the four feature selection methods with the LDA, SVM and KNN classifiers

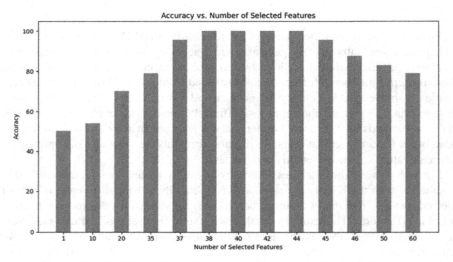

Fig. 5. Results of using Relief feature selection method with KNN classifier.

3.2 Gene Function Annotation

The retrieved information from the String database was analyzed to annotate the functions of the 38 biomarker genes acquired from the feature selection (i.e., by using the Relief algorithm) giving highest classification accuracy. These genes are involved in various essential biological activities, including but not limited to chromatin remodeling, transcriptional control, immunological modulation, and cell signaling. Nevertheless, four genes have been realized to be more effective on MS disease, so the focus will be on their function annotations. Table 4 illustrates the function of each biomarker gene and involvement with MS.

Table 4. Predicted genes from string database with its functions

Gene name	Function and Involvement
MIF	Macrophage migration inhibitory factor; Pro-inflammatory cytokine. Involved in the innate immune response to bacterial pathogens. The expression of MIF at sites of inflammation suggests a role as mediator in regulating the function of macrophages in host defense. Counteracts the anti-inflammatory activity of glucocorticoids. Has phenylpyruvate tautomerase and dopachrome tautomerase activity (in vitro), but the physiological substrate is not known. It is not clear whether the tautomerase activity has any physiological relevance, and whether it is important for cytokine activity. (115 aa)
PTGES3	Prostaglandin E synthase 3; Cytosolic prostaglandin synthase that catalyzes the oxidoreduction of prostaglandin endoperoxide H2 (PGH2) to prostaglandin E2 (PGE2). Molecular chaperone that localizes to genomic response elements in a hormone-dependent manner and disrupts receptor-mediated transcriptional activation, by promoting disassembly of transcriptional regulatory complexes. Facilitates HIF alpha proteins hydroxylation via interaction with EGLN1/PHD2, leading to recruit EGLN1/PHD2 to the HSP90 pathway. (164 aa)
CYLD	Ubiquitin carboxyl-terminal hydrolase CYLD; Deubiquitinase that specifically cleaves 'Lys-63'- and linear 'Met-1'-linked polyubiquitin chains and is involved in NF-kappa-B activation and TNF-alpha-induced necroptosis. Plays an important role in the regulation of pathways leading to NF-kappa-B activation. Contributes to the regulation of cell survival, proliferation, and differentiation via its effects on NF- kappa-B activation. Negative regulator oaf Wnt signaling. Inhibits HDAC6 and thereby promotes acetylation of alpha-tubulin and stabilization of microtubules. Plays a role in the regu [...] (956 aa)
JAK1	Tyrosine-protein kinase JAK1; Tyrosine kinase of the non-receptor type, involved in the IFN-alpha/beta/gamma signal pathway. Kinase partner for the interleukin (IL)-2 receptor as well as interleukin (IL)-10 receptor. (1154 aa)

4   Conclusion

This study shows the potential of microarray technology together with the advancements in machine learning in detecting MS. Principal Component Analysis (PCA) and four feature selection methods were utilized in this work. Yet, yielded reliable biomarkers to be introduced to the prediction model for diagnosing MS. The evaluation of these biomarkers was carried out through investigating the genes' annotations and measuring its predictive power using different classification models. Relief feature selection method yielded 38 DEGs. These DEGs achieved accuracy of 100% with KNN classifier. By investigating the gene annotation of these DEGs, they turned to be closely linked to immune and neurological functions, shedding light on the complex etiology of MS. Notably, the central roles of MIF, PTGES3, CYLD, and JAK1 in gene expression during MS pathogenesis suggest possible milestones for further research and therapeutic interventions.

References

1. Ropper, A.H., Samuels, M.A., Klein, J.P.: Multiple Sclerosis and Allied Demyelinative Disease. The McGraw-Hill Companies, New York (2014)
2. The Multiple Sclerosis International Federation (MSIF). Mapping Multiple Sclerosis around the World Key Epidemiology Findings, Atlas of MS, 3rd ed. London, UK (2020). www.atl asofms.org. Accessed 1 Dec 2020
3. Sadovnick, A.D., Baird, P.A.: Sex ratio in offspring of patients with multiple sclerosis. N. Engl. J. Med. **306**(18), 1114–1115 (1982)
4. van der Mei, I.A., et al.: Past exposure to sun, skin phenotype, and risk of multiple sclerosis: case–control study. BMJ **327**(7410), 316 (2003). https://doi.org/10.1136/bmj.327.7410.316
5. Birnbaum, G.: Making the diagnosis of multiple sclerosis. Adv. Neurol. **98**, 111–124 (2006)
6. Tang, Y., et al.: Gene expression in blood changes rapidly in neutrophils and monocytes after ischemic stroke in humans: a microarray study. J. Cereb. Blood Flow Metab. **26**, 1089–1102 (2006)
7. Lublin, F.D., Reingold, S.C.: Defining the clinical course of multiple sclerosis: results of an international survey. Neurology **46**(4), 907–911 (1996)
8. Keller, A., et al.: Multiple sclerosis: microRNA expression profiles accurately differentiate patients with relapsing-remitting disease from healthy controls. PLoS ONE **4**(10), e7440 (2009)
9. Calcagno, G., et al.: A multilayer perceptron neural network-based approach for the identification of responsiveness to interferon therapy in multiple sclerosis patients. Inf. Sci. **180**(21), 4153–4163 (2010)
10. Ratzer, R., et al.: Gene expression analysis of relapsing–remitting, primary progressive and secondary progressive multiple sclerosis. Mult. Scler. J. **19**(14), 1841–1848 (2013)
11. Zhao, C., Deshwar, A.G., Morris, Q.: Relapsing-remitting multiple sclerosis classification using elastic net logistic regression on gene expression data. Syst. Biomed. **1**(4), 247–253 (2013)
12. Guo, P., Zhang, Q., Zhu, Z., Huang, Z., Li, K.: Mining gene expression data of multiple sclerosis. PLoS ONE **9**(6), e100052 (2014)
13. DeMarshall, C., et al.: Autoantibodies as diagnostic biomarkers for the detection and subtyping of multiple sclerosis. J. Neuroimmunol. **309**, 51–57 (2017)
14. Ponce de Leon-Sanchez, E.R., Dominguez-Ramirez, O.A., Herrera-Navarro, A.M., Rodriguez-Resendiz, J., Paredes-Orta, C., Mendiola-Santibañez, J.D.: A deep learning approach for predicting multiple sclerosis. Micromachines **14**(4), 749 (2023)
15. Ikram, S.T., Cherukuri, A.K.: Intrusion detection model using fusion of chi-square feature selection and multi-class SVM. . King Saudi Saud University Comput. Inf. Sci (2016). https://doi.org/10.1016/j.jksuci.2015.12.004
16. Rachburee, N., Punlumjeak, W.: A comparison of feature selection approach between greedy, IG-ratio, Chi-square, and mRMR in educational mining. In: 2015 7th International Conference on Information Technology and Electrical Engineering (ICITEE). IEEE (2015)
17. Wu, D., Guo, S.Z.: An improved fisher score feature selection method and its application. Chinese J. Liaoning Tech. Univ. **38**(5), 472–479 (2019)

18. Kira, K., Rendell, L.: The feature selection problem: traditional methods and a new algorithm. In: Proceedings of AAAI-92 (1992)
19. Alcaraz, J., Labbé, M., Landete, M.: Support vector machine with feature selection: a multiobjective approach. Expert Syst. Appl. **204**, 117485 (2022)
20. Araveeporn, A., Banditvilai, S.: A classification study in high-dimensional data of linear discriminant analysis and regularized discriminant analysis. WSEAS Trans. Math. **22**, 315–323 (2023)
21. Ayyad, S.M., Saleh, A.I., Labib, L.M.: Gene expression cancer classification using modified K-Nearest Neighbors technique. Biosystems **176**, 41–51 (2019)
22. Nickles, D., et al.: Blood RNA profiling in a large cohort of multiple sclerosis patients and healthy controls. Hum. Mol. Genet. **22**(20), 4194–4205 (2013)

DEITS Workshop: Data Engineering in IoT Systems

Distributed and Collaborative Learning Approach for Stroke Prediction

Firas Aissaoui[1]([✉]), Imen Boudali[1,2], and Takoua Abdellatif[1,3]

[1] SERCOM Laboratory, University of Carthage, 1054 Carthage, Tunisia
firas.aissaoui@ept.ucar.tn, takoua.abdellatif@ept.rnu.tn
[2] National Engineering School of Tunis, University of Tunis ElManar, Tunis, Tunisia
imen.boudali@enit.utm.tn
[3] National Engineering School of Sousse, University of Sousse, Sousse, Tunisia

Abstract. In this paper, we focus on solving a binary classification problem for stroke prediction. The proposed approach is based on a decentralized and collaborative learning without data sharing among hospitals. This federated learning from decentralized electronic health records will provide a relevant framework for multi-institutional collaborations while maintaining data privacy for each participant. We focus on Artificial Neural Network classifier based on distributed medical data of patients. Simulation tests showed the good performances of the proposed approach, which achieves prediction accuracy of 92% in case of two centers and 95% in case of three centers.

Keywords: Federated learning · Predictive models · Classification · Clinical data · Stroke prediction

1 Introduction

As stated in [1], healthcare management has globally shifted from a disease-centered approach to a patient-centered approach. To meet the requirements of this approach and deliver efficient patient-centered care, it is essential to analyze and manage healthcare big data. A vast amount of data and electronic health records are continually generated by various types of sensors and through social media.

This big data encompasses various types of information, such as medical images, laboratory tests, genomic data, and more. Proper utilization of this abundant data would provide robust support for clinical decision-making and health management.

One major challenge in dealing with clinical data is data quality. In fact, the quality of results from analytical tools highly depends on the quality of medical data. Moreover, the size of datasets in a single center may vary considerably, while analytical tools require additional validation with larger and more diverse patient populations in a multicenter context. Another critical concern in the medical field is data privacy. Patient identity and sensitive information must be protected by healthcare institutions.

M. Mosbah et al. (Eds.): MEDI 2023, CCIS 2071, pp. 159–171, 2024.
https://doi.org/10.1007/978-3-031-55729-3_13

In this work, our primary focus is on addressing the following challenges:

- Data is stored in different locations: hospitals, clinical units, etc.
- Infeasible and impractical solutions for aggregating data into a single database due to the size and privacy of medical data.

To address these challenging issues, we propose a distributed computational scheme that preserves the distribution of data and their privacy without sharing patient-specific data. The main purpose of this paper is to develop a federated approach to predict strokes and identify risk factors for patients based on previous experiences stored in different locations. This approach will provide a collaborative framework for different parties to develop a global prediction model. The problem we address is binary classification, and the machine learning method we use is Artificial Neural Network (ANN). This method involves learning algorithms that can independently adjust when receiving new inputs, making it an effective tool for predictive analysis.

Our focus is on stroke diseases, as they represent one of the leading causes of morbidity and mortality worldwide. This disease has resulted in a significant proportion of hospitalizations, with over 12 million new strokes occurring each year worldwide [2]. For many decades, research has primarily focused on diagnosing and treating these diseases. However, efforts have recently shifted toward the early prevention of these conditions. This objective has a significant impact on public health, as well as considerable socioeconomic consequences. In fact, preventing stroke conditions by identifying risk factors, providing early treatment, and intensifying follow-up could improve patient survival and ensure long-term health stability.

The remainder of this paper is organized as follows. In Sect. 2, we present a literature review on stroke prediction and highlight the main limitations and challenging issues. Then, in Sect. 3, we present the proposed collaborative approach for stroke prediction. Simulation results on federated databases are discussed in Sect. 4. Finally, conclusions and future works are presented in Sect. 5.

2 Literature Review

In the literature, concerted efforts have been focused on stroke diseases to improve patient care management. Given the growing synergy between technology and the medical field, new opportunities have emerged for better health management using data mining techniques on electronic health records.

Previous studies have considered various aspects of stroke prediction. In the early work of [3], a decision tree model was developed on a cardiovascular health database to predict strokes. In [4], the authors focused on the probability of strokes by studying the risk factors. For this purpose, a support vector machine model was used to identify the impact of each factor on strokes. The prediction of strokes using laboratory tests of patients was proposed by [5].

Machine learning models, such as random forest, decision trees, and naive Bayes, were developed and compared after employing different data selection techniques, including data resampling and data imputation. Moreover, in the study conducted by [6], machine learning models, including artificial neural networks, support vector machines, boosting, bagging, and random forest, were developed and compared based on a centralized dataset of patient records.

In addition to classical machine learning models, deep learning has also been involved in stroke prediction. In [7], the authors compared the performances of deep learning models and classical machine learning models to predict strokes from a centralized medical database. Deep learning was also used in [8] to predict stroke patient mortality. In this work, the authors employed principal component analysis to extract relevant features and developed deep neural networks for the classification task based on a single medical database. Long short-term memory was proposed for stroke prediction in [9]. In this study, a comparison of different deep learning architectures, including propagation neural networks, recurrent neural networks, and long short-term recurrent neural networks, was performed, and high accuracy was achieved with the long short-term recurrent neural networks model.

Distinct time series-based approaches were also proposed in [10] for the prediction of early strokes based on biosignals. These deep learning approaches are mainly based on long short-term memory, gated recurrent unit, and feed-forward neural networks.

A hybrid deep learning approach was proposed by [11], considering convolutional neural networks and long short-term memory models. The aim of this study is to predict strokes from biomedical signals through a mobile health platform.

Consequently, in the literature, various machine learning techniques and models have achieved good performance in dealing with stroke prediction [11]. Nevertheless, some issues are still faced and need to be tackled. External validations of these models in a multicenter context are recommended for generalizability purposes. These validations require multicenter collaborations based on data sharing. At this level, data privacy represents a significant concern. In fact, medical data are very sensitive and require privacy protection, confidentiality, and security. These significant hurdles limit the accessibility of medical data in a multicenter context. Thus, it is essential to facilitate multicenter collaborations without sharing patient data.

3   Proposed Approach

In this work, we propose a collaborative and distributed approach for stroke prediction while preserving data privacy. The proposed approach is based on federated learning, which is a recent paradigm for collective learning. Federated learning, initially suggested by Google [12, 13], allows on-device learning without sharing local data.

This approach provides decentralized data for machine learning models and protects confidential data. Federated learning has gained increasing interest in real applications where data privacy is vital [14]. In this section, we present the basic architecture of our approach. Then, we discuss the implementation details.

3.1 Architecture

The basic idea of our approach is to train a model at different centers on local data and share only model parameters with a central entity or server. Aggregation of system parameters creates an updated global model on the server, which benefits from the collective knowledge without compromising data privacy.

The training process of federated learning is iteratively performed to converge towards a good global model. Thus, users do not have to share their private data; instead, they share the parameters of the locally learned model with the server (see Fig. 1).

This approach is particularly promising in the context of stroke prediction, where healthcare institutions may have valuable patient data that must remain confidential. By adopting federated learning, we empower these institutions to contribute to a collaborative effort to improve stroke prediction without the need to expose sensitive patient information. Our work represents a significant step toward leveraging advanced machine learning techniques while respecting data privacy in healthcare.

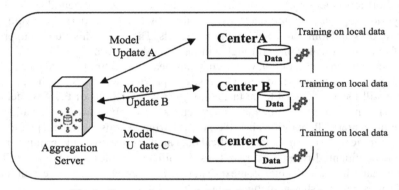

Fig. 1. Proposed Approach for Collaborative Learning

3.2 Implementation

In our approach, we used Artificial Neural Network (ANN) as a stroke prediction model. The architecture of this model is constructed using the Keras Sequential API (Application Programming Interface) [15] and encompasses several layers, forming a moderately neural network tailored for binary classification tasks. The initial layer serves as the input layer with 128 neurons and rectified linear unit (ReLU) activation, configured to match the dimensionality of the input features in the dataset. Subsequently, a Dropout layer with a dropout rate of 30% is introduced, functioning as a regularization technique to mitigate overfitting by randomly excluding a fraction of neurons during training. Following this, a second dense hidden layer with 64 neurons and ReLU activation is incorporated, succeeded by another Dropout layer featuring a higher dropout rate of 50%. The network further deepens with a third dense hidden layer containing 32 neurons and ReLU activation. Finally, a dense output layer with a single neuron and sigmoid activation is added, making it suitable for binary classification problems (see Fig. 2).

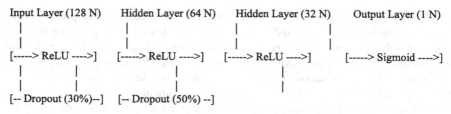

Fig. 2. Architecture of the ANN model

The choice of the number of layers often involves empirical experimentation and consideration of the specific characteristics of the dataset. The depth of the architecture is a trade-off, as deeper networks can capture more intricate patterns but may also be prone to overfitting, if not properly regularized. In this context, the model was compiled using the Adam optimizer [15], reflecting a choice made during the configuration of the neural network's training process. The Adam optimizer is known for its effectiveness in optimizing neural networks, striking a balance between capturing complex patterns and preventing overfitting. •

4   Simulation and Results

In order to assess the performances of the proposed approach, we provide in this section the simulation details and we discuss the obtained results.

4.1 Electronic Health Records

The provided dataset is accessible to the public on Kaggle [16]. It encompasses electronic health records containing the medical histories of patients that have or not experienced a stroke. Each patient's medical history includes demographic details and laboratory test results. This dataset comprises records from 40910 patients, featuring a total of 10 input attributes and 1 output feature. The output variable is binary, indicating whether a patient has encountered a stroke or not. The 10 input features in the electronic health records (EHR) are as follows:

- Sex: gender of the patient (1: male; 0: female).
- Age: age of the patient in years.
- Hypertension: presence (1) or absence (0) of hypertension.
- Heart_disease: presence (1) or absence (0) of heart disease.
- Ever_married: marital status of the patient (1: married; 0: not married).
- Work_type: Job type of the patient, categorized as (0): never_worked, (1): children, (2): govt_job, (3): self-employed, (4): private.
- Residence_type: patient's residential area, categorized as (1): urban, (0): rural.
- Avg_glucose_level: Average blood sugar level of the patient.
- BMI: Body Mass Index.
- Smoking_status: Smoking status of the patient, categorized as (1): smokes, (0): never smoked.

Before the construction of the model, it is crucial to engage in data preprocessing to eliminate undesirable noise and outliers from the dataset. The presence of these elements has the potential to lead the model astray from its intended training path. This preprocessing stage involves tackling all factors that impede the optimal functionality of the model. Thus, the dataset requires comprehensive cleaning and preparation to establish a solid foundation for effective model development.

It's noteworthy that the dataset exhibits a high degree of balance concerning the occurrence of stroke events.

4.2 Performance Evaluation

During the assessment of our approach, we used the most common performance metrics [17]. These metrics include:

- Sensitivity: It measures the proportion of actual positive cases (stroke) that the model correctly identifies as positive.
- Specificity: It measures the proportion of actual negative cases (no stroke) that the model correctly identifies as negative.
- Accuracy: It represents the overall correctness of the model's predictions across both positive and negative cases.
- Precision: It quantifies the proportion of true positive predictions among all positive predictions made by the model.
- F1-Score: It is the harmonic mean of precision and sensitivity, providing a balance between the two. It is particularly useful when dealing with imbalanced datasets.

These metrics collectively offer a comprehensive evaluation of a model's performance, taking into account both its ability to correctly identify positive and negative cases and its capacity to minimize false positives and false negatives.

4.3 Experimental Results

To study the effectiveness of our approach, we conducted two distinct experiment scenarios.

A. Scenario 1: Collaboration of two centers

In this scenario, we partitioned the global dataset into two distinct data centers, each receiving a specific portion of the data, as outlined in Table 1.

Table 1. Data Distribution between Two Centers

Center	Dataset size
Center 1	29413
Center 2	11438

The two centers collaborated to develop an aggregated global model over the span of 20 rounds, without sharing data between them. Additionally, we evaluated the model's performance after training on a test dataset containing 8824 instances. Figure 3 illustrates the accuracy evaluation of the aggregated model throughout the collaboration, providing insights into its performance across multiple rounds of collaborative learning.

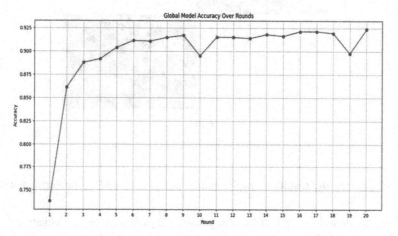

Fig. 3. Global Model Accuracy over rounds in Scenario 1

This evaluation curve shows overall growth during the training process. Notably, the model converges after 20 rounds, indicating that further rounds may not be necessary.

The graph illustrates a reduction in the accuracy of the federated model by creating local minima. These variations can be attributed to the impact of the weight averaging technique employed in local models.

The global model's performance metrics after evaluation on the test dataset are as follows:

- Accuracy: 0.92
- Precision: 0.87
- Recall: 0.999
- F1-Score: 0.93
- AUC: 0.92

The model's test performance is summarized using a confusion matrix as depicted in Fig. 4.

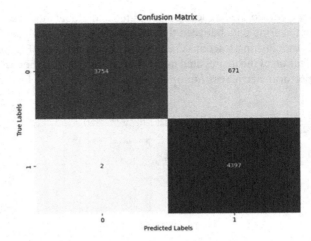

Fig. 4. Confusion matrix for the two centers

By considering the results on both centers, our global model's performance shows that:

- It correctly identified 3754 cases as negative, and they were indeed negative.
- It misclassified 671 cases as positive when they were actually negative.
- It missed only 2 positive cases by classifying them as negative.
- It correctly identified 4397 cases as positive, and they were indeed positive.

Furthermore, we conducted a comparative analysis between the global model created through the collaboration of the two centers and the locally trained models developed by each individual center. The local models share the same architecture as the global model but are trained using center-specific local data.

As illustrated in Table 2, the obtained results clearly indicate that predictions made using the aggregated global model outperform those of the centralized model. These results are more obvious in Fig. 5.

Table 2. Obtained results for the two centers

Center	Local model	Global model
Center 1	Accuracy: 0.93 Loss: 0.19	Accuracy: 0.93 Loss: 0.16
Center 2	Accuracy: 0.88 Loss: 0.28	Accuracy: 0.92 Loss: 0.16

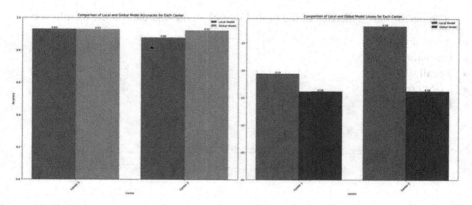

Fig. 5. Comparison of local and global model for each center according to accuracy and loss rate

B. Scenario 2: Collaboration of three centers

In this scenario, we partitioned the global dataset into three distinct data centers, each receiving a specific portion of the data, as outlined in Table 3.

Table 3. Data Distribution between Three Centers

Center	Dataset size
Center 1	13072 instances
Center 2	6944 instances
Center 3	20834 instances

We maintained a fixed number of rounds (i.e., 20 rounds) to create the aggregated global model through collaboration among the three centers. Furthermore, we assessed the global model's performance on a test dataset consisting of 6251instances.

Figure 6 visually portrays the accuracy evaluation of the aggregated model throughout the collaborative process, providing valuable insights into its performance across multiple rounds of collaborative learning.

The performance metrics of the global model on the test dataset are as follows:

- Accuracy: 0.95
- Precision: 0.92
- Recall: 0.98
- F1-Score: 0.95
- AUC: 0.95

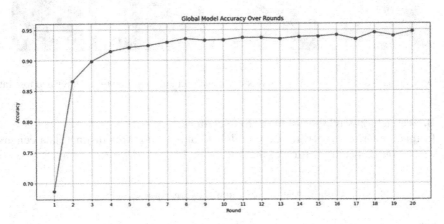

Fig. 6. Global Model Accuracy over rounds in Scenario 2

Using a similar approach as outlined in the previous scenario, the comparison between the predictions made by the global model outperforms those of the centralized models from the three centers. The obtained results as provided in Table 4 shows the good performances of the global model.

Table 4. Obtained results with three centers

Center	Local model	Global model
Center 1	Accuracy: 0.89 Loss: 0.26	Accuracy: 0.95 Loss: 0.13
Center 2	Accuracy: 0.86 Loss: 0.33	Accuracy: 0.95 Loss: 0.14
Center 3	Accuracy: 0.91 Loss: 0.23	Accuracy: 0.95 Loss: 0.14

C. Scenario 3: Centralized and Federated Models

By considering that the different centers share their datasets with each other, we created a centralized model with all the datasets, and then we compare the performance metrics between the federated models already trained in the previous scenarios and the centralized model.

As depicted in Table 5, the obtained results provide clear evidence that generated predictions by the aggregated global models surpass those produced by the centralized model. These differences become even more pronounced in Fig. 7.

Table 5. Obtained Results for centralized and federated model

Centralized model	Federated model (Scenario 1)	Federated model (Scenario 2)
Accuracy: 0.913	Accuracy: 0.924	Accuracy: 0.948
Precision: 0.889	Precision: 0.869	Precision: 0.925
Recall: 0.944	Recall: 0.999	Recall: 0.976
F1-Score: 0.916	F1-Score: 0.929	F1-Score: 0.950

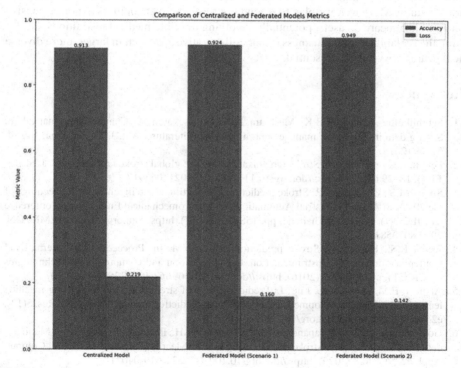

Fig. 7. Comparison of centralized and federated models (Scenario 1, 2) according to accuracy and loss rate

5 Conclusions

Our research has unveiled valuable insights into the world of healthcare data analysis using advanced machine learning techniques. By leveraging a robust electronic health record dataset and employing a sophisticated federated learning model, our experimental results demonstrated the superiority of the aggregated global model over the centralized models in two different scenarios: two and three centers. This superiority was evident in terms of higher accuracy, lower loss, and other critical performance metrics. The collaborative nature of our approach proved effectiveness in optimizing model performance while preserving data privacy and confidentiality. Our study underscores the importance of balancing model performance with data security, making strides toward a future where cutting-edge technology can coexist harmoniously with the healthcare industry's stringent privacy requirements. While our study yields promising results, there are several avenues for future research and improvement. First, exploring more complex machine learning architectures and techniques could enhance model performance further. Additionally, investigating the impact of varying the number of rounds in the federated learning process on model convergence and performance is a valuable area of study. Moreover, we plan to extend our research to encompass a more extensive range of healthcare datasets, potentially involving multiple medical institutions. Evaluating the scalability and robustness of our collaborative approach in larger, more diverse healthcare ecosystems is essential.

References

1. Senthilkumar, S.A., Rai, B.K., Meshram, A.A., Gunasekaran, A., Chandrakumarmangalam, S.: Big data in healthcare management: a review of literature. Am. J. Theor. Appl. Bus. **4**, 57–69 (2018)
2. Feigin, V.L., et al.: World Stroke Organization (WSO): global stroke fact sheet. Int. J. Stroke **17**(1), 18–29 (2022). https://doi.org/10.1177/17474930211065917
3. Singh, M.S., Choudhary, P.: Stroke prediction using artificial intelligence. In: Proceedings of the 2017 8th Annual Industrial Automation and Electromechanical Engineering Conference (IEMECON), Bangkok, Thailand, pp. 158–161 (2017). https://doi.org/10.1109/IEMECON.2017.8079581
4. Jeena, R.S., Kumar, S.: Stroke prediction using SVM. In: Proceedings of International Conference on Control, Instrumentation, Communication and Computational Technologies (ICCICCT), pp. 600–602 (2016). https://doi.org/10.1109/ICCICCT.2016.7988020
5. Alanazi, E.M., Abdou, A., Luo, J.: Predicting Risk of stroke from lab tests using machine learning algorithms: development and evaluation of prediction models. JMIR Form Res. **5**(12), e23440 (2021). https://doi.org/10.2196/23440
6. Govindarajan, P., Soundarapandian, R.K., Gandomi, A.H., Patan, R., Jayaraman, P., Manikandan, R.: Classification of stroke disease using machine learning algorithms. Neural Comput. Appl. **32**, 817–828 (2020). https://doi.org/10.1007/s00521-019-04041-y
7. Hung, C.-Y., Chen, W.-C., Lai, P.-T., Lin, C.-H., Lee, C.-C.: Comparing deep neural network and other machine learning algorithms for stroke prediction in a large-scale population-based electronic medical claims database. In: 2017 39th Annual International Conference of the IEEE Engineering in Medicine and Biology Society (EMBC),pp. 3110–3113. IEEE (2017)
8. Cheon, S., Kim, J., Lim, J.: The use of deep learning to predict stroke patient mortality. Int. J. Environ. Res. Public Health **16**, 1876 (2019)

9. Chantamit-o-pas, P., Goyal, M.: Long short-term memory recurrent neural network for stroke prediction. In: Perner, P. (ed.) Machine Learning and Data Mining in Pattern Recognition: 14th International Conference, MLDM 2018, New York, NY, USA, July 15-19, 2018, Proceedings, Part I, pp. 312–323. Springer, Cham (2018). https://doi.org/10.1007/978-3-319-96136-1_25

10. Kaur, M., Sakhare, S.-R., Wanjale, K., Akter, F.: Early stroke prediction methods for prevention of strokes. Behav Neuro. Hindawi. (2022). https://doi.org/10.1155/2022/7725597

11. Elbagoury, B.M., Vladareanu, L., Vlădăreanu, V., Salem, A.B., Travediu, A.M., Roushdy, M.I.A.: Hybrid stacked CNN and residual feedback GMDH-LSTM deep learning model for stroke prediction applied on mobile AI smart hospital platform. Sensors. **23**(7), 3500 (2023). https://doi.org/10.3390/s23073500

12. Konecêny, J., McMahan, H.B., Yu, F.X., Richtarik, P., Suresh, A.T., Bacon, D.: Federated learning: strategies for improving communication efficiency. arXiv preprint arXiv:1610.05492 (2016)

13. Bonawitz K., et al.: Towards federated learning at scale: System design. arXiv preprint arXiv: 1902.01046 (2019)

14. Rahman, A., et al.: Federated learning-based AI approaches in smart healthcare: concepts, taxonomies, challenges and open issues. Cluster Comput. **17**, 1–41 (2022). https://doi.org/10.1007/s10586-022-03658-4

15. Documentations from Tensorflow Keras. https://www.tensorflow.org

16. Health Dataset (Stroke Data). https://www.kaggle.com/datasets/prosperchuks/health-dataset?select=stroke_data.csv

17. Hossin, M., Sulaiman, M.N.: A review on evaluation metrics for data classification evaluations. Int. J. Data Min. Knowl. Manag. Process **5**, 1 (2015)

IoT Technologies for Smart Healthcare Buildings with Distributed Deep Learning Techniques

Hassen Hamdi[1]([✉]), Rim Zarrouk[2], Ramzi Mahmoudi[2,3], and Narjes Bennour[4]

[1] MIRACL (Multimedia, Information Systems and Advanced Computing Laboratory), University of Sfax, Sfax, Tunisia
hhassen2006@yahoo.fr
[2] Laboratoire Technologie Imagerie Médicale - LTIM-LR12ES06, FMM, University of Monastir, 5019 Monastir, Tunisia
ramzi.mahmoudi@esiee.fr
[3] Laboratoire d'Informatique Gaspard-Monge,Unité Mixte CNRS-UMLV-ESIEE UMR8049, ESIEE Paris Cité Descartes, BP99, Noisy Université Paris-Est Le Grand, 93162 Noisy-Le-Grand, France
[4] Laboratory of Biophysics and Medical Technologies, El Manar University, Tunis, Tunisia

Abstract. The integration of Internet of Things (IoT) technologies into healthcare buildings has recently shown to be a considerable problem. These buildings, commonly known as "intelligent" or "automated" buildings, employ several intelligent technologies such as building management systems, energy efficiency measures, automated systems, adaptive energy systems, wireless technologies, remote monitoring, digital infrastructure, and information and communications networks. However, the term "intelligent buildings" is not specific and can refer to various structures. The goal of this paper is to highlight the advantages of using distributed deep learning and IoT technologies to improve the intelligence and responsiveness of healthcare facilities, hence improving their overall performance. The findings of this research have practical implications, especially in the development of Smart Building applications for the healthcare sector. The objective of this study is to demonstrate that distributed deep learning and IoT technology can serve as a strong foundation for constructing efficient and scalable Smart Building applications in healthcare. The experimental results confirm that distributed deep learning and IoT technologies provide a suitable infrastructure for creating powerful and intelligent healthcare buildings. The study also reveals that smart technology offers a promising framework for enhancing the robustness and performance of intelligent buildings, leveraging the capabilities of distributed deep learning and IoT technologies.

Keywords: Healthcare building · Distributed deep learning · IoT

1 Introduction

Advancements in technology have made it possible to control and manage electrical appliances remotely using laptops, computers, and internet connections. This has resulted in increased convenience and flexibility in regulating devices in various settings, such as households, universities, and industrial environments worldwide. The Internet of Things (IoT) has facilitated the control of different devices, including lighting fixtures, power plugs, fans, computers, security systems, and other appliances. The primary goal of IoT is to aid individuals with disabilities and the elderly by simplifying the management of electrical appliances and enhancing security.

The integration of physical objects into computer-based systems has improved efficiency, accuracy, and economic benefits by enabling the remote control of objects enabled by IoT. Combining IoT with sensors and actuators results in a cyber-physical system that encompasses technologies such as smart environment grids, smart homes, intelligent transportation, and smart cities. Each IoT-enabled object has a unique identifier and can interoperate within the existing Internet infrastructure.

Deep Learning (DL), a machine learning framework that has demonstrated exceptional performance in various fields, including smart buildings based on IoT technology, eliminates the need for extensive feature engineering, a time-consuming process typical of traditional machine learning methods. Moreover, DL is adaptable to new challenges and utilizes techniques such as convolutional neural networks, recurrent neural networks, long short-term memory, and other approaches that make it an ideal option for smart city applications.

The deployment of smart buildings that rely on IoT technology necessitates a substantial amount of data, and training deep learning models can be computationally expensive, with the most complex models requiring weeks to train using multiple machines with expensive GPUs. This paper examines how deep learning can be distributed in a multi-core and distributed setup, specifically within the context of IoT technologies in smart buildings.

The paper is organized as follows: Sect. 2 introduces the concepts of smart buildings based on IoT technologies. Section 3 presents the problem statement. The proposed solution is presented in Sect. 4. Results and discussion of the study are presented in Sect. 5. Finally, the last section provides the main conclusions.

2 Smart Building Based on IoT Technologies

2.1 Smart Building

Smart building refers to a structure that utilizes automated processes to autonomously control various operational aspects such as heating, ventilation, air conditioning, lighting, security, and other systems. This is achieved using sensors, actuators, and microchips that collect and manage data based on the specific functions and services of the building. By leveraging this infrastructure, owners, operators, and facility managers can enhance asset reliability and performance, reduce energy consumption, optimize space utilization, and minimize the environmental impact of the building [1–3, 31, 32].

In contrast, traditional buildings that lack connectivity remain unchanged over the years, providing basic functionalities such as shelter, temperature control, and safety without the ability to adapt. In contrast, smart buildings, whether newly constructed or retrofitted from older structures, are dynamic entities interconnected through intelligent and adaptable software, constantly evolving to meet the changing demands of modern facilities management [4, 5].

2.2   Regenerate Response Smart Building Based on IoT Technologies

The rapid population growth and increased density in urban areas have created a demand for services and infrastructure to meet the needs of city dwellers. Consequently, there has been a notable increase in the use of embedded devices like sensors, actuators, and smartphones, creating immense opportunities for businesses in the era of the Internet of Things (IoT), where devices can connect and communicate with each other over the Internet. Internet technologies provide a way to integrate and share a common communication platform. In this paper, we present a unified system that leverages IoT for the advancement of smart buildings [6–9]. Figure 1 illustrates the Smart Building Based on IoT Technologies.

Fig. 1. Smart Building Based on IoT Technologies

3   Problem Statement

Smart building development based on IoT technologies necessitates a significant volume of data, particularly when dealing with thousands of examples. The term "big data" can be challenging to grasp as it can have different meanings to different people. Essentially, big data refers to two key phenomena: the extraordinary speed at which data is being generated and the need to enhance the capacity for storing, processing, and analyzing such data. Consequently, the tools and platforms utilized for managing big data differ significantly from those used for traditional data management [10].

Furthermore, training complex models for smart buildings is computationally intensive and time-consuming. The most advanced models require weeks of training on multiple machines equipped with costly GPUs [11–16]. As a result, deep learning may not necessarily outperform other approaches in this context.

4 Proposed Approach

The current system for monitoring and controlling buildings to enable smart features is based on traditional methods. However, one major drawback is that it lacks an IoT-based electronic device that serves as the foundation for smart buildings. The difference between a traditionally built home and a smart home is significant. In a traditionally built home, you must manually perform tasks like turning on the TV, closing window shades, and switching off lights, and then switch sources for additional devices. But in a smart home based on deep learning, you can simply press one button to automate all these [17, 18].

4.1 Deep Learning

Big data analytics and Deep Learning are two prominent areas of focus in the field of data science. The significance of Big Data has grown due to the massive amounts of domain-specific information being collected by organizations, both public and private. This data can contain valuable insights for various domains, such as national intelligence, cyber security, fraud detection, marketing, and Smart building development. Companies like Google and Microsoft are leveraging the analysis of large data volumes for business analysis and decision-making, influencing current and future technologies. On the other hand, Deep learning algorithms work in a way that mimics how humans learn, using a hierarchical process to extract complex and meaningful representations from data. Machine learning is a subset of AI, which enables the machine to automatically learn from data, improve performance from past experiences, and make predictions. Machine learning contains a set of algorithms that work on a huge amount of data. Data is fed to these algorithms to train them, and on the basis of training, they build the model & perform a specific task. These ML algorithms help to solve different business problems like Regression, Classification, Forecasting, Clustering, and Associations, etc. Based on the methods and way of learning, machine learning is divided into mainly four types, which are: Supervised Machine Learning, Unsupervised Machine Learning, Semi-Supervised Machine Learning and Reinforcement Learning [19–24].

4.2 Distributed Deep Learning Techniques for Smart Building Based on IoT Technologies

The application of large-scale smart buildings involves the learning of complex abstractions at different levels of a hierarchy, building upon simpler abstractions formulated in preceding levels. Distributed Deep Learning (DDL) offers a key advantage in analyzing and learning from massive amounts of unsupervised data, making it a valuable tool for big Data Analytics where data is often unlabeled and uncategorized. The concept of DDL aims to parallelize and distribute deep learning in multi-core and distributed settings [25].

In our approach, we aim to use distributed deep learning to overcome significant challenges in the field of big data analytics. This includes tasks like extracting complex patterns from massive amounts of data, semantic indexing, data tagging, fast information retrieval, and simplifying discriminative tasks. We also investigate areas of deep learning

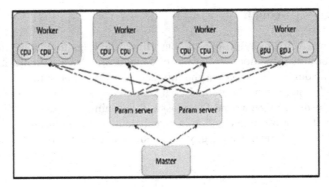

Fig. 2. Distributed Deep Learning.

research that need further exploration, especially in the context of big data analytics, such as handling streaming data, high-dimensional data, model scalability, and distributed computing. Figure 2 illustrates the overall strategy used in our approach.

Figure 3 describe the whole architecture of our application:

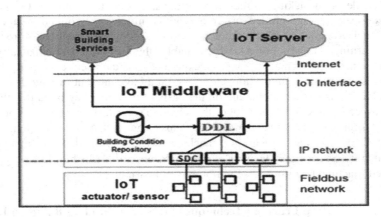

Fig. 3. Distributed Deep Learning Techniques for Smart Building Based on IoT Technologies.

The Clustering algorithm is applied as Unsupervised Machine Learning model in our approach to group or categories the unsorted dataset according to the similarities, patterns, and differences. Machines are instructed to find the hidden patterns from the input dataset [24].

4.3 A Secured Distributed Deep Learning Based on via the Application of Authentication as a Service (AaaS) in the Cloud

Security in a distributed learning model for Smart Building based on IoT Technologies is a critical aspect that should be considered. To resolve the security problem of our distributed Deep learning model, the new paradigm distributed platform such as the cloud computing model Software as a Service (SaaS) especially Security as a Service (SecaaS) is used for security management, via the application of Authentication as a service (AaaS) in the cloud. Based on considering Authentication as a service (AaaS) in the cloud to the Identity and Access Management (IAM) system. This application allows any devices or an entity to authenticate access to the pervasive network. Such a device may be human user, equipment, or another server. The AaaS application can be configured in addicted PC, an access point, a central server, or a LAN switch [26].

5   The Experimental Study

In this section, we will provide details about the hardware and software utilized in our evaluation of the approach. We will also outline the experimental environment, system testing process and platforms, as well as the usage of the blue serial (IoT) for data storage and analysis. Finally, we will discuss the analysis of results. The workflow diagram (Fig. 4) summarizes all the elements used in our evaluation.

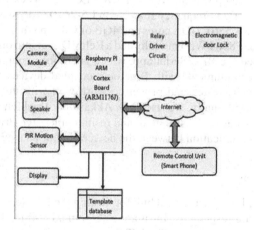

Fig. 4. Workflow of the proposed model features

5.1   Hardware Description

In this section, we present the hardware used to implement our application:

Bluetooth is the most common sense, short-range radio development to share data between mobiles, tablets, PCs and other handheld contraptions. Bluetooth keep running from 10–100 mts and influences Personal Area to organize (PAN). A plan of contraptions sharing data on same Bluetooth correspondence channel shapes "Piconet".

Arduino Uno board: is equipped with digital and analog input/output pins that can be connected to various expansion boards and circuits. It also features a serial communication interface, including USB, which allows programs to be loaded from a computer.

Voltage regulator: is a device used to maintain a constant voltage level and regulate AC or DC voltages. It may utilize a negative feed-forward design or negative feedback control loops.

WiFi Module: is typically used for wireless communication between devices. However, it may not be capable of shifting logic levels from 5V to 3V and may require an external logic level converter.

PIR Sensor: also known as a motion sensor, can detect human motion through infrared (IR) radiation. When a person passes through the sensor's field of view, it automatically senses the motion and sends data to the microcontroller.

Relay Driver (IC ULN2803 APG): used in the circuit has the following characteristics: 500mA rated collector current, high voltage outputs of up to 50V, output clamp diodes for protection, and inputs that are compatible with the microcontroller.

5.2 Software Description

For our analysis, we used powerful Amazon AWS EC2 instances with GPUs [27, 28]. These instances had 8 High Frequency Intel Xeon E5-2670 Processors and an NVIDIA GRID K520 GPU with 1,536 CUDA cores and 4GB of video memory. We also integrated an Arduino Uno, an ESP8266 WiFi module, and a Relay Driver into our setup. To connect these devices, we used the Blue Serial app, which is an open-source app designed for Android devices to communicate with Bluetooth-enabled devices like Arduino. This app has been extensively tested and proven to work well with the JY- MCU module and other devices. Additionally, we used the Akka toolkit, which is a powerful tool for building highly concurrent, distributed, and resilient message-driven applications in Java, to facilitate communication between the devices in our analysis.

5.3 Implementation

In this setup, the cloud acts as a central hub for hosting the IoT Server and Smart Building Services, which are responsible for managing home, building automation services and predicting power consumption. The IoT Server stores long-term data from the IoT actuators and sensors, such as condition and metering values, and controls access to these devices through a role-based access control list (ACL).

To enable communication between the cloud services and the fieldbus or wireless network, we implement a middleware layer. This middleware layer operates in near real-time conditions and includes a Smart Building Manager (SBM) and a Smart Device Controller (SDC). The SBM provides real-time status information of the building through RESTful Web Services, in addition to handling addressing functions. The SDC is responsible for mapping proprietary data to standardized data structures to ensure smooth communication and interoperability [29].

At the fieldbus and wireless network level, we use various protocols, such as "Using Sensors to Optimize Operations," "UC Irvine Laboratory Ventilation," "Controlling Multiple Zones," and "Control Hotel," to facilitate communication and control of the

IoT devices in the smart building environment. These protocols are designed to optimize operations, improve ventilation, control multiple zones, and manage hotel facilities effectively.

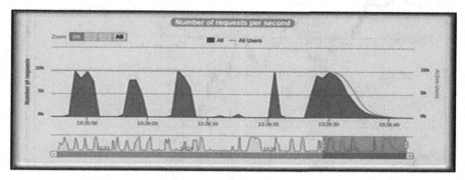

Fig. 5. Track building smart performance by using Akka-based application.

5.4 Experimental Results and Discussions

The analysis of the proposed system involves conducting critical evaluations using different approaches. However, it could become challenging to maintain separate programs for each device in the fleet. As the number of devices increases, it becomes harder to manage multiple versions of the code. Often, it is feasible to run the same program on multiple microcontrollers of the same type, even if they have different capabilities. Instead of creating separate programs for each Netduino microcontroller, a single program can be deployed on all Netduinos, with each device identifying itself based on its MAC address and performing its specific tasks accordingly. This approach allows for different behavior of the same program based on variations in IoT devices. The power consumption and power reports of all devices will be displayed in the Fig. 5.

Figures 5 and 6 depict the expenditure analysis report for home automation devices, expected to drive an increase in usage and impact the overall technological ecosystem. This is due to the inherent vulnerabilities of IoT objects and the close integration of the physical and virtual worlds through smart devices.

Figure 7 illustrates the tracking of actors and dispatcher home appliance usage using Akka-based applications, which is anticipated to drive a transformation in usage patterns and influence the surrounding technological ecosystem. This is a result of the inherent vulnerabilities of IoT objects and the interconnectedness of the physical and virtual realms through intelligent objects.

The benefits of Smart Buildings are centered around efficiency in various aspects [30]:

1. *Energy Efficiency*: Smart technologies enable effective energy management by controlling electricity consumption in households and building facilities. This includes automated activation/deactivation of lights, HVAC systems, and appliances based on

Fig. 6. IoT Spend Analysis report for all Smart Building system devices.

Fig. 7. IoT Spend Analysis report for the all-building activities.

real-time communication with other equipment such as smart windows or presence detectors. Additionally, occupancy indicators help identify energy loss in unused spaces. Studies have shown that implementing smart solutions can result in cost savings of 24–32% on electricity bills, which is a major motivation for building occupants/managers.

2. *Safety and Security Efficiency*: Enhancing safety and security is one of the key drivers for implementing smart systems in buildings. Access control systems authenticate authorized personnel, detect irregular intrusions, and can alert emergency centers in case of emergencies like fires. Monitoring services also provide warnings in case of abnormal events. Consumers and businesses are increasingly willing to invest in security measures to ensure peace of mind.

3. *Employee Productivity*: Smart solutions contribute to greater convenience, comfort, and wellness for building occupants. This includes providing thermal comfort and monitoring indicators such as air quality and humidity which can significantly impact employee productivity. A healthy and comfortable indoor environment can improve the overall well-being of employees and enhance their productivity levels.

Overall, the efficiency benefits of Smart Buildings encompass energy management, safety and security, and employee productivity, making them an attractive choice for building owners, occupants, and managers.

6 Conclusions

In our research, we talked about how using distributed deep learning and IoT can make smart building applications even better. The integration of the deep learning, distributed system and the Internet of Things provides powerful and effective solutions to many problems.

- Distributed deep learning has opened new avenues for solving complex problems in machine learning and artificial intelligence.
- By leveraging the power of distributed computing, it has become possible to train models on massive datasets that were previously impossible to handle with traditional deep-learning techniques.
- This has led to significant advances in various fields, from computer vision and natural language processing to healthcare and finance.

Looking forward, we're hoping to take things even further.

- The deployment of our approach ''IoT Technologies for Smart Healthcare Buildings with Distributed Deep Learning Techniques'' in a multi-cloud platform based on cloud broker architecture as a new alternative to address the limitations of cloud computing.
- The creation of a special cloud computing service just for smart buildings. We're calling it Smart Healthcare Buildings with Distributed Deep Learning Techniques -as-a Service SHBDDL-as-a-S in the cloud, and we think it could offer some customized solutions for this field.

References

1. Vijayan, D.S., Rose, A.L., Arvindan, S. et al.: Automation systems in smart buildings: a review. J. Ambient Intell Human Comput. 1–13 (2020). https://doi.org/10.1007/s12652-020-02666-9
2. Aelenei, L., et al.: Smart city: a systematic approach towards a sustainable urban transformation. Energy Procedia **91**, 970–979 (2016)
3. Giang, N.K., Lea, R., Blackstock, M., Leung, C.M.: On building smart city IoT applications: a coordination-based perspective. In: Proceedings of the 2nd International Workshop on Smart, pp.1–6 (2016)
4. Cook, D.J., et al.: MavHome: an agent-based smart home. In: PerCom 2003. LNCS, pp.521–524. Springer, Heidelberg (2003)

5. Bakici, T., Almirall, E., Wareham, J.: A smart city initiative: the case of Barcelona. J. Knowl. Econ. **2**(1), 1–14 (2012)
6. Avalos, M., Silva, I., Larios, V.: Application of business analytics on big data scenarios to obtain actionable insights in systems or services in mega-cities: Multiple use cases from the living lab at the smart cities innovation center at Guadalajara University. White Paper. IEEE-GDI (2015)
7. Chauhan, S., Agarwal, N., Kar, A.: Addressing big data challenges in smart cities: a systematic literature review. **18**(4), 73–90 (2016)
8. Bengio, Y., LeCun, Y.: Scaling learning algorithms towards AI. In: Bottou, L., Chapelle, O., DeCoste, D., Weston, J. (eds.) Large Scale Kernel Machines, pp. 321–360. MIT Press, Cambridge (2007)
9. Arel, I., Rose, D.C., Karnowski, T.P.: Deep machine learning - a new frontier in artificial intelligence research. Comput. Intell. **5**, 13–18 (2010)
10. Dietterich, T.G.: Ensemble methods in machine learning. In: Kittler, J., Roli, F. (eds.) MCS 2000. LNCS, vol. 1857, pp. 1–15. Springer, Heidelberg (2000). https://doi.org/10.1007/3-540-45014-9_1
11. Tsoumakas, G., Vlahavas, I.: Effective stacking of distributed classifiers. In: ECAI, pp. 340–344 (2002)
12. Amazon Web Services (2019). https://d1.awsstatic.com/whitepapers/machine-learning-foundations.pdf
13. Chen, Y., Zhang, L., Wei, M.: How does smart healthcare service affect resident health in the digital age? empirical evidence from 105 cities of China. vol. 9, pp. 833687, Public Health (2022). https://doi.org/10.3389/fpubh.2021.833687
14. Slam, M.M., Rahaman, A., Islam, M.R.: Development of smart healthcare monitoring system in IoT environment. SN Comput. Sci. **1**(3), 15 (2020). https://doi.org/10.1007/s42979-020-00195-y
15. Aliero, M.S., Asif, M., Ghani, I., Pasha, M.F., Jeong, S.R.: Systematic review analysis on smart building: challenges and opportunities. Sustainability **14**(5), 3009 (2022). https://doi.org/10.3390/su14053009
16. Lee, J., Lee, J.W., Kim, K.H.: Smart healthcare building system: from concept to reality. Sustain. Cities Soc. **23**, 15–22 (2016)
17. Kim, D., Yoon, Y., Lee, J., Mago, P.J., Lee, K., Cho, H.: Design and implementation of smart buildings: a review of current research trend. Energies **15**(12), 4278 (2022)
18. Baykasoglu, A., Koseoglu, M.A.: Smart healthcare building management systems for energy efficiency. In: Handbook of Research on Energy-Saving Technologies for Environmentally-Friendly Agricultural Development, pp. 341–356. IGI Global (2019)
19. Bhatti, A.R., Shami, A., Shah, M.A., Ali, A.: Smart healthcare building based on IoT technologies: opportunities and challenges. Futur. Gener. Comput. Syst. **91**, 291–307 (2019)
20. Choi, B., Cho, J.: Smart healthcare building: a systematic review of literature and future directions. J. Intell. Rob. Syst. **91**(3–4), 369–381 (2018)
21. Lee, H., Kim, J., Lee, S., Jung, S.: Design of a smart healthcare building system based on IoT technology and its application to a hospital. J. Healthcare Eng. 7642061 (2019). https://doi.org/10.1155/2019/7642061
22. Pouloudi, A., Lekakos, G., Giaglis, G.: Understanding the factors that affect the adoption of smart health devices: insights from a systematic review of the literature. J. Med. Internet Res. **18**(5), 128 (2016). https://doi.org/10.2196/jmir.5561
23. Ahuja, V., Sharma, N., Bhatia, S.: Internet of Things (IoT) in healthcare: a comprehensive systematic review. Int. J. Med. Informatics **98**, 116–126 (2017). https://doi.org/10.1016/j.ijmedinf.2016.11.008
24. Hasan, S.S., Padmanabhan, D.L., Zhan, X.: Internet of Things (IoT) applications in health: a literature review. J. Med. Syst. **43**(2), 26 (2019). https://doi.org/10.1007/s10916-018-1150-8

25. Zeadally, S., Chen, S., Tsang, A.H.: Internet of Things (IoT) security research: a bibliometric analysis. Futur. Gener. Comput. Syst. **92**, 376–397 (2019). https://doi.org/10.1016/j.future. 2018.10.003

26. Hassen, H., Maher, K.: A secured distributed OCR system in a pervasive environment with authentication as a service in the cloud. In: The 4th International Conference on Multimedia Computing and Systems, ICMCS'14, Marrakech, Morocco, pp.1200–1205 (2014)

27. Jin, J., Gubbi, J., Marusic, S., Palaniswami, M.: An information framework for creating a smart city through Internet of Things. Internet of Things J. **1**(2), 112–121 (2014). https://doi. org/10.1109/JIOT.2013.2296516

28. Caragliu, A., Del Bo, C., Nijkamp, P.: Smart cities in Europe. J. Urban Technol. **18**(2), 65–82 (2011). https://doi.org/10.1080/10630732.2011.601117

29. Alawad, A.M., Altalhi, A.R.: A review on smart city sensing applications and technologies. Comput. Mater. Continua **61**(2), 463–482 (2019). https://doi.org/10.32604/cmc.2019.06584

30. Giffinger, R., Fertner, C., Kramar, H., Kalasek, R., Pichler-Milanović, N., Meijers, E.: Smart cities: Ranking of European medium-sized cities, pp. 1–185. Centre of Regional Science, Vienna UT (2007)

31. Kumar, T., Srinivasan, R., Mani, M.: An energy-based approach to evaluate the effectiveness of integrating IoT-based sensing systems into smart buildings. Sustain. Energy Technol. Assess. **52**, 102225 (2022)

32. Shah, S.F.A., et al.: The role of machine learning and the internet of things in smart buildings for energy efficiency. Appl. Sci. **12**(15), 7882 (2022)

How Does Blockchain Enhance Zero Trust Security in IoMT?

Maher Boughdiri[1]($\boxtimes$), Takoua Abdellatif[1,2], and Chirine Ghedira Guegan[3]

[1] SERCOM Laboratory, University of Carthage, Carthage 1054, Tunisia
maher.boughdiri@ept.ucar.tn
[2] ENISo, University of Sousse, 4002 Sousse, Tunisia
[3] Univ Lyon, Université Jean Moulin Lyon 3, iaelyon school of Management, CNRS, INSA Lyon, UCBL, LIRIS, UMR5205, 69008 Lyon, France

Abstract. This study intends to answer the question of the benefits of using blockchain to improve the implementation of a zero trust security model in the context of Internet of Medical Things (IoMT). First, we examine the concept of zero trust security and its potential to revolutionize security in the IoMT landscape. Then, through an analysis of related research on the intersection of zero trust and blockchain, we discuss the potential advantages of a decentralized zero trust model based on blockchain technology. Finally, we provide recommendations and insights into future trends for the implementation and enhancement of the decentralized zero trust model. This research will offer cybersecurity researchers and professionals who are interested in adopting zero trust security in IoT intuitive insights into the principles, requirements, and recommendations that foster a defense-in-depth strategy.

Keywords: IoMT · Security · Decentralized Zero Trust · Blockchain

1 Introduction

The Internet of Things (IoT) has sparked good changes across a wide range of industries. One area where IoT holds immense promise is healthcare, often referred to as the Internet of Medical Things (IoMT). It has the potential to revolutionize patient care and improve services in unprecedented ways. The ever-growing number of healthcare-focused IoT devices creates numerous opportunities, and the vast amount of data they generate can transform the healthcare industry [1].

Nevertheless, the exponential growth and seamless integration of IoMT have undeniably expanded the attack surface, thereby creating the potential playground for cyber threats. With billions of interconnected IoMT devices in use, it provides cyber attackers with a gateway to pilfer sensitive personal and industrial data, thereby paving the path for potentially colossal damages [2].

The alarming surge in security breaches targeting IoMT devices has thrust the situation into a state of urgent concern. Research conducted by Check Point

M. Mosbah et al. (Eds.): MEDI 2023, CCIS 2071, pp. 184–197, 2024.
https://doi.org/10.1007/978-3-031-55729-3_15

Software Technologies[1] underscores this alarming trend. Their findings reveal that the healthcare sector endured an average of 1,684 attacks per week in the first quarter of 2023-an increase of 22% compared to the previous year. That makes healthcare the third most targeted industry in 2023, ahead of finance, insurance and communications. Also, the initial two months of 2023 witnessed a 41% surge in average weekly attacks per organization targeting IoT devices, compared to the previous year. A staggering 54% of organizations face attempted cyber attacks on IoT devices every week. The increase in the number of IoMT cyberattacks can be attributed not only to the proliferation of a vast number of devices, networks, applications, and users but also to the inherent characteristics of distributed structures. Additionally, the constrained nature of some IoMT devices adds to the intricacy of implementing robust authentication and authorization mechanisms for widely distributed edge devices, further complicated by the need to manage multiple identities. Besides, traditional security models, assuming trust within network perimeters, prove inadequate in IoMT environments where data, applications, devices, and users increasingly operate beyond these traditional boundaries, introducing security risks. Given these challenges, bolstering the security of IoMT becomes imperative. compromise them and orchestrate attacks on critical systems. In this context, the adoption of the zero-trust security model has gained traction among many organizations as a compelling paradigm for enhancing security in the IoMT landscape [3]. This revolutionary approach dismisses the notion of a trusted perimeter, operating under the premise that all entities, whether devices or users, are initially untrusted. The zero trust architecture stands resolute in its mission to thwart any potential breach. Gartner[2] believes that Zero Trust Network Access (ZTNA) is the fastest-growing form of network security, which will grow by 31% in 2023 and completely replace VPNs by 2025. Furthermore, Microsoft emphasizes that implementing this strategy not only protects important data by limiting breach risks, but also results in a spectacular 50% reduction in breaches, offering huge cost savings of up to 50% across the entire company [4]. Integrating Zero Trust principles into IoT architectures can also address distinct security challenges within the interconnected IoMT landscape, fostering heightened security for devices, users, and data [7].

Meanwhile, blockchain technology has emerged as a promising solution in the realm of cybersecurity, leading to the development of various security mechanisms, including access management, identity management, authentication, and authorization. Leveraging its capacity to enhance cybersecurity, blockchain has the potential to establish a robust zero-trust security framework. This framework can offer highly accessible and transparent security mechanisms through a visible blockchain ledger, where all transactions are recorded and made available to authorized operators. The immutability of blockchain further strengthens zero-trust models by enabling the technology to recognize, authenticate, and grant

---

[1] https://blog.checkpoint.com/.
[2] https://www.datacenterknowledge.com.

access to trusted entities [5]. Blockchain-enabled zero-trust security holds, thus, the potential to effectively address previous security challenges within the IoMT.

Motivated by the promise of zero-trust strategies in bolstering IoMT security and recognizing the transformative power of blockchain technology, this study endeavors to achieve several critical objectives:

- Highlight the fundamental components and principles of zero-trust security while underscoring its paramount significance as the foundational pillar for fortifying IoMT security.
- Explore the potential and advantages of leveraging blockchain technology to construct a resilient zero-trust security framework.
- Navigate through the existing challenges and contemplate the future trends that will empower blockchain-driven zero-trust solutions in safeguarding the IoMT landscape.

The paper's structure is as follows: Sect. 2 provides a background on key technologies. Section 3, reviews current works on zero trust frameworks. Section 4 emphasizes the zero trust security in the context of IoMT. Then, after discussing the potential of using blockchain for zero trust security, we provide some recommendations and future perspectives. Lastly, we conclude this study, summarizing key insights and findings.

2   Background on Key Technologies

In this section, we will delve into the fundamental concepts of zero trust security and blockchain technology.

2.1   Zero Trust Security

The Zero Trust security, pioneered by the National Institute of Standards and Technology (NIST) [6], presents a revolutionary shift in cybersecurity thinking. This paradigm challenges the traditional notion of implicit trust within networks and introduces the philosophy that all users and traffic should be treated as potentially malicious. It is characterized by constant and rigorous security of all activities, even within the network perimeter. At the core, Zero Trust is an architectural approach encompassing a set of policies, strategies, and technologies that prioritize defense in depth security rule. This approach is anchored in the understanding that trust should not be tied to physical location but should be established through robust identity authentication and dynamic trust evaluation [8]. Zero Trust is built on inherently not trusting users, devices, networks, and applications. It is based on the following five fundamental tenets: (1) The network is constantly in a dangerous environment; (2) The network is constantly under threat, either from the outside or from within; (3) The network's physical location is insufficient to assess the network's credibility; (4) All devices, users, and network traffic should be authenticated and authorized; (5) Security policies must be dynamic and determined using as many data sources as possible.

Based on these assumptions, the key principles for achieving zero trust architecture (ZTA) are identity management (validity of user accounts and IoT devices), Access control (access levels with least privileges), data security, devices security and security analytics. These principles are encapsulated within the five foundational pillars: user, devices, network, application & workload, and data, [9]. In an enterprise setting, a Zero Trust deployment comprises various logical components, which can operate as on-premises services or through cloud-based services. The Fig. 1 model the basic relationship between the components and their interactions, according to NIST SP800-207 Framework [10]. These components include the Policy Engine (PE), responsible for access decisions, the Policy Administrator (PA), managing communication paths, and the Policy Enforcement Point (PEP), enforcing access rules. Additionally, data sources such as network and application logs, threat intelligence, Continuous Diagnostics and Mitigation (CDM), and compliance with industry standards contribute to the policy rules used by the Policy Engine in making access decisions. This comprehensive approach ensures that Zero Trust is a dynamic, data-driven security paradigm that effectively mitigates evolving cyber threats [8,13].

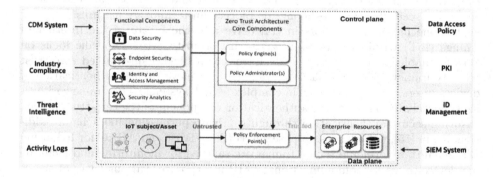

Fig. 1. Zero trust architecture for IoT (according to NIST SP 800-207 [10])

2.2 Blockchain Technology

Blockchain is decentralized and distributed ledger technology that allow data to be shared and stored in a peer-to-peer networks without the need of third parties. It is serves as a digital backbone of timestamped and hierarchical chain of blocks, logging an ever-evolving of network's transaction records. [11]. Notably, blockchain manifests its prowess through attributes such as decentralization, accountability, traceability, transparency, and data immutability. This robustness emerges from the employment of consensus protocols and cryptographic techniques. Moreover, blockchain's ability to deploy smart contracts, which execute predefined rules once conditions are met, enhances its capabilities. By design, blockchain eliminates dependence on central authorities, establishing an unassailable decentralized foundation of trust. This revolutionary feature facilitates the establishment of trust relationships between previously untrusted or suspicious entities, thus reshaping the paradigm of trust in digital ecosystems. This pivotal prowess renders blockchain an indispensable technology across diverse sectors [12].

3 State of the Art

The exploration of Zero Trust for IoT and IoMT is still in its nascent stage, with a limited number of research initiatives dedicated to developing architectures and frameworks. These endeavors aim to expand the application of the Zero Trust model to the domain of IoT. Within this landscape, ongoing research projects and practical industrial solutions are emerging. Despite the diversity in approaches, technologies, and strategies, they all revolve around a central principle: "never trust, always verify." In our work, we will focus on research that leverages blockchain and zero trust security to enhance the overall security of IoT and IoMT. These efforts can be categorized into two main groups: (1) those that utilize blockchain for zero trust security and (2) those that incorporate zero trust security principles alongside blockchain technology features.

On one hand, the authors in [14] delve into the future of the Internet of Things (IoT) within the realm of zero-trust security, with a specific focus on 5G/6G-enabled IoT networks. They introduce a blockchain-enabled zero-trust security framework called BasIoT, designed to achieve robust authentication of devices, users, and applications in complex 5GIoT systems. This framework utilizes blockchain to bolster the authentication component of the zero-trust model, ensuring secure authentication through a private permission blockchain. Additionally, in [15], the authors propose ZAIB (Zero-Trust and ABAC for IoT using Blockchain), a novel and secure framework tailored for monitoring and facilitating device-to-device communications. ZAIB incorporates various levels of access control mechanisms based on environmental parameters and device behavior. It operates under the protective umbrella of a zero-trust architecture and conducts dynamic behavioral analysis of IoT devices, calculating trust levels for each request. This framework enforces variable policies, generated for specific scenarios, through attribute-based access control (ABAC). Blockchain technology is employed to ensure anonymous device and user registrations and maintain immutable activity logs. All attributes, trust level histories, and data generated by IoT devices receive protection via the InterPlanetary File System (IPFS). A comprehensive security evaluation confirms that ZAIB effectively meets the requirements for active defense and end-to-end security enforcement of data, users, and services in smart grid networks. Alevizos et al. [16] conducted a study to explore the enhancement of zero-trust security in IoT endpoints by harnessing the capabilities of blockchain technology. Their research delves into how blockchain can be effectively employed to guarantee and enhance the integrity of shared alerts within intrusion detection systems at these endpoints. Furthermore, blockchain serves to bolster the security of backend storage for essential logs and audit trails, ensuring their integrity and immutability. The work presented in [17] introduces a blockchain-based access control scheme, specifically tailored for enabling secure and lightweight data sharing across diverse organizations characterized by a lack of mutual trust. These organizations may operate in regions with differing security and privacy regulations and cultural norms. The approach employs a consortium blockchain to create a reliable and trusted environment. Within this context, a Role-Based Access Control (RBAC) model is implemented, leveraging a multi-signature protocol and smart contract methods developed in the study. This approach aims to address the complex challenges of secure data sharing in multi-jurisdictional and culturally diverse settings.

On the other hand, the authors of [18] have developed a secure system for sharing medical images, integrating the principles of zero trust and blockchain technology. This innovative system leverages the blockchain's inherent immutability, combines it with the enhanced security of zero trust principles, and capitalizes on the scalability of off-chain data storage via the InterPlanetary File System (IPFS). Through this solution, blockchain technology guarantees data integrity by maintaining a tamper-proof record of every transaction, while zero trust principles ensure that medical data remains encrypted and is only accessible by authenticated users and authorized devices. Consequently, this proposed model effectively mitigates numerous vulnerabilities related to data security, particularly in the context of medical or health data transmission.

In [19], a comprehensive security protection scheme is introduced, featuring the integration of blockchain technology, zero trust principles, and ShangMi cryptographic (SM) algorithms. This scheme effectively combines these elements to enhance security. Hyperledger Fabric is employed for key management and to maintain trust evaluation event records, ensuring the authenticity, non-repudiation, and tamper-proof nature of keys and events. Furthermore, zero trust principles are applied to safeguard valuable resources and enforce identity and access management (IAM) for entities seeking access. The approach utilizes dynamic trust evaluation techniques to continually assess the trustworthiness of accessing entities in real-time, enabling dynamic authorization processes.

In [20], the authors put forward a comprehensive framework for enhancing the security of IoT using Zero Trust principles and blockchain technology. This framework involves risk-based segmentation of the IoT network, which enhances the uniformity of IoT device attributes and communication protocols. Zero Trust extends the scope of trust beyond the conventional boundaries, while blockchain technology is introduced to bolster the capabilities of device identification and access control within the IoT network.

To sum up, these initiatives have effectively combined blockchain and zero trust principles to bolster IoT application security. They have made substantial progress in implementing the zero trust strategy within IoT while leveraging the potential of blockchain. However, existing research often treats blockchain and zero trust as separate elements or doesn't fully harness blockchain's unique features. Additionally, some essential zero trust principles may not receive the emphasis they deserve. Table 1 compares those efforts according to the NIST zero trust principles (**P1-P8**) To address these shortcomings, our work aim to analyze the numerous benefits that blockchain can offer to enhance unaddressed zero trust principles. It thus delves into how each feature of blockchain aligns with and enhances various aspects of zero trust principles.

Table 1. Comparison of the state of the art works(**P1**: Verify and Authenticate, **P2**: Least Privilege Access, **P3**: data protection, **P4**: Micro-Segmentation, **P5**: Analytics and monitoring, **P6**: Policy Enforcement, **P7**: SIEM and incident response, and **P8**: Governance and Compliance)

Works	Methods	Zero Trust pillar	Zero Trust principles							
			P1	P2	P3	P4	P5	P6	P7	P8
Li, Shan, et al. [14]	Blockchain-based IoT device authentication and authorization for zero trust security within 5G-IoT networks	Device/Network/ application	✓	✗	✓	✓	✗	✗	✗	✗
Awan et al. [15]	Zero-Trust and attribute-based access control for IoT using Blockchain	Device/User/Data	✓	✓	✓	✓	✓	✓	✗	✗
Alevizos et al. [16]	Using blockchain to extend zero-trust architecture to IoT endpoints	Device/User	✓	✗	✗	✗	✗	✓	✓	✓
Gai, Keke, et al. [17]	A blockchain-based access control method for zero-trust data sharing	User/Data	✓	✓	✓	✗	✗	✓	✗	✗
Sultana, Maliha, et al. [18]	Combination of blockchain and zero trust concepts to create a secure medical picture sharing system	User/Data	✓	✓	✓	✗	✗	✗	✗	✗
Li, Peirong, et al. [19]	A security approach that combines blockchain, zero trust, and ShangMi cryptography (SM) algorithms.	User/Data/ application	✓	✓	✓	✓	✓	✓	✓	✗
Dhar, Suparna, et al. [20]	Using Blockchain for device identification and access control capabilities, while adhering to the zero trust principle	Device/User/ Network	✓	✓	✓	✗	✗	✓	✗	✗

4   Zero Trust Security for IoMT

The Internet of Medical Things (IoMT) is revolutionizing healthcare by connecting medical devices, healthcare systems, and technology into a seamless network. This interconnected ecosystem offers a wide range of applications, from remote patient monitoring and telemedicine to smart wearables and hospital management. IoMT enables healthcare providers to monitor patients' vital signs in real time, conduct virtual consultations, and improve medication adherence. It streamlines hospital operations, enhances emergency response, and harnesses the power of health data analytics for informed decision-making. IoMT not only improves patient care and outcomes but also reduces healthcare costs and enhances accessibility to medical services, particularly in remote or underserved areas. However, as with any transformative technology, IoMT also poses challenges related to data security, privacy, and compliance that need to be carefully addressed to ensure its continued success in the healthcare industry. However, IoMT presents challenges in terms of data security, privacy, and compliance that demand meticulous attention to ensure its sustained success in the healthcare industry. Notably, a significant concern lies in the vulnerability of many IoMT devices to security breaches due to inadequate security measures during their design and implementation. Given the critical nature of healthcare, where lives can hang in the balance, robust security is imperative [21].

When addressing IoMT security, it is crucial to emphasize a holistic cybersecurity strategy. This strategy should encompass tailored defense mechanisms, techniques, policies and principles designed to protect against cyberattacks targeting connected medical devices. IoMT security must consist of a multifaceted cybersecurity approach and protective mechanisms aimed at guarding against potential cyber threats directed at IoMT devices within healthcare networks. Additionally, it should include strategies for reducing risk and ensuring compliance with relevant standards and regulations.

An essential and effective step in securing these connected medical devices involves the adoption of a Zero Trust security framework. By embracing this approach, healthcare IT teams shift from a reactive, alert-based security stance to a proactive, prevention-oriented strategy. As shown in Fig. 2, the Zero Trust framework operates on the principle of "never trust, always verify." It necessitates continuous authentication, authorization, and verification of both internal and external users and their devices. Access to applications and data is granted strictly on a need-to-have basis and retained only as long as a valid necessity exists. Zero Trust security plays a pivotal role in addressing security challenges in the IoMT by adopting a proactive and comprehensive approach to safeguarding connected medical devices and healthcare networks. Here's how Zero Trust security helps address key IoMT security challenges:

- Continuous Authentication and Dynamic Authorization: IoMT devices are continuously authenticated and authorized, ensuring that only trusted entities gain access to sensitive medical data and resources. This mitigates the risk of unauthorized access or malicious actors infiltrating the network.
- Device Verification and evaluation: Zero Trust requires rigorous device verification, confirming the identity and security posture of each connected device. Suspicious or compromised devices are immediately identified and isolated, preventing them from compromising the network's integrity. Also, trust of device and user is continuously evaluated within the network. Thus, it is possible to evaluate the security posture and trustworthiness of devices and users before granting access (Risk-based access control).
- Least Privilege Access: IoMT security is enhanced by enforcing the principle of least privilege. Users and devices are granted the minimum necessary access rights to perform their functions. This minimizes the attack surface and limits potential damage from breaches.
- Micro-Segmentation: Zero Trust networks are segmented into smaller, isolated zones or micro-segments. This containment strategy helps contain breaches and prevents lateral movement within the network, limiting the potential impact of security incidents.

- Data Encryption: data transmitted between IoMT devices and healthcare systems is encrypted, ensuring the confidentiality and integrity of sensitive information. Encryption helps protect data both in transit and at rest.
- Continuous Monitoring and analysis: IoMT environments benefit from continuous monitoring and real-time threat detection. This proactive approach allows for the immediate identification and mitigation of potential security threats. Also, Zero Trust frameworks incorporate advanced anomaly detection and behavior analysis tools. These technologies continuously monitor network activity for deviations from established baselines, promptly identifying and responding to suspicious behavior or security incidents.
- Zero Trust Policies: Comprehensive Zero Trust policies are established and strictly enforced across the IoMT ecosystem. These policies dictate user and device access, behavior, and trust levels, ensuring that all entities adhere to predefined security standards.
- Security Automation: Automation and orchestration are integral to Zero Trust security, enabling rapid responses to security incidents and policy violations. Automated security measures can isolate compromised devices and remediate vulnerabilities in real-time.
- Compliance and Auditing: Zero Trust frameworks facilitate compliance with industry regulations and standards, such as HIPAA and GDPR. They also enable detailed auditing and logging, providing visibility into network activity and helping organizations meet compliance requirements.

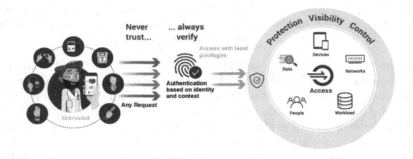

Fig. 2. IoMT Zero Trust Security

5   Blockchain-Driven Zero Trust Security

Implementing a Zero Trust architecture in IoMT significantly enhances overall security by ensuring that network access is strictly based on need and least privileges. This approach effectively reduces the attack surface by blocking unnecessary access to critical resources. However, centralized Zero Trust models can present limitations, particularly in terms of a single point of failure in the data plane. These models rely on a central control point or security gateway, and if this central point experiences a failure or is compromised, it can disrupt the entire security infrastructure.

To address this limitation, the adoption of a decentralized architecture using a peer-to-peer model is recommended. This approach is particularly suitable for flat networks, where devices can directly connect without intermediaries like gateways. The use of blockchain technology plays a crucial role in achieving this decentralized Zero Trust security model. Here are some key benefits of leveraging blockchain in this context:

- Immutable Identity Management: Blockchain provides a tamper-resistant ledger for identity management. Each device, user, or entity can have a unique digital identity stored on the blockchain. This identity is immutable, ensuring that once it's established, it cannot be altered or forged. This helps in verifying the trustworthiness of entities within the network, a fundamental aspect of Zero Trust. Moreover, blockchain can enable secure device onboarding and management. Devices can be registered on the blockchain with their unique identities and certificates. When a device requests access to the network or specific resources, it must present its credentials and satisfy predefined criteria, enhancing security.
- Decentralized Authentication: Blockchain enables decentralized authentication mechanisms. Devices and users can prove their identity without relying on a central authority. Smart contracts can be used to establish trust relationships and automate access control based on predefined rules.
- Audit Trails and Transparency: Every transaction and access request in a blockchain is recorded in a transparent and immutable manner. This creates a robust audit trail that can be crucial for monitoring and verifying actions in an IoT network. Security administrators can use this audit trail to track any suspicious activity and ensure compliance with security policies.
- Access Control and Permissions: Smart contracts on a blockchain can enforce access control policies based on the principles of least privilege. Devices and users are only granted access to the resources and data they need for their specific functions. Access permissions can be defined and updated in a transparent manner.
- Policy Enforcement and Automation: Security policies and configurations can be stored on a blockchain in a tamper-proof manner. Any changes to policies must be recorded as transactions, and alterations can be easily identified and addressed. This ensures that security policies remain consistent and cannot be manipulated by unauthorized parties. Thus help in decentralized the governance of a system's security. Also, executing smart contracts will help in enforcing these policies and rules without the need of third parties.
- Decentralized Intrusion Detection: Blockchain can facilitate decentralized intrusion detection mechanisms, where devices collectively contribute to monitoring network behavior and identifying anomalies. Suspicious activities can trigger automated responses or alerts based on predefined consensus rules.

The advantages of the decentralized zero trust model over the centralized and traditional perimeter-based models are highlighted in Table 1 (Table 2).

Table 2. Comparison perimeter-based, centralized and decentralized zero trust models

Aspects	Decentralized Zero Trust	Centralized Zero Trust	Traditional Perimeter-Based
Device Trust Verification	Distributed trust	Centralized trust	Trust based on perimeter No frequent device validation
	Trust is frequently updated and verified		
Access Control	Grant access with least privileges to accomplish a specific task Dynamically updated based on subject trust and context Expired by the end of request		No frequent trust evaluation Predominantly network-based Everything in the organization is trusted No further verification's required
	Decentralized management	Manged by centralized entity	
Authentication	Crucial in service delivery Continuously authenticate Single Sign On (SSO)/Multi Factor authentication		Once at the initial request Use of single factor
	Decentralized management Immutable log of every authentication request	Managed by centralized entity (identity and access management (IAM) system).	
Authorization	Dynamic, device-centric Automated by smart contract	Dynamic, role-based. Policies must be manually enforced through IAM systems. Automated by Policy Decision Point.	Static, network-based, rule-based, requiring manual adjustments.
Threat Detection	Distributed immutable ledger for auditing Real-time detection through smart contracts	Centralized Response to threats may not be as immediate	Perimeter-focused malicious activity identification Post-intrusion detection capabilities
	Continuous monitoring/auditing/ user and devices behavior analytics proactive detection of malicious attacks		
Automation and policies enforcement	Self-adaptive measures and policies Smart contract based enforcement and automation	Centralized policies Enforcement point	Limited automation Perimeter protection via firewalls, VPNs and network access control
	Adaptive and dynamic policies Micro-segmentation : smaller and manageable zones		
Confidentiality	End-to-end encryption		Prone to data theft and loss
	Every data access is stored in immutable ledger data storage is distributed	single point of failure	
Resilience	Distributed architecture	Centralized resilience	Single point of failure Attack can not occur in trusted zone Attack Lateral movement possibility
	Always assume breach and attack Continuous monitoring and analysis		
Identity Management	Decentralized, device-centric Self sovereign identity management capabilities Pseudo anonymity identity possibilities	Single point of failure Centralized, role-based	Network-based Certificate based management

6 Recommendations and Future Perspectives

Numerous challenges can arise when implementing a blockchain-driven zero trust strategy for IoMT. While blockchain offers significant benefits, it can also introduce vulnerabilities and expand the attack surface if not carefully selected, implemented, and configured. To establish a robust and resilient zero trust security model based on blockchain, the following recommendations are essential: First (1) Select the Right Blockchain Platform by Choosing a blockchain platform tailored for IoT, one that offers scalability, security, low latency, high transaction per second (TPS), and low gas fees. Platforms with Zero-Knowledge EVM (ZK EVM) capabilities, such as Ethereum with zkRollup or other Layer 2 solutions, can be particularly suitable. (2) Ensure that the chosen blockchain technology is compatible with the resource limitations and power constraints of IoT devices. Optimizing blockchain protocols for IoT can help reduce resource consumption. (3) Develop the framework in compliance with relevant data protection and privacy regulations, such as GDPR (General Data Protection Regulation) or HIPAA (Health Insurance Portability and Accountability Act). This is crucial, especially when handling sensitive medical data in IoMT. Finally, Configure traditional Security Information and Event Management (SIEM) and log management tools to read data from the blockchain ledger. This integration ensures that blockchain-based security events and logs are monitored alongside other security information, providing a comprehensive view of the security landscape.

Building upon the recommendations and best practices for implementing a blockchain-driven zero trust security framework in IoMT, several promising future perspectives and trends can further enhance this framework:

- Decentralized Identity Management: The rise of decentralized identity solutions, often based on blockchain technology, is gaining momentum. Embracing Web3 and W3C standards such as decentralized identifiers (DIDs) and verifiable claims (VCs) can be seamlessly integrated into decentralized identity management for IoMT. This approach allows patients, healthcare providers, and devices to establish self-sovereign identities, greatly enhancing trust and reducing the vulnerability to identity-related attacks. However, a notable challenge lies in efficiently implementing these identifiers, especially on resource-constrained IoT devices.
- Zero-Knowledge Proofs (ZKPs): The incorporation of zero-knowledge proofs (ZKPs) into IoMT blockchains holds immense promise. ZKPs are cryptographic techniques that enable one party to prove knowledge of specific information to another party without revealing the information itself. When applied within the IoMT blockchain, ZKPs can significantly elevate data privacy while still facilitating robust verification. This is particularly valuable when sharing sensitive health data, ensuring confidentiality is maintained throughout the process. Yet, a potential challenge lies in optimizing and adapting ZKP algorithms to function efficiently on devices with limited processing power and memory. Addressing this challenge requires the development of lightweight ZKP protocols tailored specifically for IoT devices. These

protocols should minimize computational overhead while still providing a robust level of privacy and security.

– Zero Trust Edge Security: As IoMT devices increasingly operate at the network's edge, the principles of zero trust should seamlessly extend to edge computing environments. Implementing zero trust edge security guarantees that all devices, even those located in remote or challenging-to-reach locations, adhere to stringent access controls and authentication protocols. This proactive approach minimizes the risk of breaches and unauthorized access. Furthermore, the incorporation of trust elevation and verification algorithms at the edge can substantially reduce network latency while enhancing security. However, a notable challenge in this context is to balance the security requirements with the resource constraints of edge devices and to consider their potential role as blockchain nodes.

7 Conclusion

The promise of blockchain technology in enhancing cybersecurity cannot be overstated, primarily due to its fundamental attributes of decentralization, transparency, and immutability. Blockchain, with its proven effectiveness, has the potential to serve as the pillar of a zero trust security framework, offering highly accessible and transparent security mechanisms that can revolutionize IoMT cybersecurity. In this study, we endeavor to address the question of how blockchain can benefit the implementation of zero trust security. While existing research has explored the intersection of blockchain and zero trust principles, it often treats them as separate entities or fails to fully exploit the unique features of blockchain technology. To bridge these gaps, our work sheds light on the multitude of advantages that blockchain can bring to the realm of zero trust security. We do so by first dissecting the core components and benefits of zero trust security for IoMT systems, then illustrating how blockchain complements and enhances this approach. Furthermore, we provided recommendations and insights into the challenges associated with leveraging this synergy between blockchain and zero trust security. Our aim is to optimize and refine the blockchain-driven zero trust framework for maximum effectiveness.

Looking ahead, our future work will leverage the insights gained from this study to implement a comprehensive zero trust security framework. This framework will incorporate blockchain technology, decentralized identifiers, and zero-knowledge proofs (ZKP) at the edge, thereby promoting a security-in-depth and privacy-by-design approach at the edge of IoMT.

References

1. Shah, V., Alex, K.: Internet of medical things (IoMT) driving the digital transformation of the healthcare sector. In: Data-Centric AI Solutions and Emerging Technologies in the Healthcare Ecosystem. CRC Press (2023)
2. Saxena, A., Sangeeta, M.: Internet of medical things (IoMT) security and privacy: a survey of recent advances and enabling technologies. In: Proceedings of the Fourteenth International Conference on Contemporary Computing (2022)

3. Gellert, G.A., et al.: Zero Trust and the future of cybersecurity in healthcare delivery organizations. J. Hosp. Adm. 12(1) (2023)
4. Jakkal, V.: Microsoft zero trust solutions deliver 92 percent return on investment, says new forrester study (2022). https://www.microsoft.com/security/blog/; last acceded September 15, 2023
5. Alkatheiri, S., et al.: Blockchain-assisted cybersecurity for the internet of medical things in the healthcare industry. Electronics **12**(8), 1801 (2023)
6. Stafford, V.A.: Zero trust architecture. NIST Spec. Publ. **800**, 207 (2020)
7. Xiaojian, Z., Chen, L., Fan, J., Xiangqun, W., Qi, W.: Power IoT security protection architecture based on zero trust framework. In: IEEE 5th International Conference on Cryptography, Security and Privacy (CSP) (2021)
8. Shore, M., Zeadally, S., Keshariya, A.: Zero trust: the what, how, why, and when. Computer **54**(11), 26–35 (2021)
9. He, Y., Daochao, H., Lei, C., Yi, N., Xiangjie, Ma.: A survey on zero trust architecture: Challenges and future trends. Wirel. Commun. Mob. Comput **2022** (2022)
10. Rose, S., et al.: NIST special publication 800–207 zero trust architecture. National Institute of Standards and Technology, US Department of Commerce: Washington, DC, USA (202sectors0)
11. Boughdiri, M., Abdellatif, T., Abdellatif, T.: Blockchain survey for security and privacy in the e-health ecosystem. In: Kallel, S., Jmaiel, M., Zulkernine, M., Hadj Kacem, A., Cuppens, F., Cuppens, N. (eds.) CRiSIS 2022. LNCS, vol. 13857, pp. 69–84. Springer, Cham (2023). https://doi.org/10.1007/978-3-031-31108-6_6
12. Sharma, P., Wilfred Godfrey, W. Trivedi, A.: When blockchain meets IoT: a comparison of the performance of communication protocols in a decentralized identity solution for IoT using blockchain. Cluster Comput. (2022)
13. Dimitrakos, T., et al.: Trust aware continuous authorization for zero trust in consumer internet of things In: IEEE 19th International Conference on Trust, Security and Privacy in Computing and Communications (TrustCom), China (2020)
14. Li, S., Muddesar, I., Neetesh, S.: Future industry internet of things with zero-trust security. Inf. Syst. Front. (2022)
15. Awan, S.M., Azad, M.A., Arshad, J., Waheed, U., Sharif, T.: A blockchain-inspired attribute-based zero-trust access control model for IoT. Information **14**, 129 (2023)
16. Alevizos, L., et al.: Augmenting zero trust architecture to endpoints using blockchain: a state-of-the-art review. Secur. Priv. **5**, e191 (2021)
17. Gai, K., et al.: A blockchain-based access control scheme for zero trust cross-organizational data sharing. ACM Trans. Internet Technol. (2023)
18. Sultana, M., et al.: Towards developing a secure medical image sharing system based on zero trust principles and blockchain technology. BMC Med. Inform. Decis. Making **20**(1), 1–10 (2020)
19. Li, P., et al.: A zero trust and blockchain-based defense model for smart electric vehicle chargers. J. Netw. Comput. Appl. **213**, 103599 (2023)
20. Dhar, S., et al.: Securing IoT devices using zero trust and blockchain. J. Org. Comput. Electron. Commer. **31**, 18–34 (2021)
21. Bhushan, B., et al.: Towards a secure and sustainable internet of medical things (IoMT): requirements, design challenges, security techniques, and future trends. Sustainability **15**(7), 6177 (2023)

HIPAA and GDPR Compliance in IoT Healthcare Systems

Abdelmlak Said[1]([✉])[iD], Aymen Yahyaoui[1,2][iD], and Takoua Abdellatif[1,3][iD]

[1] SERCOM Lab, University of Carthage, 1054 Carthage, Tunisia
abdelmlaksaid@outlook.com
[2] Military Academy of Fondouk Jedid, 8012 Nabeul, Tunisia
[3] ENISO, University of Sousse, 4023 Sousse, Tunisia

Abstract. Data privacy in the Internet of Things (IoT) remains a challenging topic in all industries, including healthcare services. The introduction of new data privacy regulations: the Health Insurance Portability and Accountability Act (HIPAA) and the European General Data Protection Regulation (GDPR) enables users to control how their data is accessed and processed, requiring consent from users before any data collection from smart devices or sensors. Consequently, the implementation of these regulations in IoT infrastructures is still a major concern for all researchers. Since these laws don't only apply to doctors and nurses, IT personnel must comply too. In this work, a novel IoT architecture is proposed to protect users' privacy and comply with both regulations using edge computing and encryption techniques for healthcare infrastructure.

Keywords: IoT · Security · Privacy · HIPAA · GDPR · Healthcare · Edge computing

1 Introduction

Healthcare systems are strongly dependent on recent technologies for the purpose of improving the quality of human services. Hence, IoT plays a major role in offering smooth and seamless ubiquitous services for the healthcare sector [1]. With the ability to interconnect numerous devices, from sensors to cloud services, it allows the exchange of healthcare information as an Electronic Health Record (EHR) over the network. Therefore, patient confidential data becomes accessible, often without the patient's or the medical staff's consciousness [2]. The rising security threats that target IoT healthcare systems underscore the critical importance of examining security and privacy topics. Different privacy standards are presented to preserve patients' privacy; these include HIPAA [3] in the United States and GDPR [4] in Europe. In the EU, GDPR controls all processing of individuals' data. Thus, any organization that handles Personally Identifiable Information (PII), including health information, can be subject to GDPR regulations. In contrast, HIPAA's scope is limited to entities that manage protected health information (PHI) within the US. Organizations that transfer US health-related data to the EU must comply with both sets of rules [8].

M. Mosbah et al. (Eds.): MEDI 2023, CCIS 2071, pp. 198–209, 2024.
https://doi.org/10.1007/978-3-031-55729-3_16

1.1 The IoT Healthcare System

Smart hospital infrastructures are hospitals that optimize, redesign, and/or build new methods, processes, and management systems, all enabled by improving and enhancing the networking infrastructure of interconnected resources. In order to provide a reliable and more effective service for better patient care and operational efficiency [5]. Smart hospital infrastructure offers multiple sensors: (1) Environmental sensors to collect environmental data such as: room temperature, humidity, lightning level, etc. (2) Context data that can be inserted by administrative workers and contain information about patient identity: name, address, birth date, etc.; (3) Health sensors to collect data related to patients health status, as we mention:

- Blood pressure sensor: Sphygmomanometer.
- Pulse and Oxygen in Blood Pressure: SPO2.
- Body temperature Sensor.
- Galvanic Skin Response Sensor: GSR-Sweating.
- Electromyography Sensor: EMG.
- Electrocardiogram Sensor: ECG.
- Airflow Sensor: Breathing.

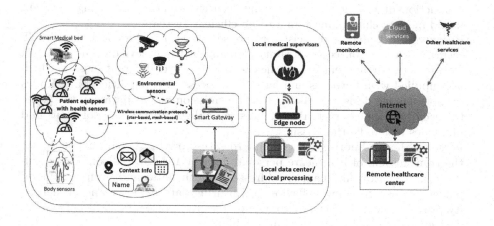

Fig. 1. Smart hospital ecosystem

After gathering this useful information, they will be sent to an intermediate border router or edge router. The edge router forwards data to a central server for further stream processing [6]. Data analysis may take place at the edge, or data may be sent to servers over the Internet for storage and advanced analysis. Then, this data can be used by other organizations.

Smart hospital infrastructures, as depicted in Fig. 1, encompass a wide range of physically distinct resources that are vital for sustaining operations, patient care, employee support, and ensuring the safety of the facility.

1.2 Security/Privacy Challenges

Contrary to traditional IT systems, where all devices or machines have wired connections (Ethernet, optical fiber, ...), IoT infrastructure in general and IoT healthcare infrastructure in specific need extra research in terms of security and privacy. Multiple challenges that are pursued threaten the security and privacy of devices, individuals, and companies. Below are the main IoT challenges [7] :

- Remote exposure: IoT networks have an exceptionally large attack surface due to their radio connectivity between different entities. It grants malicious users the possibility to execute a broad spectrum of intrusions and attacks. In addition to communication, the IoT is composed of different layers and a large number of entry points. Databases, Clouds, Servers, and sensors, and others are vulnerable components, and their exploitation can sorely affect the progression of the system or even more by causing interruptions and violations of the system.
- Interportability and evolution: With many industries presenting different devices to monitor a specified area, transmit data through the network, store and save data in a database or data center, or analyze collected information, research needs to offer reliable contributions that can handle this great technological evolution. Industries and healthcare have recently ballooned their production of IoT devices. Managing security solutions in a single system would be very challenging to afford an efficient system.
- Resource constraints and decision response: Another major concern with IoT security is the resource constraints of many of these devices. The common feature between different IoT applications is the use of different sensors, which are supplied with batteries and have low processing capabilities. Since nodes cannot manage decision making, the transmission of this data can take time to reach the cloud server. Researchers are obliged to propose solutions and find clues to handle those issues.
- Personal Health Information (PHI): Protecting privacy is paramount due to the transmission of healthcare personal data by IoT devices containing sensitive information like names, addresses, health data, and even behavioral patterns (Diet, Sleeping behavior...). Ensuring data integrity and authenticity proves difficult in IoT environments, as alterations can lead to erroneous decisions and compromise system reliability.

Those challenges can complicate the work of researchers in implementing the privacy and security aspects. In this context, regulatory compliance can help to achieve and confidently indicate to its users that it has met specific standards. Healthcare organizations should follow regulations to guarantee the security and privacy of patient data.

1.3 HIPAA Privacy/Security Regulations

HIPAA or the Health Insurance Portability and Accountability Act, is a US federal law enacted in 1996 that identifies the control of personal healthcare information. These regulations set limits on patients' privacy and uphold their rights to comprehend and manage the usage and disclosure of protected identifiable information (PII). This includes any information that can distinguish individuals as unique entities, distinct from all others, such as name, address, email, telephone number, date of birth, passport number, and other critical data. Many researchers have set guidelines concerning HIPAA rules and safeguards [8].

HIPAA Security Components. Within the HIPAA framework, the Security Rule constitutes one of four essential rules. This comprehensive framework outlines the necessary controls and protocols that healthcare providers and related businesses must adhere to implement. They can be concluded on the following points:

Administrative Safeguards

1. **Security Management Process:** The measures to prevent, detect, contain, and correct security breaches including risk analysis and management program.
2. **Security Personnel:** Entities delegate responsibilities to security officers for developing and implementing threat management procedures.
3. **Information Access Management:** Entities must establish role-based access to ePHI, where access is appropriate for only authorized users.
4. **Workforce Training and Management:** Enforcing accountability for security across the organization with authorization and supervision to access to e-PHI.
5. **Evaluation:** Regular technical and nontechnical evaluations must be performed according to security policies and taking corrective action when necessary.

Physical Safeguards

1. **Facility Access and Control:** Restrict physical access to facilities containing ePHI (or networks and servers that host ePHI) to individuals who are authorized to access the data. These measures must also guarantee convenient access to ePHI for the authorized users.
2. **Workstation and Device Security:** Restrictions to physical devices, workstations, and media controls that house or are connected to servers that house ePHI by policies and procedures regarding transfer, removal, disposal, and reuse.

Technical Safeguards

1. **Access Control:** Apply technical controls (including 2FA (2-Factor Authentication), MFA (Multi-Factor Authentication, ...) to allow access to only authorized users.
2. **Audit Controls:** Access across all software and hardware must be monitored and take appropriate action if misuse is detected.

3. **Integrity Controls:** Improving ePHI integrity by ensuring no undue alterations or deletions, and with backups prepared at regular intervals.
4. **Transmission Security:** Protect and control the transmission of ePHI across wired and wireless networks.

HIPAA Privacy Guidelines. The privacy guidelines prioritize safeguarding an individual's rights and their capacity to manage and retrieve their own PHI. It comprehends a set of requirements that must be satisfied:

1. Patients' understanding: Patients have a right to understand how their personal Health information is stored, used, and kept by healthcare providers;
2. Patients' control: Patients may determine who can access and use their health data;
3. Confidentiality: A patient's health data must be kept away from people who have no right to access it;
4. Data integrity: Shared patient health data must be safeguarded against unauthorized tampering or deletion and must remain unchanged;
5. Consent exception: Access to a patient's health data without his/her consent is permitted only in emergencies;
6. Non-repudiation: All pertinent activities must be recorded to avoid controversy and to guarantee that authorities fulfill their responsibilities regarding patient information;
7. Auditing: Information and logs of all activities must be constantly monitored to ensure that patient health data are properly protected.

1.4   GDPR Privacy Principles

GDPR or the General Data Protection Regulation laws is a European standard that came out on 26 May 2018. They are laws that regulate personal data sharing in the European Union. It focuses on compliance, data protection, and personal data of European residence. There are four main entities in the regulation as shown in Table 1.

GDPR sets out the following seven key privacy principles for the processing of personal data :

1. Lawfulness, fairness, and transparency: Organizations must inform data subjects about the handling of their data in a lawful, fair, and transparent manner.
2. Purpose limitation: Personal data should be collected only for specified, explicit, and legitimate purposes. Controllers should define and document the purpose of data usage.
3. Data minimization: The storage and collection of personal data must be adequate, relevant, and limited to satisfy the stated purpose.
4. Truth and Accuracy: Created or updated data should be accurate with the right of rectification.

Table 1. GDPR entities.

GDPR entities	Roles
Data Subject (DS)	An individual who can be identified, directly or indirectly. Their rights include consent/opt out, access data, know where data are, how data are processed, where data are communicated, and request data erasure (employee or customer).
Controller	The controller determines the purpose, conditions, and means of personal data processing the data. It guarantees compliance with GDPR rules: Personal data processing, Accuracy, and data protection strategies and data security proceedings, inform data subjects on their rights, inform supervisory authority in the case of a breach, and prevent the transfer to insecure processors (organization).
Processor	The processor processes data on behalf of the controllers and takes additional measures. The processor collects personal data under the instructions of the controller. It has a signed agreement and erases data once services are terminated.
Supervisory Authority (SA)	A public authority that is responsible for monitoring regulated entity compliance with GDPR

5. Storage Limitation: Controllers should consider which data to store, why, and for how long. They should be deleted as soon as they are no longer needed.
6. Integrity and confidentiality: Personal data may be processed only with appropriate security measures. Records are needed to demonstrate compliance.
7. Accountability: Controllers assume responsibility for their actions concerning personal data and their adherence to the other principles.

1.5 Organization

This study is organized as follows: Sect. 2 describes the related works concerning privacy and compliance in IoT systems. Section 3 presents the proposed architecture alongside the security model components. Section 4 analyzes the security of the scheme and its compliance with privacy regulations. Section 5 draws conclusions.

2   Related Works

In the past decade, IoT privacy has attracted lots of research attention and a number of privacy-preserving mechanisms have been developed for protecting data in IoT systems. Related works can be split into two major fields: Privacy-preserving solutions in modern technologies and HIPAA/GDPR compliance.

2.1   Privacy-Preserving Solution in Modern Technologies

There are different proposed solutions to protect health data by providing security and privacy. Those solutions are using several techniques such as encryption, anonymization, and access control. Authors in [9] propose a stream data anonymization method based on k-anonymity for data collected by IoT devices. The experiment results show that the proposed techniques can well preserve privacy without significantly affecting the value of the data. Authors in [10] present an encryption solution for IoT sensors based on homomorphic strategy and DES algorithm. A novel Big data-based system called PRIAH which stands for PRIvate Alerts in Healthcare is presented in [11]. Using pseudonymization for privacy implementation and a Big data streaming system for scalability will improve the privacy of overall architecture without any significant overhead compared to non-secure systems. Another work [12] focuses on media image in the healthcare systems. It shows that the use of 3D chaotic systems to generate a key stream is secure against statistical attacks.

This work describes the privacy implementation, but this solution lacks conformity with privacy standards.

2.2   HIPAA/GDPR Compliance

In [13], authors propose a mechanism for preserving Blockchain-based healthcare information that considers data generation through transmission by wearable devices to mobile devices and then to a medical center server. This process is protected in a manner that complies with HIPAA privacy and security regulations. Propose a sustainable and analytical approach to maintain patients' medical records in a well-preserved and suitable setting complying with the HIPAA regulation. In [15], authors made a first attempt to test the validation of GDPR on the healthcare sector. Authors in [16–18] proposed a framework for GDPR compliance verification and implementation. An e-health application is considered to validate the framework, which shows that the implementation respected GDPR without significant overhead on system performance. The framework was the first step towards GDPR-compliance which is used to evaluate the proposed solution of this work. Meanwhile, in [19], the authors examined the effectiveness of GDPR on storage systems and extracted security requirements and adequate storage features to provide GDPR compliance. Few works discuss compliance with both the HIPAA privacy/security regulations and the GDPR privacy principles. In [20], authors reviewed the compliance of Blockchain EHR systems with GDPR and HIPAA regulations, where blockchain systems can provide both encryption and pseudonymization techniques which are essential for GDPR and HIPAA compliance. In the reference [8], the authors create an innovative, secure, and efficient certificateless authentication and key agreement scheme using extended Chebyshev chaotic maps. The suggested scheme resolves security issues including unauthorized access to patient information while they prove that their solution is compliant with HIPAA and GDPR regulations

3   Architecture and Security Model

Based on previous sections, compliance and privacy in IoT infrastructure is a recent research directive. In this context, we present a security model for data privacy and an original solution that complies with HIPAA/GDPR regulations, alongside its main components in IoT healthcare architecture as shown in Fig. 2.

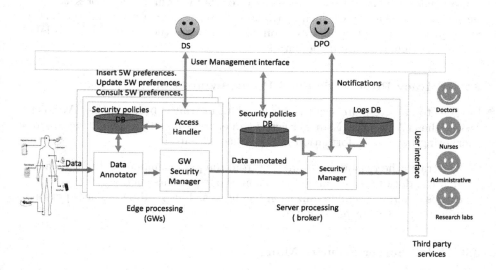

Fig. 2. Proposed IoT Healthcare architecture.

We suppose in our architecture that the communication channel between the GW and the server is secured. We concentrate on addressing the privacy concern, which involves managing data dissemination in accordance with the user-expressed preferences following the 5W format and the access to this data.

3.1   5W Labels Annotation

To overcome the constraints of earlier solutions, security labels are associated with the collected data. These security labels are metadata information attached to the collected data and give extra information about them [21]. The metadata contains the 5W constraints to restrict access control to the associated data and control authorization as follows: L=O:data owner identifier, who: "principles having the right to access data", what: "data being transferred and processed", when: "when the transfer takes place", where: "where data is to be stored", why: "purpose for collecting data" where O is the data subject ID and the value is a String. To provide the uniqueness of the data subject ID, we concatenate the unique user ID or patient ID with the sensor ID. In particular, patients are equipped with multiple sensors and each sensor has its unique function: SPO2 sensor can only control the oxygen saturation. Every W should have a default value. An example of the label of collected data is : L=O:ID, who= "Cardiology's doctor", what= "Heart rate" when= "15h" , where= "Cardiologist-DB" , why= "diagnostic" .

This annotation process is executed at the GW level. With a friendly user interface, the patient or the data subject DS has the capability to express his 5W preferences and also the capability to update them. The Access Handler component translates user preferences into JSON format and stores them in the security policies DB, which is available in both the gateway and the server. Subsequently, the data annotator component utilizes these preferences to label all events originating from the data source.

3.2   Privacy Preservation and Pseudonymization

In order to achieve more security for the data-in-transit between the GW to the server, the GW security Manager acts as an encryption engine by extracting and encrypting personal information in the collected data [11]:

- It extracts the personal information from the patient name field in the packet or if the data type reveals information about patients such as address.
- It uses different pseudonymization techniques. This module replaces personal information with a pseudonym.

3.3   Edge/Server Security Manger

Multiple GWs can connect to the same server. The edge/server security manager can establish authentication between the two components for reliable and secure communication. Meanwhile, multiple users will access to the data. The server security manager uses tokens that store the who and when policies. Tokens are attributed to data consumers (services and persons in our case) to access the healthcare data sent by the server. After a successful authentication, wherein the consumer is identified in the who list and the data processing target aligns with the specified policy, a unique token is issued to the data consumer. The token provides access to decryption services during the authorized period as stipulated by the policy. When this duration expires, the encryption keys are invalidated, and the user loses the capability to decrypt incoming events.

The log DB contains the history of streams and all notifications of 5W preferences updates and data tracking. We can rely on third-party services for the security manager such as Hashicorp Vault [22].

4   Security and Performance Analysis

This section analyzes the security requirements of the proposed scheme. It shows that the proposed scheme complies with HIPAA privacy/security regulations and GDPR privacy principles.

4.1   Compliance with HIPAA Privacy/Security Regulations

(1) Patient's Understanding: In the registration phase of the proposed scheme, the patient needs to sign the consent form and apply his preference.
(2) Patient's Control: The patient can control all the access to his data alongside notification in case of beaches. Token sessions are established thanks to the security manager services and the logs database can track all data streams.
(3) PHI's Confidentiality: All data are kept away only from authorized persons with "who" preferences, otherwise everything is encrypted.
(4) Data Integrity: Encryption enforces the ownership and the who policy by providing integrity principle.
(5) Consent Exception: The DPO can allow access to the patient data in case of an emergency with the help of the security manager.

4.2   Compliance with GDPR Privacy Principles

(1) The Principles of Lawfulness, Fairness, and Transparency: In the registration phase of the proposed scheme, the patient must sign a privacy contract, which includes the patient's information and instructions to ensure that the patient is transparent about the process of personal data processing. Even more, with the user interface the DS can track all steps and access history.
(2) The Principle of Purpose Limitation: Furthermore, in the registration phase of the proposed scheme, the patient must sign a privacy contract to ensure that the patient is transparent about the process of personal data processing. Additionally, with the proposed solution only specific persons have access to specific data thanks to the "why" preference.
(3) The Principle of Data Minimization: In the proposed scheme, the patient is the one to define who has access to each type of data with the "who" preference.
(4) The Principle of Trueness, Accuracy: Data subject can upload data and verify all the transferred data with the "what" preference .
(5) The Principle of Storage Limitation: Stored data in the database can be kept in a form and limited to its necessity of the original purpose with the DS consent and both the "when" and "where" preferences.
(6) The Principle of Integrity and Confidentiality: Encryption enforces the ownership and the "who" policy by providing both integrity and confidentiality principles.
(7) Accountability: The administrator can act as the data protection officer DPO that evaluates the Compliance.

5 Conclusion

This work presents a novel security architecture for healthcare IoT systems for data privacy preservation under HIPAA/GDPR regulations. The idea of this work is to translate both HIPAA and GDPR principles into technical requirements. By introducing new components on the edge and server sides, the data subject and the data protection officer can monitor all aspects of privacy in the healthcare infrastructure. The data subject will introduce his 5W preferences into the IoT system, which will be used for annotation. The security manager at the edge and at the server will ensure the security of data transfer and data access by using encryption techniques and access control. This work considers new challenges in IoT system compliance. For future work, we plan to implement this solution with simulation and hardware to assess performance overhead and evaluate the efficiency of this solution.

References

1. Elhoseny, M., et al.: Security and privacy issues in medical internet of things: overview, countermeasures, challenges and future directions. Sustainability **13**(21), 11645 (2021)
2. Riahi Sfar, A., Natalizio, E., Mazlout, S., Challal, Y., Chtourou, Z.: Privacy preservation using game theory in e-health application. J. Inf. Secur. Appl. **66**, 103158 (2022)
3. U.S. Department of Health and Human Services. Health Insurance Portability and Accountability Act of 1996 (1996). https://aspe.hhs.gov/report/health-insurance-portability-and-accountability-act-1996
4. European Union. General Data Protection Regulation GDPR (2016). https://gdpr-info.eu/
5. Said, A.M., Yahyaoui, A., Abdellatif, T.: Efficient anomaly detection for smart hospital IoT systems. Sensors **21**(4), 1026 (2021)
6. Yu, W., et al.: A survey on the edge computing for the Internet of Things. IEEE Access **6**, 6900–6919 (2017)
7. Sfar, A.R., Natalizio, E., Challal, Y., Chtourou, Z.: A roadmap for security challenges in the Internet of Things. Digit. Commun. Netw. **4**(2), 118–137 (2018)
8. Lee, T.F., Chang, I.P., Su, G.J.: Compliance with HIPAA and GDPR in certificateless-based authenticated key agreement using extended chaotic. Electronics **12**(5), 1108 (2023)
9. Ren, W., et al.: Privacy enhancing techniques in the Internet of Things using data Anonymisation. Inf. Syst. Front., 1-12 (2021)
10. Tianhe, G., et al.: A medical healthcare system for privacy protection based on IoT. In: Seventh International Symposium on Parallel Architectures. Algorithms and Programming (PAAP), p. 2015. IEEE (2015)
11. Said, A.M., Yahyaoui, A., Abdellatif, T.: PRIAH: private alerts in healthcare. In: Kallel, S., Jmaiel, M., Zulkernine, M., Hadj Kacem, A., Cuppens, F., Cuppens, N. (eds.) Risks and Security of Internet and Systems. Lecture Notes in Computer Science, vol. 13857, pp. 47–61. Springer, Cham (2023). https://doi.org/10.1007/978-3-031-31108-6_4

12. Sarosh, P., Parah, S.A., Bhat, G.M.: An efficient image encryption scheme for healthcare applications. Multimedia Tools Appl. **81**, 7253–7270 (2022)
13. Lee, T.F., Chang, I.P., Kung, T.S.: Blockchain-based healthcare information preservation using extended chaotic maps for HIPAA privacy/security regulations. Appl. Sci. **11**(22), 10576 (2021)
14. Mbonihankuye, S., Nkunzimana, A., Ndagijimana, A.: Healthcare data security technology: HIPAA compliance. Wirel. Commun. Mob. Comput. **2019**, 1–7 (2019)
15. Yuan, B., Li, J.: The policy effect of the general data protection regulation (GDPR) on the digital public health sector in the European union: an empirical investigation. Int. J. Environ. Res. Public Health **16**(6), 1070 (2019)
16. Rhahla, M., Allegue, S., Abdellatif, T.: A framework for GDPR compliance in big data systems. In: Kallel, S., Cuppens, F., Cuppens-Boulahia, N., Hadj Kacem, A. (eds.) Risks and Security of Internet and Systems. Lecture Notes in Computer Science(), vol. 12026, pp. 211–226. Springer, Cham (2020)
17. Rhahla, M., Abdellatif, T., Attia, R., Berrayana, W.: A GDPR controller for IoT systems: application to e-health. In: 2019 IEEE 28th International Conference on Enabling Technologies: Infrastructure for Collaborative Enterprises (WETICE), pp. 170-173. IEEE (2019)
18. Rhahla, M., Allegue, S., Abdellatif, T.: Guidelines for GDPR compliance in big data systems. J. Inf. Secur. Appl. **61**, 102896 (2021)
19. Shah, A., Banakar, V., Shastri, S., Wasserman, M., Chidambaram, V.: Analyzing the impact of GDPR on storage systems. In: 11th USENIX Workshop on Hot Topics in Storage and File Systems (2019)
20. Shuaib, M., Alam, S., Alam, M.S., Nasir, M.S.: Compliance with HIPAA and GDPR in blockchain-based electronic health record. Mater. Today: Proc. (2021)
21. Allegue, S., Rhahla, M., Abdellatif, T.: Toward GDPR compliance in IoT systems. In: Yangui, S., et al. (eds.) Service-Oriented Computing – ICSOC 2019 Workshops. Lecture Notes in Computer Science(), vol. 12019, pp. 130–141. Springer, Cham (2020). https://doi.org/10.1007/978-3-030-45989-5_11
22. Vault. https://www.vaultproject.io

A Secure IoT Architecture for Industry 4.0

Aymen Wali[1(✉)], Hichem Mrabet[1], and Abderrazek Jemai[2]

[1] SERCOM Laboratory, University of Carthage, 2078 Carthage, Tunisia
aymen.wali@ept.ucar.tn
[2] INSAT and SERCOM Laboratory, University of Carthage, 2078 Carthage, Tunisia

Abstract. This paper proposes a secure and smart IoT architecture for monitoring and automating industrial production processes emulated by flexible manufacturing simulators (FMS) while ensuring data security and privacy. The proposed architecture extends the current FMS architecture with two additional layers. The application layer incorporates an MQTT broker and Domoticz's dashboard for monitoring and controlling FMS-related data. The cloud layer leverages Google Cloud for secure data archiving and sharing. The solution undergoes a security analysis, demonstrating its dependability, exceptional performance, and robust protection against ARP spoofing and session hijacking.

Keywords: IoT · IIoT · Security · Industry 4.0 · FMS

1 Introduction

The Internet of Things (IoT) paradigm is expanding quickly [1] with the innovative design, development, and integration of numerous technologies. It has presented a potential chance to create potential industrial systems and applications. IoT, which allows everything to be connected at any time or place, has grown to be a very active study area [2]. It has been used to connect previously unheard-of numbers of devices for consumer applications (home appliances, transportation, mobile devices, etc.). These consumer applications, such as smart homes, smart cities, smart grids, and smart transportation, can offer customers convenience, efficiency, and intelligence to help them manage their time and resources more effectively. The adoption of IoT for use in manufacturing, kown as Industrial-IoT (IIoT) has the potential to significantly increase productivity, efficiency, safety, and the intelligence of industrial factories and plants. Consequently, IIoT enables the interconnection of "everything" (sensors, actuators, controllers, production lines, equipment, etc.) in industrial production and automation environment. The sector has benefited from IoT adoption in a several ways, including cost reduction, worker safety, product anomaly detection, and more. Despite this achievement, numerous problems still exist [3]. The primary concern that could impede the adoption of IoT among them is security. In secure designs, architectures, and deployments are caused by the heterogeneity of protocols, operating systems, and devices, as well as a lack of widespread use of standard solutions.

M. Mosbah et al. (Eds.): MEDI 2023, CCIS 2071, pp. 210–223, 2024.
https://doi.org/10.1007/978-3-031-55729-3_17

IoT applications are also frequently linked to sensitive data, key infrastructures, and assets, making them more vulnerable to data breaches and denial-of-service assaults. Unfortunately, the resource constraints of IoT devices and the decentralized nature of IoT designs make conventional security measures frequently inapplicable in the IoT.

In manufacturing, virtual commissioning is a well-liked technique in the industrial sector for testing and validating the behavior of the target control system based on a virtual model. It may genuinely imitate and aid in the study of the behavior of shop floor components, which are distinguished by a physical layer and low-level control functions. The flexible manufacturing system is a method for assisting with the virtual commissioning of the flexible manufacturing system, including the separate but consistent modeling of their low- and high-level control functions. It entails gradually creating an emulator of the shop floor to which a several potential high-level control techniques can link via a common interface layer. Numerous manufacturing and supply chain processes can be simulated using this simulator. But, it lacks smart control and automation.

This research's main objective is to examine, analyze, and discuss how to meet the privacy and security concerns of industry 4.0 applications. Indeed, the goal is to propose a smart and secure IoT architecture for an industrial manufacturing process simulated using a manufacturing emulator.

The remainder of this work is as follows. Section 2 presents a background on industry 4.0. In Sect. 3 presents the literature-related works. In Sect. 4 we will discuss the proposed solution. Then we will present the implementation and performance evaluation of our architecture. Finally, a conclusion is drawn and future work is fixed.

2 Industry 4.0: A Background

2.1 IoT and Smart IoT for Industry 4.0

In recent decades, the industrial sector has seen a transformative shift known as Industry 4.0, driven by digitization and adherence to strict standards. This transformation has led to substantial investments in intelligent production systems, reshaping the industrial value chain. Industry 4.0 encompasses vital elements such as enterprise resource planning, big data, social product creation, logistics, and cloud manufacturing. The adoption of cutting-edge technologies like AI, machine learning, and IoT has revolutionized manufacturing, enhancing product quality and reducing downtime. Industrial Internet of Things (IIoT) and automation have become instrumental in boosting collaboration, productivity, early issue detection, cost efficiency, and regulatory compliance. By leveraging IoT, Industry 4.0 connects industrial equipment, facilitating seamless data exchange and fostering collaboration among personnel. IIoT, with its real-time data and predictive diagnostics capabilities, significantly improves manufacturing efficiency. While establishing IoT-based factories involves an initial investment, it leads to substantial operational cost reductions over time. Automation, system integration, and IIoT's data management and optimization features contribute to cost savings in manufacturing and shipping processes. Furthermore, these advancements offer real-time insights for better decision-making, ultimately enhancing the profitability of production cycles. Industry 4.0 also empowers companies to meet government requirements automatically through advanced tracking, consumer profiling, and comprehensive information recording [4].

2.2 Security Challenges and Requirements

Security in IoT is vital as it can disrupt entire industries like manufacturing, transport, and healthcare. IoT's diversity in devices, protocols, and technologies increases vulnerabilities, expanding the attack surface. In Industry 4.0, IoT connects diverse items, requiring a flexible 5-layer architecture: the physical sensing, the network/protocol, the transport, the application, and the data/cloud services. Each layer has its security concerns due to distinct functions and technologies. Data from multiple IoT devices is sensitive and prone to privacy risks in Industry 4.0, increasing the threat of cyberattacks [5]. Therefore, safeguarding this data is essential, involving robust defenses, data encryption, user authentication, access control, and adherence to evolving security regulations. In the context of Industry 4.0, security entails several crucial requirements. Firstly, there's the need for **confidentiality**, ensuring that sensitive information remains protected from unauthorized access. **Integrity** comes next, focusing on safeguarding data from any unauthorized or unintentional alterations. **Authenticity** is vital as it ensures both the data and its source can be trusted. Additionally, **availability** guarantees that information is accessible whenever required by a device user. Furthermore, **traceability** plays a significant role as it logs all actions within the Industry 4.0 system in chronological order. **Access control** is essential for establishing authorization policies that dictate who is authorized to carry out activities on resources like databases or IoT devices. Lastly, **unlinkability** of data is crucial to prevent the identification of connections between various parts of the system [6].

3 State of the Art

This section reviews the most recent state-of-the-art work that has proposed solutions and architectures to improve data security and privacy in Industry 4.0. These works are compared and evaluated in light of the above security and privacy requirements and our proposed architecture to enhance FMS security against ARP spoofing and session hijacking attacks. Thus, it serves as a benchmark against which our proposed solution can be measured, and helps distinguish our contribution.

This study [7], which is based on blockchain technology and machine intelligence, proposes a secure architecture for the Industrial Internet of Things (IIoT) in smart manufacturing. It is meant for sensor access control systems in these situations. The proposed architecture makes use of blockchain to provide a secure and decentralized system for limiting access to sensor data, as well as machine learning to improve process efficiency and accuracy. The paper examines the advantages of this technique and offers a case study that proves its efficiency in a real-world industrial scenario.

This paper [8] proposed the architecture, incorporating SDN (Software Defined Networking) with NFV (Network Function Virtualization) technology, an IoT-SDN model with multiple controller execution in order to manage an automated industrial system during the spread of the virus SARS-COV-2 condition. Due to the outbreak, the present world is depending on the internet and performing almost every important activities over the cloud. In this context. The authors propose a system model able to provide enormous automation while maintaining security and privacy within the networking system, so making the industry 4.0 application efficient and reliable in order to properly manage the pandemic crisis. They also propose a three-layer architecture, such as perception layer, SDN and NFV environment, and cloud layer.

The work in [9] describes the design and implementation of a digital platform for small and medium-sized enterprises (SMEs) to collaborate on Industry 4.0 initiatives. The platform includes various components such as front-end interfaces, back-end infrastructure, integration with Industry 4.0 technologies, and collaboration tools to enable effective communication. The paper outlines the architecture of the platform, which is intended to provide SMEs with a scalable and secure environment for collaboration, data analysis, and decision-making in the context of Industry 4.0.

In [10], the authors propose a traceability system for the textile manufacturing industry that combines blockchain technology and the Internet of Things (IoT) in the context of Industry 4.0. The authors demonstrate how the suggested system may handle the different challenges faced by the textile industry, such as quality control, supply chain management, and counterfeit products. The technology employs RFID sensors to collect data at various stages during the production process, which is subsequently saved on a blockchain to ensure data integrity and transparency. This study includes a full technical description of the system design and implementation, and evaluates its performance using various metrics such as data retrieval time and system scalability. Ultimately, the paper highlighted the potential of combining blockchain and IoT technology to allow efficient and secure traceability systems in the textile sector, which might aid in addressing a number of industry-specific challenges (Table 1).

Despite these initiatives' efforts, there are no solutions or strategies in place that use IoT and FMS for testing and assessing industrial processes in IIoT. Moreover, these works do not discuss the security issues in IIoT-based systems. To these end, this study presents a method that combines IoT and FMS to analyze a manufacturing process. It proposes a five-layer safe and intelligent IoT architecture for monitoring and automating an industrial production process modeled by FMS while retaining security and privacy. The suggested design extends FMS's present architecture by two levels to enable monitoring, control,

Table 1. Related works based on secure IoT architecture for industry 4.0

Years	Authors	Focus
2022	Mrabet et al. [7]	Authors proposed an architecture wich makes use of blockchain to provide a secure and decentralized system for limiting access to sensor data
2022	Rahman et al. [8]	Authors proposed a SDN-IoT intelligent framework for Industry 4.0 during COVID-19 that leverages the capabilities of SDN and IoT to create an adaptive network infrastructure
2022	LIU et al. [9]	The paper describes the architecture of a digital platform for SME collaboration on Industry 4.0 initiatives, which includes front-end interfaces, back-end infrastructure, integration with Industry 4.0 technologies, and collaboration tools for effective communication
2021	Faridi, M.S. et al. [10]	Authors proposed a system that combines blockchain and IoT to create a traceability system for the textile manufacturing industry

and sharing of FMS-related data. Further, the proposed architecture is secure by design against ARP spoofing and session hijacking.

4   A Secure IoT Architecture for an Industrial Manufacturing Process

This section goes over the suggested solution for an industrial manufacturing process scenario, including its architecture and key components.

4.1   System Architecture Layers

The proposed solution enables the monitoring and control of data related to an industrial manufacturing process that is being simulated using a manufacturing emulator. This five-layers architecture allow an end-to-end monitoring and automation of the industrial process while maintaining data security and privacy. As shown in Fig. 1, this architecture can be divided into two parts:

The first part includes the three layers which such as the Physical Sensing Layer, the Network/ Protocol Layer, and the Transport Layer. The manufacturing emulator manages or ensures the first part. Indeed, it simulates a scenario of an IIoT supply chain in industry 4.0, with no interactions with external applications and tools required for data monitoring and management. With a local data base, it is not a smart solution. It is devoid of automation and connectivity.

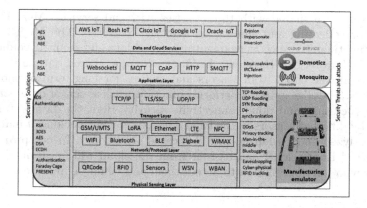

Fig. 1. Proposed Solution Layered Architecture

The second part includes the 4th and 5th layers which are the Application Layer and the Data and Cloud Services. This part describes our work's solution, which consists of implementing these two layers using two services such as Mosquitto as a message broker and Domoticz as a monitoring dashboard for the application layer and cloud services, resulting in a smart architecture for Industry 4.0. This architecture enables the manufacture to simulate a supply chain scenario and monitor its data in a secure manner.

4.2 System Description

The main goal of the proposed architecture is to address the issue of connecting and self-monitor of and IIoT system based on IoT and FMS while maintaining the previously specified security requirements. In this approach, data collected from IoT gadgets in traditional IoT architecture is emulated using the FMS. These sensors are part of the first layer (Physical Sensing Layer) and provide data on the shuttle position in our manufacturing process use case. Ethernet is utilized as the communication protocol between the Physical Sensing Layer and the Transport Layer in the network/protocol layer. Due to its tremendous consistency during data transfer, the TCP/IP protocol is utilized in the transport layer. The collected data is then broadcast to the MQTT broker for storage and eventual usage. To make our system highly reliable, the MQTT broker keeps the information received by the sensors on a local or cloud-based database. In this scenario, the MQTT protocol is selected in the Application Layer. As previously indicated, the data acquired by the MQTT Broker is stored locally on the system for local analysis and cannot be accessed externally. To accomplish this, Google Cloud services was chosen as a cloud service, giving remote access to data collected via the MQTT broker. So we're talking about the Data and Cloud Services layer. The data life cycle of this architecture is as follows: In **data collection** phase, sensors monitor physical objects, and data is shared, stored, and retrievable in real time through IoT devices. Then, in the **Data sharing**, gathered data are shared with third parties API and services. MQTT Broker cis used for collecting and sharing data to the database. The MQTT Broker provides functionality, such as aggregating sensor data and securing connectivity to the local data base or the cloud. In **Data storage**, shared data are stored at the edge or in the cloud from sensors and devices for long-term or short-term applications. The edge gateway performs functions such as sensor data gathering, data pre-processing, and cloud connectivity security. Here, the data is stored and collected by different sensors in the local data base or in the cloud. Finally, data will be analyzed and visualized in a dedicated Dashboard. In our project, any data received from a local database or from the cloud will be available to the end-users who have permission to access them and could be analyzed.

4.3 System Workflow

First, we will provide an overview of the solution's workflow for the use case of an industrial manufacturing process. To do so, we will enhance an industrial manufacturing process simulator with two new layers: Mosquitto as an MQTT broker and Domoticz as an automation and management dashboard. Therefore, ensure intelligent control and monitoring of the industrial chain while maintaining its security. The proposed solution maintains the security in an industrial system emulated using a manufacturing emulator while ensuring intelligent monitoring and handling of the industrial chain following these steps:

Step 1. Start the emulator in offline mode to create a log file called "F2.log," which will be protected from accidental overwriting (Read only).

Step 2. Start an emulator scenario while adding the two previously mentioned layers, resulting in the creation of a log file called "F1.log."

Step 3. Following that, the two log files will be compared using a Python script. Thus, we ensure the integrity of the data and that there is no alteration or attempt of modification by malicious parties.

Step 4. The Hash function ("SHA256" of the "F1.log" file) will be sent to the cloud, ensuring traceability and authenticity.
These two acts are only performed at the level of the emulator.

Step 5. We will launch another Python script that will remotely project all emulator operations to the Domoticz dashboard through Mosquitto as an MQTT Broker, ensuring confidentiality and security of the data to be sent.

Step 6. The connection between the emulator and Mosquitto is made through an already created topic called "Test" that contains connection credentials such as the username and password ensuring the confidentiality.

Step 7. To connect to Domoticz, we need a login and a password as connection credentials. Domoticz also allows us to track all devices in the emulator activity by creating a log file called "Domoticz.log". Then this file will be sent to the cloud.

This workflow is shown on the picture depicted in Fig. 2:

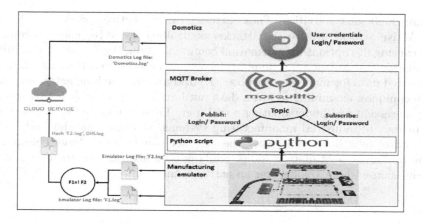

Fig. 2. Proposed Solution WorkFlow

4.4   A Potential Attacks Scenarios

Given that we have a connection between our IoT devices and the cloud to transfer and store their states in the cloud, the manufacturing emulator log file might be a target of several cyberattacks aimed at disrupting or destabilizing the system, ARP Spoofing, and Session Hijacking attacks are possible.

ARP Spoofing: is a spoofing attack used by hackers to intercept data by tricking a device into sending data to the hacker instead of the intended receiver as shown in Fig. 3. This allows hackers to access sensitive data, such as passwords and credentials, and can be used for eavesdropping, man-in-the-middle attacks, and denial-of-service attacks [11]. The hacker can alter IP addresses in the log file, potentially containing ransomware, and disrupt the supply chain.

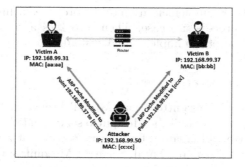

Fig. 3. ARP spoofing attack

Session Hijacking: As demonstrated in Fig. 4, Session hijacking attacks involve an attacker gaining a valid session ID, impersonating a legitimate user, and performing malicious activities. These attacks can be active, passive, or hybrid [12]. Active attacks involve the attacker controlling an active network connection, causing disruptions in information communication. Passive attacks monitor information transmission but do not take over an active connection, intercepting transferred data for malicious purposes. Hybrid attacks combine active and passive techniques, examining network data until an issue is identified, then taking over the session and impersonating a real user. These attacks affect the security and privacy of industrial manufacturing systems, allowing unauthorized access and control over industrial data. The attacker can transmit large volumes of traffic to disrupt legitimate sessions, while passive attacks monitor information transmission without taking over an active connection.

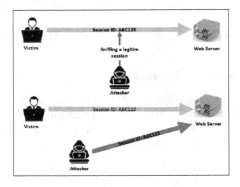

Fig. 4. Session hijacking attack

5 Implementation and Security Analysis

This chapter presents the implementation of the proposed solution for the industrial manufacturing process use case. Then, provides a security analysis and performance evaluation of the implemented system.

5.1 System Implementation

Mosquitto. To install Mosquitto as an MQTT broker in our system: First, update Ubuntu's package, install the Mosquitto server and client. Second, create a configuration file.We will create a backup file to prevent any modification or damage to the main file "conf.d". Third, Securing Mosquitto: Controlling Access to MQTT Broker using User Permissions as shown in Fig. 5

> "allow_anonymous false": to deny anonymous connection
>
> "password_file /etc/mosquitto/pwfile":to create password file
>
> "listener 1883" : port listener

Fig. 5. Mosquito security: Deny anonymous connection

Domoticz. To configure Domoticz, we need to follow these main steps: configure the Mosquitto server in Domoticz, set up the switches and shuttles, and review the Domoticz log file for configuration issues. After, accessing Domoticz web page, we have to configure the MQTT broker that is already installed on our machine as "MQTT Client Gateway with LAN interface", then we have to give the address of our machine "10.0.2.15" while mentioning the port that is by /default "8080". After that, we will give the login and the password which are already configured on our broker in the "pwfile" file in " /etc ". Second, to create a new device, such as a switch or workstation sensor, you need to select the appropriate option sensor type and gateway. We can have two possible states of the configured switches "1" or "0. So, to change these states manually we will run the command:

mosquitto_ pub -h 10.0.2.15 -u test1 -P test1 -t " Domoticz /in" -m " idx" : 1 , " nvalue " : 1 . This command is used to activate switch number 1.

mosquitto_ pub -h 10.0.2.15 -u test1 -P test1 -t " Domoticz /in" -m " idx" : 1 , " nvalue " : 0 . This command is used to disable switch number 1.

Notes: "idx" indicates the index of the switch in Domoticz and "nvalue" indicates its state.

Finally, Domoticz allows us to ensure the traceability of all actions executed on the switches while listing them in a log file that can be displayed directly on the Domoticz dashboard, or in the file "/var/snap/Domoticz-gm/341/Domoticz.log". We can also have visibility and traceability of the said switches one by one and display a report whether daily or weekly. The purpose of this implementation is to run Domoticz from the manufacturing emulator log file ensuring security and privacy requirements like confidentiality, integrity, authenticity, availability, traceability, access control, unlinkability of data, and accountability.

Cloud Services. Google is used as cloud services due to its simplicity and security. Google Cloud is a part of the 5th layer, which is the Data and Cloud Services layer. All files log sent from Domoticz and manufacturing emulator will be stored in Google Cloud. After the configuration of Google Cloud environment, we activate the "Google Cloud API" to be allowed to automate our workflows by using our favorite language. Use these Cloud APIs with REST calls or client libraries in popular programming languages [13]. Then, we will create an OAuth client ID called "Aymen." Authentication is the process of confirming access's credential. It is also the process of demonstrating that you are who you claim to be. Google offers several APIs and services that require authentication before use. Google also offers a variety of services for hosting apps built by our clients; these applications must also recognize the identity of their users.

We can always access the client ID and secret code via the "Identifiers" section of the "API and Services" webpage. During the client creation process, a ".json" file is created. Data types used by APIs (JSON) RESTful APIs use the XML or JSON (JavaScript Object Notation) file format for data contained in the body of an HTTP request method. This file, called "code_secret_client.json" can be used by Google Drive components and data assistants to get access to Google Drive using the OAuth Service Account method. Following the setting of the Google Cloud environment, a Python script called "Cloud.py" will be launched to automate the sending of the manufacturing emulator's log file "F1.log" to Google Cloud. The execution of the script will result in a verification of the security and connectivity parameters of the Google Cloud service. To accomplish this task, we must authorize access to our operating system and the cloud services. Finally, following the update of our Google Drive, the files "F1.log", "Domoticz.log", and "Log.txt" are now in the cloud.

5.2   Security Analysis and Performance Evaluation

ARP Spoofing Attack Prevention. All MAC addresses in a network should be statically mapped to their respective IP addresses. This method is quite successful in avoiding ARP Poisoning assaults; as is the case with the manufacturing emulator log file. We must determine when an IP address is falsified and what the attacker is doing. We may examine abnormal activity on our system and try to figure out what information they are targeting.

The method implemented to compare the two log files of the manufacturing emulator can alert us when there is a change in the log file. This can also indicate what types of data are vulnerable to any attack, not simply ARP spoofing.

Session Hijacking Attack Prevention. Some of the most common methods for preventing session hijacking attempts are as follows:

- **Share session IDs with only trusted sources:** Sharing links or sending requests to websites may include session IDs, requiring limited sharing of identity-related data and ensuring connection security. Domoticz can protect against session hijacking by canceling the user's connection to the session as a precautionary measure as represented in Fig. 6.

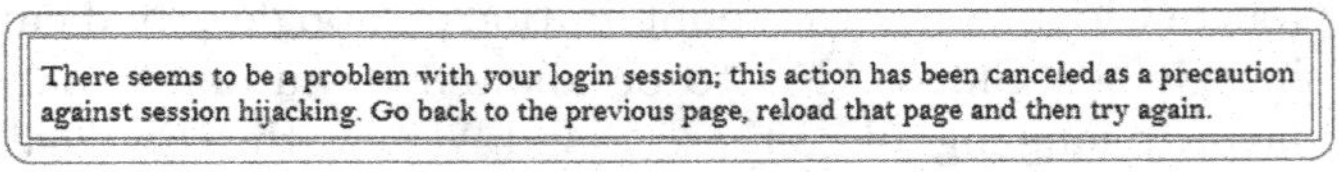

> There seems to be a problem with your login session; this action has been canceled as a precaution against session hijacking. Go back to the previous page, reload that page and then try again.

Fig. 6. Protection against session hijacking

- **Don't log in on open wireless networks:** To protect your data from malicious hackers, avoid using public, unencrypted Wi-Fi networks and use a secure VPN or trusted network for localhosting in your project.
- **Keep software updated:** Install the latest security patches and updates to prevent attackers from exploiting vulnerabilities to access user sessions, using the latest version of Domoticz and our Linux operating system.
- **Install firewall software:** Install a firewall on your system to detect and remove viruses, protect against malware attacks, and prevent session hijacking. Use Linux's default firewall managed by "iptable" tools. Choose Google Cloud for secure and transparent connections between your manufacturing emulator and server. A token is requested, and a response token is provided.

Protect the Log File. We are currently facing threats that can act on our system and our data integrity. For this reason, it is necessary to set up a tool or an approach for the protection of our log file against all attempts of crashes or modifications, whose goal is the disturbance of our chain of production. We have set up a script to check the integrity of our log file's data. First, we use the command "chmod 400 /tmp/F2.log" to protect our source file against accidental overwriting. Second, we move the manufacturing emulator's log source file "F2.log" to a different location to ensure the file's availability. Third, after extracting the manufacturing emulator log file "F1.log," the script "log.py" will be run to verify the integrity of the data in our log file. Following the execution of the script, there are three possible outcomes:

The two files are identical, and there has been no data alteration in the log file as represented in Fig. 7.

Fig. 7. Same file

A change in the content of the log file that may disrupt the proper operation of our work chain and result in data traceability as shown in Fig. 8.

Fig. 8. File is modified

As shown in Fig. 9, deleting lines from the log file might potentially disturb our work chain's appropriate execution and result in data traceability.

Fig. 9. line modified in file

Security Analysis. In our solution, confidentiality is ensured at the application and transport layer with the MQTT protocol to enhance the security of our model. Integrity is guaranteed by comparing the two log files to ensure that the data has not been altered at the Data and Cloud Services layer. Authenticity and traceability is ensured by hashing the log file with SHA256 for full visibility and control over FMS activities. Data availability is ensured, at the application layer, by data storage in the cloud through the Domoticz dashboard and the protection of the first log file in our proposed solution. When connecting the application layer to the data and cloud services layers, access control can be provided to end users who have authorization to access it. Additionally, access control is ensured throughout the connection between the transport layer and the application layer by connecting to the topics using the appropriate credentials.

6   Conclusions and Future Works

The adoption of the Internet of Things (IIoT) in the industrial sector has transformed unconnected systems into smart, automated ones. The need for industrial sensors is crucial, but reliability and security are also important concerns. A flexible manufacturing system can help virtualize control systems, but it is not connected and automated. This research aims to identify security and privacy requirements, determine how to connect, automate, and monitor a manufacturing emulator, and design a secure IoT architecture for industrial manufacturing processes. The study provides an analysis of security concerns and proposes a secure IoT architecture that enables smart monitoring and automation while preserving industrial data security. The architecture's security analysis demonstrates its reliability and high performance. We added two other layers to the manufacturing emulator architecture, which simulate only the physical sensing layer, Network/ Protocol layer, and Transport layer. These two layers are: (1) the application layer implementing an MQTT broker and Domoticzs dashboard for monitoring and control of manufacturing emulator-related data, (2) the cloud layer adopting Google Cloud, enabling secure storage and sharing manufacturing emulator data. The security analysis of this architecture demonstrates its reliability and high performance towards current works.

In future work, several areas need to be explored to improve this work, we propose to implement a blockchain and SDN-based architecture to enhance the security and privacy of an IIoT systems.

References

1. Atzori, L., Iera, A., Morabito, G.: Understanding the Internet of Things: definition, potentials, and societal role of a fast evolving paradigm. Ad Hoc Netw. **56**, 122–140 (2017)
2. Aleksic, S.: A survey on optical technologies for IoT, smart industry, and smart infrastructures. J. Sens. Actuator Netw. **8**(3), 47 (2019)
3. Kumar, A.S., Iyer, E.: An industrial IoT in engineering and manufacturing industries benefits and challenges. Int. J. Mech. Prod. Eng. Res. Dev. (IJMPERD) **9**(2), 151–160 (2019)
4. Hofmann, E., Rusch, M.: Industry 4.0 and the current status as well as future prospects on logistics. Comput. Ind. **89**, 23–34 (2017)
5. ElMamy, S.B., et al.: A survey on the usage of blockchain technology for cyber-threats in the context of industry 4.0. Sustainability **12**(21), 9179 (2020)
6. Ervural, B.C., Ervural, B.: Overview of cyber security in the industry 4.0 era. Ind. 4.0: Manag. Digit. Transform., 267–284 (2017)
7. Mrabet, H., et al.: A secured industrial internet-of-things architecture based on blockchain technology and machine learning for sensor access control systems in smart manufacturing. Appl. Sci. **12**(9), 4641 (2022)
8. Rahman, A., et al.: SDNIoT empowered intelligent framework for industry 4.0 applications during COVID-19 pandemic. Cluster Comput. **25**(4), 2351–2368 (2022)
9. Liu, Z., et al.: The architectural design and implementation of a digital platform for Industry 4.0 SME collaboration. Comput. Ind. **138**, 103623 (2022)
10. Faridi, M.S., Ali, S., Duan, G., Wang, G.: Blockchain and IoT based textile manufacturing traceability system in industry 4.0. In: Wang, G., Chen, B., Li, W., Di Pietro, R., Yan, X., Han, H. (eds.) Security, Privacy, and Anonymity in Computation, Communication, and Storage. Lecture Notes in Computer Science(), vol. 12382, pp. 331–344. Springer, Cham (2021). https://doi.org/10.1007/978-3-030-68851-6_24
11. Girdler, T., Vassilakis, V.G.: Implementing an intrusion detection and prevention system using software-defined networking: defending against ARP spoofing attacks and blacklisted MAC addresses. Comput. Electr. Eng. **90**, 106990 (2021)
12. Nastase, L.: Security in the internet of things: a survey on application layer protocols. In: 2017 21st International Conference on Control Systems and Computer Science (CSCS) (2017)
13. Alqahtani, A.: Usability testing of google cloud applications: students' perspective. J. Technol. Sci. Edu. **9**(3), 326–339 (2019)

From Functional Requirements to NoSQL Database Models: Application to IoT Geospatial Data

Fatimata Dia[1]([envelope])[ID], Nawel Bayar[2][ID], and Takoua Abdellatif[1][ID]

[1] SERCOM - Polytechnic School of Tunisia, University of Carthage,
La Marsa, Tunisia
fatimaata.dia@gmail.com, takoua.abdellatif@ept.rnu.tn
[2] Horizon School of Digital Technologies, Sousse, Tunisia
nawel.bayar@horizon-tech.tn
http://www.ept.rnu.tn/, https://horizon-university.tn/fr

Abstract. The design of optimal geospatial NoSQL databases is complex and depends on application requirements and query patterns. This paper presents a top-down methodology for IoT applications, starting with data-related requirements defined using a UML class diagram and expected queries. Subsequently, a set of rules is applied to create a geospatial NoSQL database model. This approach is illustrated with an example of soil moisture detection.

Keywords: UML · NoSQL Modeling · Iot Application · Geospatial data · Document-oriented database

1 Introduction

The importance of geospatial data is undeniable, representing a significant portion of the data volume generated daily [1]. They originate from sources such as satellites, telescopes, and sensor networks, and their production is constantly expanding [2]. As a result, effective management of this data has become a central research challenge, demanding swift resolution. Currently, the field of geospatial databases is divided into two main categories: relational databases and NoSQL databases [1]. The management of this geospatial data is mostly carried out through relational databases equipped with spatial extensions [2]. While NoSQL databases have gained popularity for various reasons, including their ability to handle data characterized by high variety, velocity, volume, and variability, commonly grouped under the term Big Data, their heterogeneity and flexibility, combined with limited developer skills in NoSQL, have at times resulted in the creation of subpar NoSQL database structures [3].

To address this issue, NoSQL databases modeling is of paramount importance, as it establishes the structure and interrelationships of data to ensure efficient storage, effective management, and streamlined querying for essential information within a given system. Numerous modeling techniques have been developed, including UML, which has emerged as a widely accepted standard in both industry and academia, including within the geomatics community [4].

However, modeling geospatial databases has always faced numerous challenges. Despite many proposals to improve modeling formalisms for NoSQL document-oriented geospatial databases in recent years (see Sect. 2), these proposals have generally focused primarily on data-related requirements often leaving aside the functional requirements of users. It has been demonstrated [5] that considering functional requirements during the database design leads to better performance in terms of execution time and input/output. Nevertheless, to the best of our knowledge, these functional requirements are rarely taken into account in the modeling of a NoSQL document-oriented geospatial. Thus, it is this gap and the significant potential for improving the design of NoSQL document-oriented geospatial databases by integrating functional requirements that motivated us to undertake this contribution.

In this paper, we present a method for modeling a NoSQL document-oriented geospatial database based on a UML data conceptual model, taking into account both data-related and user functional requirements. We also highlight the significant impact of integrating functional requirements into the database design process. We propose a methodology based on a top-down approach: the designer defines user data requirements using a UML class diagram and then a set of expected queries. Subsequently, a set of rules is applied to arrive at a NoSQL geospatial database model. We illustrate this approach by applying it to a document-based NoSQL database and providing an example of an Internet of Things (IoT) soil moisture detection case study. We show that defining two functional requirements leads to two different NoSQL database models.

Section 2 is dedicated to review existing work in the literature, while Sect. 3 focuses on the presentation of a concrete case study. In Sect. 4, we detail our contribution, while Sect. 5 demonstrates the practical application of our approach through a sample application. Finally, Sect. 6 concludes our document.

2   Related Works

The geospatial applications, like many IoT applications, are data-driven decision-making ones in which geospatial data plays a crucial role in enhancing their capabilities and their effectiveness. Indeed, they add a spatial context to the information collected from the various connected sensors and devices [6].

Geospatial applications generate massive amounts of data, including geospatial information. NoSQL databases can handle the high velocity and volume of incoming data. They allow for flexible schema design to accommodate different types of data, making it easier to store and retrieve location-based information [1].

In most cases, the design of NoSQL databases incorporating geospatial data relies primarily on best practices and practitioners' experience [5,12]. However, a few references propose modeling approaches. Among the references we consulted, some explain how to design document-oriented NoSQL databases, while others detail the process of transitioning from a UML class diagram to a document-oriented NoSQL database. It is worth noting that some of these references take geospatial data into account, while others do not. We mention below a few of the consulted sources.

2.1   Modeling Document-Oriented NoSQL Geospatial Databases

In this section, we present the papers that demonstrate how to model document-oriented NoSQL databases for geospatial data.

Basmi et al. [7] are interested in modeling collected data from smart cities. In their approach, not only electronic devices like temperature or nose sensors are tracked, but also every abnormal event like accidents, population concentration, etc. They proposed a data model in the form of an entity-relationship schema inspired from the OGC (Open Geospatial Open Consortium) API to represent collected data from smart cities.

Ferreira et al. [8] explain the dynamicity criteria of a geo-object which is related with the change over time of spatial or non-spatial attributes of that object. They present various categories of geospatial applications and list the frequently demanded queries in each category. After that they investigate the existing geospatial-temporal database models.The authors enumerate the disadvantages of each presented model taking into account only the dynamicity criteria. They overlooked the analysis of each model's efficiency when changing the application category or the system functionalities.

Wagner et al. [2] propose a set of rules to standardize the building of diagrams for conceptual data modeling for documents-based NoSQL databases. Proposed diagrams include the representation of geo-spacial data. Their proposal is inspired from the OMT-G model [9] which provides primitives to model the geometry of geographic data.

Imam et al. [3] introduce new cardinality notations and three types of relationships (referencing, integration, and bucketing) for the modeling of document-oriented NoSQL databases. They also conducted an evaluation to determine the most suitable relationship style for each level of cardinality. However, the authors did not give particular attention to spatial data.

2.2   Mapping of a UML Class Diagram to a Document-Oriented NoSQL Database Model

In the papers cited in the previous section, attention is only given to conceptual modeling. All papers missed indications about the translation of proposed models to suitable data structures able to be stored in appropriate NoSQL databases. In this section, we present the papers that demonstrate how to start from a UML class diagram to model a document-oriented NoSQL database.

Abdelhedi et al. [10] propose the UMLtoNoSQL approach, which is based on Model-Driven Architecture (MDA). In this approach, the authors define a set of rules from which they automatically translate a UML class diagram into multiple NoSQL physical models, including the MongoDB physical model. They proposed five solutions to transform the relationships between two classes, but they have not specified the specific cases in which each solution should be applied.

In [11], Maicha et al. present another approach called UML4NoSQL. This approach uses UML use case and class diagrams to enhance data manipulation strategies in document-oriented NoSQL databases. It is based on four fundamental pillars, including a data-up technique to create a use case diagram for system behavior visualization and guidelines for transitioning from a class diagram to a NoSQL document-oriented model.

Benmakhlouf presents in [12] an approach that uses UML class diagrams to create a logical structure for a NoSQL database, specifically relying on the document-oriented model. This approach aims to eliminate the use of joins by implementing comprehensive and structured integration within the collections of the document-oriented database. Additionally, the paper introduces rules for transitioning from UML class diagrams to the Logical oriented-document model to facilitate the transformation of various types of class associations. An illustrative example is provided within the context of an e-commerce organization.

Roy-Hubara et al. [5] propose a method for designing document-oriented databases. The authors suggest design methods for these databases that take into account both data-related and functional requirements. They present a set of rules for transforming user needs into logical data models for these databases. The idea is to enhance performance and reduce query complexity directed at the databases. The contribution of this study is to provide a common model for user-centric database design and to evaluate the benefits of these design methods. The results demonstrate that databases perform better in terms of runtime and input/output operations when functional requirements are considered during design, as opposed to when they are not.

Shin et al. [13] present a NoSQL database design using the UML conceptual model based on Peter Chen's framework. The transformation from the UML conceptual data model to a document-oriented database model took into consideration both the application's functional requirements and the data requirements.

None of the papers we reviewed addressed the modeling of geospatial data. The last two papers [5,13], however, caught our attention as they considered functional requirements in data modeling. Nevertheless, they did not give particular attention on geospatial data modeling. Our contribution aims to fill this gap by proposing an approach that takes into account both data-related requirements and functional requirements for geospatial applications.

3   Application to IoT Case Study

This section marks the starting point of our contribution by introducing a fundamental element: a standard UML class diagram specifically tailored for IoT data modeling. This diagram serves as the foundation for our approach, enabling us to delve deeply into how functional requirements influence the design of document-oriented NoSQL databases for geospatial data.

3.1   IoT Data Modeling: The UML Class Diagram

In Fig. 1, we propose a UML class diagram consisting of multiple geographical zones, each of which contains a set of sensors distributed across various locations. These sensors can vary in type, including temperature sensors, humidity sensors, or cameras. In real-time, multiple objects can be detected within a given zone, and the sensors can collect multiple data values from different locations.

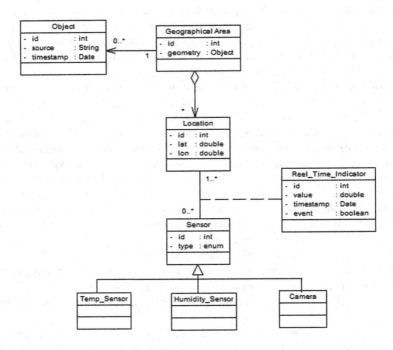

Fig. 1. Standard UML class diagram for modeling geospatial data

3.2   Functional Requirements

In this section, we explore the fundamental functional requirements applicable to any geospatial application. These requirements define essential functionalities and capabilities that the application must encompass to meet user needs. It's worth noting that the example queries provided below are generic and can vary according to specific use cases. Nevertheless, they serve as a foundational perspective to comprehend how functional requirements can impact the design of geospatial databases.

1. **Spatial selection** : Find all the objects and events taken within a specific zone.
2. **Spatial join** : Display sensors values within a zone at the time of capturing an object.
3. **Spatial analysis** : Identify the areas where a specific sensor's value is above a critical threshold.
4. **Spatial aggregation** : Identify the zone most prone to a given event.
5. **Spatial clustering** : Identify geographic areas where low levels of sensors values are clustered.
6. **Geospatial temporal queries** : Find all objects taken on a specific date and time.
7. **Network analysis** : Identify the distance between two specific locations.
8. **Geospatial visualization** : Create a map showing the objects positions within a given zone.
9. **Location-based services** : Find the five nearest locations to a given point.
10. **Geospatial data transformation** : Convert geographic coordinates (latitude, longitude) into a format readable by GPS navigation systems.

4   Generating NoSQL Database Model for IoT

In this section, we illustrate how to start from the definition of functional requirements to arrive to the design of the NoSQL database. We apply the approach on the IoT functional requirements defines in the previous sections. Indeed, taking into account the generic functional requirements listed in Sect. 3.2, we execute a set of rules to transit from the standard UML class diagram, that is proposed in Sect. 3.1, to arrive to the document-oriented NoSQL database model. This process will highlight how functional requirements influence the design of document-oriented NoSQL geospatial databases.

4.1   Adjusting the Original Class Diagram

Before modeling our document-oriented NoSQL geospatial database, we must first adjust it to make it simpler. According to Roy-Hubara et al. [5], we can adjust the UML class diagram by applying the rules below.

Inheritance Relationships (R1)
If all the necessary information can be obtained by focusing solely on the superclass as a whole, it's recommended to remove the subclasses. Conversely, if each object strictly belongs to a single subclass, and no query requires the presence of the superclass, then it is advisable to remove the superclass.

Composition and Aggregation Relationships (R2)

The suggestion is to transform an aggregation into a many-to-many relationship and a composition into a one-to-many relationship

Association Classes (R3)

An association class is translated into a regular class with two composite relationships, each connecting to the respective classes involved.

After applying the transformation rules R1, R2 and Rch13, we get the following adjusted class diagram (see Fig. 2).

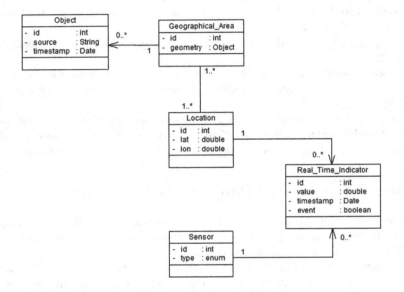

Fig. 2. Adjusted UML class diagram

4.2   Transforming the Adjusted Class Diagram to a Document Databases Schema

Once the class diagram has been adjusted, the transition to the document database must adhere to the rules inspired by [5], as stated below. Before delving into this, it's important to note that [2,9] :

– A conceptual model of a document-oriented NoSQL database consists of documents and collections. We depict their graphical representation in Fig. 3.
– There are two types of relationships between documents: embedding and referencing. A document can embed one or more other documents (collections), just as it can reference one or more documents. These relationships

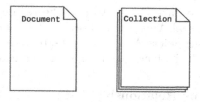

Fig. 3. Graphic representation of a document and a collection

are referred to as one-to-one or one-to-many embedding and referencing relationships, respectively. These relationships are illustrated in Fig. 4.

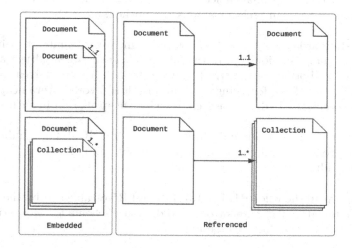

Fig. 4. Graphical representation of one-to-one and one-to-many relationships for embedded and referenced documents.

- The distinction between a georeferenced document and a non-georeferenced document lies in the addition of symbols located in the upper right corner of the document. Specifically, a point is represented by a star, a line by a solid line, and a polygon by a square.
- The association between two georeferenced documents is represented by a dashed line, whereas when two non-georeferenced documents are involved, the association is symbolized by a solid line.

Mapping Many-to-Many Relationship (R4)
It is recommended to avoid encapsulating many-to-many relationships and, instead, to favor establishing bidirectional connections.

However, in our case, we have chosen to add the reference in only one direction between "Geographical_Area" and "Location" because adding the "Location" reference in "Geographical_Area" would be redundant since the geometry attribute encompasses all the locations belonging to a geographical area.

Mapping One-to-Many Relationship (R5)
When two classes are queried simultaneously, the choice between encapsulation and referencing hinges on how frequently each class is solicited as the subject of queries. If one of the classes appears less frequently, it is encapsulated within the class that is more frequently the subject of queries, provided the minimum cardinality is 1.
However, if the first class is often the subject of independent queries, encapsulation might not be the optimal choice. In cases where encapsulation isn't feasible, a bidirectional referencing relationship is established.

In our standard adjusted UML class diagram, we encounter two instances of the one-to-many relationship. In the first scenario (between Object and Geographical_Area), both classes actively interact with each other. Given this active interaction, we opt for referencing. This approach is favored over encapsulation due to the potentially high cost associated with encapsulation in such a specific context.
Nevertheless, in the second and third cases where "Real_Time_Indicator" is more query-prone, we will encapsulate the "Sensor" and "Location" within the "Real_Time_Indicator."

After applying the rules R1, R2, R3, R4, and R5 established by the authors, here is the foundational document-oriented database schema for geospatial applications that we have obtained - see Fig. 5.

5   Experience

This section, show how functional requirements define the optial model in the design of document-oriented NoSQL databases for geospatial data. Indeed, we consider, two different functional requirements and we show that they lead to two different NoSQL models. As IoT application, we use a soil moisture detection as an example.
In this phase of implementing our approach, we have developed two sets of functional requirements, each containing geospatial queries. We will demonstrate how these diverse functional requirements can lead to distinct modifications in the database structure, despite starting from the UML class diagram - See Fig. 6.

5.1   Functional Requirements (Type 1)

1. **Spatial selection**: Retrieve all humidity values captured within a specific area.

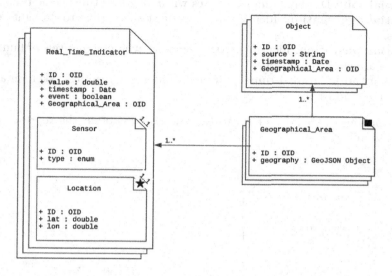

Fig. 5. Document-oriented database schema for geospatial applications

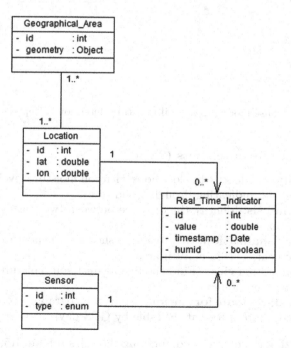

Fig. 6. UML class diagram for soil moisture data

2. **Spatial join**: Display humidity values within a zone at a specific time.
3. **Spatial aggregation**: Identify the area most susceptible to drought conditions.
4. **Spatial clustering**: Identify geographic areas where high levels of humidity values are clustered in soil.
5. **Geospatial temporal queries**: Find all humidity readings taken on a specific date and time.

By applying rules R4 and R5 to the queries, we obtain the representation illustrated in Fig. 7.

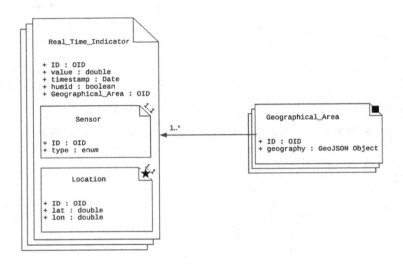

Fig. 7. Database modeling for soil moisture detection – Representation 1

5.2   Functional Requirements (Type 2)

1. **Spatial analysis**: Identify the locations with soil moisture levels falling below a given threshold, indicating drought conditions.
2. **Network analysis**: Identify the distance between two specific soil moisture measurement locations.
3. **Geospatial visualization**: Create a map showing the positions of soil moisture measurements within a given area.
4. **Location-based services**: Find the five nearest soil moisture measurement locations to a given point.
5. **Geospatial data transformation**: Convert geographic coordinates (latitude, longitude) into a format readable by GPS navigation systems.

Upon analyzing the queries and applying the rules R4 and R5, it's noticeable that the resulting representation takes a different form. This variability is entirely expected – See Fig. 8.

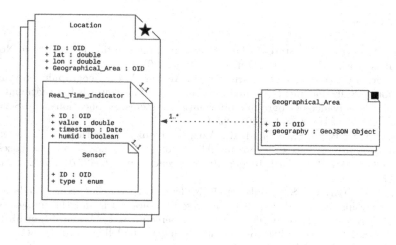

Fig. 8. UML class diagram for soil moisture data – Representation 2

5.3   Results' Analysis

To study the functional requirements' impact, we developed two separate lists of geospatial queries. In the first list, we determined that "Sensor" and "Location" should be integrated into "Real_Time_Indicator" due to the high number of queries expected for this part of the application. However, for the second list of queries, we noticed that the resulting representation took a different form. This variability was anticipated, as the nature of data representation is closely tied to the specific characteristics of the queries themselves.

The results of our experimentation clearly highlight that NoSQL document-oriented database modeling heavily depends on the specific functional requirements of the application. These findings underscore the crucial importance of a deep understanding of functional requirements during the database design phase.

6   Conclusion

The primary objective of this study was to present a method for modeling a NoSQL document-oriented geospatial database based on a UML data conceptual model. We also emphasized the significant influence of functional requirements from an application on the design of a database, especially when dealing with geospatial data. Despite starting from the common foundation provided by the UML class diagram, we observed that different functional requirements led to distinct transformations in the database structure, which is particularly relevant in the context of geospatial data. We focused solely on the phase of transforming the UML conceptual data model into the NoSQL document-oriented database. The performance evaluation of each model based on queries will be addressed in an upcoming paper. These findings underscore the crucial importance of a deep understanding of functional requirements during the database design phase.

References

1. Guo, D., Onstein, E.: State-of-the-art geospatial information processing in NoSQL databases. ISPRS Int. J. Geo-Inf. **9**(5), 331 (2020)
2. Wagner, B.F., Harley, V.O., Maristela, H., Aleteia, A. F.: Geographic data modeling for NoSQL document-oriented databases. In: The Seventh International Conference on Advanced Geographic Information Systems, Applications, and Services. IRIA (2015). ISBN: 978-1-61208-383-4
3. Imam, A.A., Basri, S., Ahmad, R., Aziz, N., González-Aparicio, M.T.: New cardinality notations and styles for modeling NoSQL document-store databases. In: TENCON 2017–2017 IEEE Region 10 Conference, pp. 2765–2770. IEEE, Malaysia (2017)
4. Bédard, Y., Larrivée, S., Proulx, M.-J., Nadeau, M.: Modeling geospatial databases with plug-ins for visual languages: a pragmatic approach and the impacts of 16 years of research and experimentations on perceptory. In: Wang, S., et al. (eds.) ER 2004. LNCS, vol. 3289, pp. 17–30. Springer, Heidelberg (2004). https://doi.org/10.1007/978-3-540-30466-1_3
5. Roy-Hubara, N., Sturm, A., Shoval, P.: Designing NoSQL databases based on multiple requirement views. Data Knowl. Eng. **145**, 102149 (2023)
6. Kamilaris, A., Ostermann, F.: Geospatial analysis and the Internet of Things. ISPRS Int. J. Geo-Inf. **7**(7), 269 (2018). https://doi.org/10.3390/ijgi7070269
7. Basmi, W., Boulmakoul, A., Karim, L., Lbath, A.: Modern approach to design a distributed and scalable platform architecture for smart cities complex events data collection. J. Ambient Intell. Humanized Comput. **12**(1), 75–83 (2020)
8. Ferreira, K., Camara, G., Monteiro, A.: Towards a Dynamic Geospatial Database Model. Copyright (c) 2011 EDB 2011. 62 (2011)
9. Borges, K.A., Davis, C.A., Laender, A.H.: OMT-G: an object-oriented data model for geographic applications. GeoInformatica **5**, 221–260 (2001). https://doi.org/10.1023/A:1011482030093
10. Abdelhedi, F., Brahim, A.A., Atigui, F., Zurfluh, G.: UMLtoNoSQL: automatic transformation of conceptual schema to NoSQL databases. In: 14th International Conference on Computer Systems and Applications, pp. 272–279, IEEE/ACS, Hammamet, Tunisia (2017). https://doi.org/10.1109/AICCSA.2017.76
11. Maicha, M.E., Ouinten, Y., Ziani, B.: UML4NoSQL: a novel approach for modeling NoSQL document-oriented databases based on UML. Comput. Inform. **41**, 813–833 (2022). 10.31577/cai_2022_3_813
12. Benmakhlouf, A.: NoSQL implementation of a conceptual data model: UML class diagram to a document-oriented model. Int. J. Database Manage. Syst. **10**(2), 1–10 (2018)
13. Shin, K., Hwang, C., Jung, H.: NoSQL database design using UML conceptual data model based on peter chen's framework. Int. J. Appl. Eng. Res. **12**(5), 632–636 (2017). ISSN 0973-4562

A Survey on Intrusion Detection Systems for IoT Networks Based on Long Short-Term Memory

Nour Elhouda Oueslati[1]([✉]), Hichem Mrabet[1], and Abderrazak Jemai[1,2]

[1] Faculty of Sciences of Tunis, University of Tunis El Manar, Tunis, Tunisia
`{nourelhouda.oueslati,hichem.mrabet}@fst.utm.tn`
[2] National Institute of Applied Sciences and Technology, Tunis, Tunisia
`abderrazak.jemai@insat.tn`

Abstract. The Internet of Things (IoT) network is a promising technology that links both living and nonliving things in a worldwide fashion. Due to the wide availability and usage of connected devices in IoT networks, the number of attacks on these networks is continually increasing. Various types of cyber-security-enabled mechanisms have been developed to limit these attacks. Intrusion detection system (IDS) is among these mechanisms. IDS has two different functions: intrusion alarming, which represents the first function and detects malicious activity in the system, and the site security office (SSO), which represents the alarm and takes the appropriate action. Since sensitive data is more easily targeted and can be used immediately, the IDS works well while machine learning (ML) and especially deep learning (DL) algorithms are employed to identify and prevent various threats. Long Short-Term Memory (LSTM) is mainly utilized because it can forecast data held in long-term memory and provide more accurate predictions based on current information. In this paper, a comprehensive survey about using LSTM as a key solution for intrusion detection is provided, followed by a comparison of the most modern and extensive data sets used to detect intrusion attacks in the IoT environment.

Keywords: Internet of Things (IoT) · Cyber-Security · Intrusion Detection System (IDS) · Deep Learning · Long Short Term Memory (LSTM) · Recurrent Neural Network (RNN)

1 Introduction

Due to the exponential data generation, which ranges from zettabytes to petabytes, there has been a significant increase in computer networks and Internet of Things (IoT) networks globally over the past ten years. Consequently, with the expansion of the network, security vulnerabilities have also surfaced, Network viruses, eavesdropping and malicious attacks are on the rise, causing network security to become the focus of attention of society and government departments. However, it can be difficult to detect intrusions in such large data sets.

M. Mosbah et al. (Eds.): MEDI 2023, CCIS 2071, pp. 237–250, 2024.
https://doi.org/10.1007/978-3-031-55729-3_19

There are many sophisticated uses of the developing networks, including smart homes, cities, grids, gadgets, and objects as well as e-commerce, e-banking, e-government, etc. Fortunately, intrusion detection may effectively overcome these issues. Intrusion detection plays an important part in ensuring network information security. However, as Internet commerce booms, network traffic kinds increases daily, and network behavior features become more complicated, intrusion detection is faced with enormous difficulties.

A major issue that cannot be ignored is how to recognize different hostile network traffics, especially unanticipated malicious network traffics. Actually, there are two types of network traffic (normal traffics and malicious traffics). Therefore, it is possible to think about intrusion detection as a categorization issue. Accuracy of intrusion detection can be significantly increased by enhancing classifier performance in accurately recognizing malicious traffic. In modern studies, researchers focus on machine and deep learning techniques to provide accurate intrusion detection schemes the reason behind using these techniques, especially deep learning, is to reduce the effort for input preprocessing. Deep learning (DL) [1,2] can extract features of data from the input data itself, which may fit schemes that need real-time processing.

Classic ML techniques have been utilized in this sector for over 20 years. However, when the technology boom begins, the assault categories are expanding on their own. As a result, the potential of any traditional ML model is significantly less than the scope of the intrusion. Furthermore, while the hybrid technique based on these models has performed effectively for a long time, it eventually falls short in comparison to contemporary DL models. The richness of the dataset available to us greatly influences machine learning. Furthermore, the inability to scale the data appropriately limits the extensive use of any ML model. To address such challenges, deep learning methods such as ANN (Artificial Neural Networks) were developed. The model is based on neurons that are controlled by parameters and hyper-parameters. To scale the input and use it on extensive scale, the number of layers are kept accordingly to get maximum efficiency. In terms of accuracy, precision, and the ability to handle massive volumes of data, DL methods have proven to be considerably superior to ML models. ANN, CNN (Convolutional Neural Networks) [19], RNN (Recurrent Neural Networks), FDN (Feed Forward Deep Networks) are many examples of DL architectures.

Many survey papers on intrusion detection systems [29] and anomaly detection [4,30] have focused on security and risk analysis in different domains such as wireless sensor networks (WSN) and IoT using statistical and machine learning techniques [8–19]; fraud detection [20], and credit risk analysis [21]. To our knowledge, no survey or review is focusing specifically on Intrusion Detection Systems in IOT using Deep Learning Technique "Long short-term memory (LSTM)" [23]. In this study, the use of the LSTM to provide intrusion detection schemes has been conducted. This methodology is a subset of RNN [24].The most notable feature of LSTM is the ability to save information/parameters for subsequent usage in the system. They can deal with data that is time series and may be varied over time. The key reason for employing LSTM is that it is not constrained by the constraints of traditional DL (neural networks) [52] methodologies.

Contribution. Our major contributions in the under contention research study are enlisted as follows:

- A new taxonomy of IoT IDS is proposed.
- A comparative study is performed between existing works using LSTM presenting the advantages and drawbacks for each work.
- A comparative parameter of the common LSTM models is proposed as a function of Layers (number), Neurons/Kernel, AF (Activation function), Epochs, Optimizer, and batch size.
- A comparative analysis of various LSTM models as a function of various performance metrics such as Accuracy, Recall, F1-Measure, and Precision.

Organization. This survey paper is organized in a systematic order in which, Sect. 2 contains the taxonomy of IoT IDS architecture, Sect. 3 includes a comparative study of the common LSTM models, and finally, the study is concluded in Sect. 4 of this paper.

2 Taxonomy of IoT IDS Architecture

Intrusion Detection System(IDS) [32] play an important role in IoT network security, as they are designed to identify and report suspicious or malicious activity on a network. In the context of IoT networks, IDS can detect attacks [31] such as data theft, malicious code injection or sensor manipulation, and help prevent potential damage. There are several types of(IDS) [18] for IoT networks: including Signature-based IDS (SIDS), Anomaly-based IDS (AIDS), Specification-base IDS, Hybrid-based IDS(HIDS), Host-based IDS, Network-based IDS (NIDS), Distributed-based IDS (DIDS) (see Fig. 1).

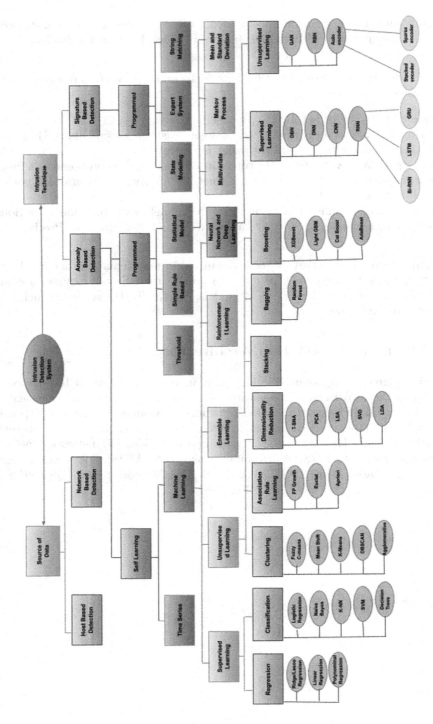

Fig. 1. A hierarchical taxonomy of Intrusion Detection System (IDS).

2.1   Signature-Based Intrusion Detection Systems (SIDS)

SIDS is also referred to as knowledge-based detection. It compares network communication and activities to analyse and evaluate networks based on well-known patterns or corresponding signatures for detecting attack signatures in signature databases. It saves each attack's behaviour and signature within a network. When the attack signature is identified or matched against the stored signature database, an alert is generated.

2.2   Anomaly-Based Intrusion Detection Systems (AIDS)

Because new anomalous behaviours are concerned with pattern databases, the primary goal of AIDS is to detect zero-day attacks. It is capable of learning deviant behaviour within networks. For example, if any unauthorised activity or stealing from an account occurs, the alarm is triggered [4,5].

Machine Learning-Based AIDS. Machine Learning (ML) has seen widespread use in the field of cybersecurity [24]. Many specialised branches of ML , including as Data Mining [25], Deep Learning [26,27], Deep Reinforcement Learning, and, more recently, Adversarial Learning [28], have been used to develop an AIDS. Machine Learning models are used in ML-based AIDSs to automatically learn a representation of the computing system's normal circumstances.

Statistics-Based AIDS. During the learning phase, a statistically based IDS constructs a probability distribution model of the computer system's nominal behaviour. The model is constructed by taking measurements of various parameters and events occurring in the computing system. When the IDS is deployed, it analyses the probability of all the system's monitored events and issues alerts for low probability events. The "Univariate" technique is the simplest way to design a statistical model since it considers each measurement independently of the others. The "Multivariate" technique, which consists on discovering correlations and relationships between two or more measurements, is an evolution of it.

2.3   Host-Based Intrusion Detection Systems

The HIDS is software that is installed on the network's host computer and investigates, analyses, gathers, and monitors data actions within the network and host network on a consistent basis by reviewing firewall, server, or database logs. HIDS is confined to identifying aberrant assaults on a particular host while detecting uninvolved attacks throughout the network.

2.4   Network-Based Intrusion Detection Systems(NIDS)

NIDS monitors network communications by collecting packet capture and other information via NetFlow. Its fundamental function is to defend the networks from the outer threats causing an alert/alarm when a harmful attack occurred. This IDS operates with numerous hosts across the networks and external firewalls by monitoring and analyzing network communications using software or hardware. Software is installed on servers for monitoring, while sensors are attached to servers to analyze the network's communications. As a result, NIDS detects malicious attacks very effectively and securely. Due to high bandwidth and speed traffic flow, NIDS cannot process and analyse large amounts of network data. NIDS also does not support encrypted network packets.

2.5   Distributed-Based Intrusion Detection Systems (DIDS)

DIDS consists of many IDS deployed across a large network to analyse communication monitoring management, malicious attack information, and incidents. To manage intrusion detection and prevention, information is combined utilising several sensors (NIDS and HIDS-based) and a central analyzer.

3   Comparative Study of the Common LSTM Models

3.1   Public Cyber-Security Datasets of IoT

The development of a dataset used to train the IDS detection models is a very important task. Over the years, different datasets have been created, and the ones that are most commonly used in the field of IDS are briefly explained below.

Bot-IoT Dataset: The dataset consists of both legitimate and simulated IoT traffic and various attack types. It provides full packet capture information with corresponding labels. The dataset is highly imbalanced, with very records. The full dataset consits of 37,360,900 rows and has a size of over 69 GB.

N-BaIoT Dataset: The dataset is made up of real-world IoT network traffic collected from nine commercial IoT devices. The dataset has been infected with two well-known and dangerous IoT batnets, Mirai and BASHLITE (also known as Gafgyt).The dataset is unbalanced, with benign records being far smaller than malicious records.

CICIDS-2017 Dataset: The CICIDS-2017 dataset is made up of multiple network traffic captures taken from a realistic network environment with a mix of normal and malicious activities. It comprises several sorts of assaults such as DoS, DDoS, port scans, and brute force attacks. Researchers and cybersecurity experts can use the information to design and test intrusion detection systems and related algorithms.

UNSW-NB15 Dataset: Dataset is designed based on a synthetic environment for generating attack activaties. The dataset is not IoT-specific and was created by gathering real benign network traffic as well as synthetically manufactured attacks. It contains around an hour of anonymized traffic traces from a 2007 DDoS assault. The increased number of classes (10 in NB15 vs 5 in KDD) and higher Null Error Rate in NB15 versus in KDD have a mitigating effect on total classification accuracy [3].

IoT-23: is a network traffic dataset containing 20 malware subsets and three benign subsets. The Stratosphere Laboratory in Czechia first made the dataset available in January 2020. The dataset's goal is to present a large dataset of labeled malware and benign traffic from real-world captures in order to develop intrusion detection systems that use machine learning methods.

Table 1 lists the different cyber-security datasets in the context of IoT. We highlight the attacks captured, total features, total benign records, and total malicious records.

Table 1. Comparative Cyber-security Datasets of IoT

Ref	Dataset	Attacks captured	Total Features	Total Benign Records	Total Malicious Records
[33]	Bot-IoT	DoS, DDoS, Reconnaissance, Theft	43	477	3668045
[17]	N-BaIoT	Gafgyt combo, Gafgytjunk, Gafgytscan, GafgytTCP, GafgytUDP, Mirai ack, Mirai scan, Mirai syn, MirainUDP, and Mirai-Udpplain	115	555932	7134943
[34]	CICIDS-2017	DoS Hulk, Port scan, DDoS, DoS GoldenEye, FTP-Patator, SSH-Patator, DoS Slowloris, DoS Slowhttptest, Bot, Web Attack Brute Force, Web Attack XSS, Infiltration, Web Attack SQL Injection, Heartbleed	83	2271320	556556
[35]	UNSW-NB15	Generic, Exploits, Fuzzers, DoS, Reconnaissance, Analysis, Backdoor, Shellcode, Worms	49	1867614	232389
[36]	IoT-23	Mirai, Hide & seek, Muhstik, IRCBot, Hakai, Hajime, Torli, torjan, Kenjiro, Okiru, Gagfyt	23	5063238	4697805

3.2   LSTM Architecture

LSTM solves the traditional RNN's vanishing gradient issue, it can be used to simulate the long-term dependencies of IoT traffic. An input layer, a recurrent hidden layer whose fundamental unit is a memory block (instead of a conventional neuron node), and an output layer make up the LSTM architecture [21,22]. A collection of frequently connected subnets make up memory blocks. Three multiplicative units the input, output, and forget gates provide the continuous analogs of write, read, and reset operations on the memory cells, and each block has one or more interconnected memory cells. Multiplicative gates enable LSTM memory cells to retain and access information over lengthy periods of time. However, due to the chain structure of the memory blocks, the performance of LSTM deteriorates rapidly as the length of the sequence increases.

Table 2 compares the different LSTM models that are used often, with the huge of cyber-security "Datasets" to train and test aiming to attain a high accuracy rate, "Advantages", "Drawbacks", and "Solution compared with".

The Systematic architecture of each LSTM model is detailed as a function of Layers(number), Neurons/Kernel, AF(Activation Function), Epochs, Optimizer, and Batch-size can be witnessed in Table 3. In [6], the model consists of 3 BLSTM layers possessing 500, 300, and 200 neurons, 3 dense layers possessing 200, 100, and 50 neurons, and 1 output layer that occupies 02 neurons. Softmax is used as an Activation Function (AF) in consanguinity with the Adamax optimizer, and the simulations are performed until 10 epochs with a batch size of 32. In [7], the model consists of 3 BLSTM layers that possess 400, 300, and 200 neurons, 3 dense layers, and 1 output layer that occupies 09 neurons. Softmax is used as an AF and the simulations are performed until 20 epochs with a batch size of 64. In [8], the model consists of 1 Convolutional layer possessing a 3D kernel, 1 Pooling layer, 1 LSTM layer, 1 dense layer, and 1 output layer occupying 01 neuron. Sigmoid is used as an AF in consanguinity with the Adam optimizer, and the simulations are performed until 100 epochs. In [9], the model consists of 2 Embedding layers that possess 100, and 150 neurons, 4 convolutional layers that possess 3 kernels, 2 BLSTM layers that possess 128, and 64 neurons, 2 Dropout layers possess 0.2, 1 Dense layer and 1 output layer occupies 1 neuron. Softmax is used as an AF in consanguinity with the Adam optimizer, and the simulations are performed until 05 epochs with a batch size of 32. In [10], the model consists of 1 LSTM layer possessing 100 neurons, 4 dense layers possessing 100, 100, 100, and 100 neurons, and 1 output layer occupying 05 neurons. Softmax is used as an Activation Function (AF) in consanguinity with the Nadam optimizer, and the simulations are performed until 20 epochs with a batch size of 64. Table 3 conscripts detailed the rest information of [12,14–16]. No information is provided For [11] and [13].

Table 2. Comparative study of the common LSTM models.

Year	Proposed work	Classifier/Dataset	Advantages	Drawbacks	Solution compared with
2022	Cyber threats Detection in Smart Environment using SDN-Enabled DNN-LSTM Hybrid Framework [6]	Cu-DNNLSTM/ CICIDS-2018	-High accuracy -low False Positive Rate	-It is not real-time IDS	Cu-DNNGRU Cu-BLSTM
2022	An AI-Driven Hybrid Framework for Intrusion Detection in IoT-Enabled E-Health [7]	Cu-BLSTM+GRU/ CICIDSDoS2019	-High accuracy	-It is not real time IDS	Cu-BLSTM, Cu-GRU +Dnn
2019	Deep Learning Models for cyber-security in IoT Networks [8]	CNN+LSTM/DDoS attack CICIDS-2017	-High accuracy	-Few type of attacks	SVM, Byes, Random Forest, LSTM, 1d-CNN
2019	A deep learning-based static taint analysis approach for IoT software vulnerability location [9]	CNN+BLSTM/NVD and SARD	-High accuracy -Low False Positive Rate	-High training time	RNN, LSTM, BLSTM
2020	Hybrid Deep Learning for Botnet Attack Detection in the Internet of Things Networks [10]	LAE-BLSTM/Bot-IoT	-High accuracy	-Few type of attacks	PCE-FNN, PCE-SNN, IFG-CSVM
2020	A technical review and comparative analysis of machine learning techniques for intrusion detection systems in MANET(Mobile Ad Hoc Network) [11]	BLSTM/NSL-KDD	-High precision	-high False Positive Rate	Inception -CNN, DBF
2020	Flow-Based and Packet-Based Intrusion Detection Using BLSTM [12]	BLSTM Flow-based model/UNSW-NB15	-High accuracy -Low resource consumption	-The model caused a performance bottleneck	BLSTM packet-based model
2020	Explainable Software Vulnerability Detection based on Attention-based Bidirectional Recurrent Neural Networks [13]	ABLSTM/NVD and SARD	-High accuracy -Low False Positive Rate	-Computational complexity	MLP, CNN, LSTM, GRU, BLSTM
2022	LBDMIDS: LSTM-based Deep Learning Model for Intrusion Detection Systems for IoT Networks [14]	LBDMIDS/UNSW-NB15 Bot-IoT	-High accuracy	-High training time	ARM, Decision Tree, DNN, Naive Bayes, RNN
2022	IoT Intrusion Detection System Based on LSTM Model [15]	LSTM/CTU-13 + CICIDS-2017	-High accuracy -low false alarm rate	-high energy "CPU"	1D CNN, 2D CNN, CNN-LSTM
2022	M-LSTM: Multiclass Long Short-Term Memory Approach for Detection of DDoS Attacks [16]	M-LSTM/ CICDDoS2019	-High accuracy -low resource consumption	-Few types of attacks -It is not real-time IDS	

Table 3. Comparative parameters of the common LSTM models

Ref	Layers(number)	Neurons/Kernel	AF	Epochs	Optimizer	Batch-size
[6]	BLSTM Layer(3)	500, 300, 200	Relu	10	Adamax	32
	Dense Layer(3)	200, 100, 50	-			
	Output Layer(1)	02	Softmax			
[7]	BLSTM Layer(3)	400, 300, 200	Relu	20	-	64
	Dense Layer(3)	- - -	-			
	Output Layer(1)	09	Softmax			
[8]	Convolutional Layer(1)	3D	Relu	100	Adam	-
	Pooling Layer(1)	-	-			
	LSTM Layer(1)	-	Relu			
	Dense Layer(1)	-	-			
	Output Layer(1)	01	Sigmoid			
[9]	Embedding Layer(2)	100, 150	-	05	Adam	32
	Convolutional Layer(4)	3 Kernel	-			
	BLSTM Layer(2)	128, 64	-			
	Dropout Layer(2)	0.2	-			
	Dense Layer(1)	-	-			
	Output Layer(1)	01	Softmax			
[10]	LSTM Layer(1)	100	Relu	20	Nadam	64
	Dense Layer(4)	100, 100, 100, 100	Relu			
	Output Layer(1)	05	Softmaw			
[11]	-	-	-	-	-	
[12]	BLSTM Flow-based model					
	BLSTM Layer(1)	-	Relu	30	Adam	32
	Dropout(1)	0.2	-			
	Dense Layer(3)	50, 50, 50	Relu			
	Output Layer(1)	01	Sigmoid			
	BLSTM Packet-based model					
	BLSTM Layer(1)	-	Relu	30	Softmax	32
	Dropout(1)	0.2	-			
	Dense Layer(3)	50, 50, 50	Relu			
	Output Layer(1)	10	Softmax			
[13]	-	-	-	-	-	
[14]	Sacked LSTM with UNSW-NB15					
	LSTM Layer(4)	40, 128, 128, 64	-	50	-	-
	Output Layer(1)	64	Softmax			
	Sacked LSTM with Bot-IoT					
	LSTM Layer(2)	32, 32	-	50	-	-
	Output Layer(1)	32	Softmax			
	BLSTM with UNSW-NB15					
	LSTM Layer(1)	64	-	50	-	-
	Output Layer(1)	64	Softmax			
	BLSTM with Bot-IoT					
	LSTM Layer(1)	12	-	05	-	-
	Output Layer(1)	12	Softmax			
[15]	LSTM Layer(2)	128, 128	-	-	-	-
	Dropout Layer(2)	0.5	-			
	Output Layer(1)	01	SOftmax			
[16]	LSTM Layer(1)	50	Relu	20	Adam	64
	Dense Layer(3)	32, 16, 8	-			
	Output Layer(1)	04	Softmax			

3.3 Evaluation Indicators

In the specified detection findings,T (True) and F (False) reflect the data classified correctly or inaccurately, respectively. The detection system's prediction results are represented as aberrant or normal data, respectively, by the letters P (Positive) and N (Negative). Any one of the four categories-TP, TN, FP, or FN-must be applied to every piece of data in the dataset. TN indicates that the classification result of the system is positive and correct; FP indicates that the system predicts the data as anomalous attack data, but the classification result is wrong; FN indicates that the system predicts the data as constant data, but the classification result is wrong.

$$Accuracy = \frac{TP + TN}{TP + FP + TN + FN} \tag{1}$$

$$Precision = \frac{TP}{TP + FP} \tag{2}$$

$$Recall = \frac{TP}{TP + FN} \tag{3}$$

$$F1 - Measure = \frac{2 * Precision * Recall}{Precision + Recall} \tag{4}$$

3.4 Comparative Analysis of a Various LSTM Model as Function of Various Performance Metrics

Table 4. Comparative Accuracy, Recall, F1-measure, and Precision of the common LSTM model.

Ref	Accuracy	Recall	F1-measure	Precision
[6]	98.90%	98.71%	98.82%	98.64%
[7]	98.53%	98.43 %	98.68 %	98.71 %
[8]	97.16%	99.12%	-	97.41%
[9]	CWE-119 97.32%	-	-	-
	CWE-399 97.21%	-	-	-
[10]	99.49%	-	-	-
[11]	84.03%	86.01%	-	93.98%
[12]	FBID 96%	96%	96%	96%
	PBID 76%	76%	72%	70%
[13]	96.70%	-	92.40%	90.90%
[14]	Stacked LSTM(UNSW-NB15) 96.60%	96%	96%	97%
	Stacked LSTM(Bot-IoT) 99.99%	100%	100%	100%
	BLSTM(UNSW-NB15) 96.41%	96%	96%	97%
	BLSTM(Bot-IoT) 99.99%	100%	100%	100%
[15]	99.84%	99.96%	99.58%	99.20%
[16]	-	97.50%	98%	98.75%

In Table 4 We used the assessment measures Accuracy, Recall, F1-measure, and Precision to evaluate the prediction accuracy of all the LSTM models shown in Table 2 to one another. The performance of the two LSTM models (Stacked LSTM and BLSTM) used in [14] with the Bot-IoT dataset is significantly better than other models, according to the evaluation results in Table 4. These models achieve the best detection Accuracy, Recall, F1-measure, and Precision, which are 99.99%, 100%, 100%, and 100% respectively.

4 Conclusion

This study present a complete survey on intrusion detection systems for IoT network based on the LSTM model, where we have proposed a new taxonomy of IoT IDS. Then, we presented a comparative study performed between the existing works using LSTM while focusing on their advantages and drawbacks. Likewise, the common LSTM models in the state of the art are compared in terms of number of layers, number of neurons, activation function, epoch's number, optimizer and batch size. Finally, the performance of the existing works based on LSTM are evaluated on diverse performance metrics such as accuracy, precision, recall, and f1-measure.

References

1. Ghumro, A., Memon, A.K., Memon, I., Simming, I.A.: A review of mitigation of attacks in IoT using deep learning models. Quaid-E-Awam Univ. Res. J. Eng. Sci. Technol. Nawabshah. **18**(1), 36–42 (2020)
2. Rodriguez, E., Otero, B., Gutierrez, N., Canal, R.: A survey of deep learning techniques for cybersecurity in mobile networks. IEEE Commun. Surv. Tutorials **23**(3), 1920–1955 (2021)
3. Altunay, H.C., Albayrak, Z.: A hybrid CNN+ LSTMbased intrusion detection system for industrial IoT networks. Eng. Sci. Technol. Int. J. **38**, 101322 (2023)
4. Wang, Y.C., Houng, Y.C., Chen, H.X., Tseng, S.M.: Network anomaly intrusion detection based on deep learning approach. Sensors **23**(4), 2171 (2023)
5. Alabadi, M., Celik, Y.: Anomaly detection for cyber-security based on convolution neural network: A survey. In: International Congress on Human-Computer Interaction, Optimization and Robotic Applications (HORA), pp. 1–14. IEEE (2020)
6. Al Razib, M., Javeed, D., Khan, M.T., Alkanhel, R., Muthanna, M.S.A.: Cyber threats detection in smart environments using SDN-enabled DNN-LSTM hybrid framework. IEEE Access, **10**, 53015–53026 (2022)
7. Wahab, F., et al.: An AI-driven hybrid framework for intrusion detection in IoT-enabled E-health. Comput. Intell. Neurosci. (2022)
8. Roopak, M., Tian, G.Y., Chambers, J.: Deep learning models for cyber security in IoT networks. In 2019 IEEE 9th Annual Computing and Communication Workshop and Conference (CCWC), pp. 0452–0457 (2019)
9. Niu, W., Zhang, X., Du, X., Zhao, L., Cao, R., Guizani, M.: A deep learning based static taint analysis approach for IoT software vulnerability location. Measurement **152**, 107139 (2020)

10. Popoola, S.I., Adebisi, B., Hammoudeh, M., Gui, G., Gacanin, H.: Hybrid deep learning for botnet attack detection in the internet-of-things networks. IEEE Internet Things J. **8**(6), 4944–4956 (2020)
11. Laqtib, S., El Yassini, K., Hasnaoui, M.L.: A technical review and comparative analysis of machine learning techniques for intrusion detection systems in MANET. Int. J. Electr. Comput. Eng. **10**(3), 2701 (2020)
12. Andreas, B., Dilruksha, J., McCandless, E.: Flow-based and packet-based intrusion detection using BLSTM. SMU Data Sc. Rev. **3**(3), 8 (2020)
13. Mao, Y., Li, Y., Sun, J., Chen, Y.: Explainable software vulnerability detection based on attention-based bidirectional recurrent neural networks. In IEEE International Conference on Big Data (Big Data), pp. 4651–4656. IEEE (2020)
14. Saurabh, K., et al.: LBDMIDS: LSTM based deep learning model for intrusion detection systems for IoT networks. In IEEE World AI IoT Congress (AIIoT), pp. 753–759. IEEE (2022)
15. Li, W., Chang, C.: IoT intrusion detection system based on LSTM model. In 3rd International Conference on Artificial Intelligence and Education (IC-ICAIE), pp. 1404–1409. Atlantis Press (2022)
16. Gaur, M.V., Kumar, R.: M-LSTM: multiclass long short-term memory based approach for detection of DDoS attacks. Math. Stat. Eng. Appl. **71**(3s2), 1375–1394 (2022)
17. Al-Sarem, M., Saeed, F., Alkhammash, E.H., Alghamdi, N.S.: An aggregated mutual information based feature selection with machine learning methods for enhancing IoT botnet attack detection. Sensors **22**(1), 185 (2022)
18. Albulayhi, K., Smadi, A.A., Sheldon, F.T., Abercrombie, R.K.: IoT intrusion detection taxonomy, reference architecture, and analyses. Sensors **21**(19), 6432 (2021)
19. Ordóñez, F.J., Roggen, D.: Deep convolutional and LSTM recurrent neural networks for multimodal wearable activity recognition. Sensors **16**(1), 115 (2016)
20. Inayat, U., Zia, M.F., Mahmood, S., Khalid, H.M., Benbouzid, M.: Learning-based methods for cyber attacks detection in IoT systems: a survey on methods, analysis, and future prospects. Electronics **11**(9), 1502 (2022)
21. Kim, J., Kim, J., Thu, H.L.T., Kim, H.: Long short term memory recurrent neural network classifier for intrusion detection. In: International Conference on Platform Technology and Service (PlatCon), pp. 1–5. IEEE (2016)
22. Elsayed, R., Hamada, R., Hammoudeh, M., Abdalla, M., Elsaid, S.A.: A hierarchical deep learning-based intrusion detection architecture for clustered internet of things. J. Sensor Actuator Netw. **12**(1), 3 (2022)
23. Khan, A.R., Yasin, A., Usman, S.M., Hussain, S., Khalid, S., Ullah, S.S.: Exploring lightweight deep learning solution for malware detection in IoT constraint environment. Electronics **11**(24), 4147 (2022)
24. Amit, I., Matherly, J., Hewlett, W., Xu, Z., Meshi, Y., Weinberger, Y.: Machine learning in cyber-security-problems, challenges and data sets. In: arXiv preprint arXiv:1812.07858 (2018)
25. Dua, S., Du, X.: Data mining and machine learning in cybersecurity. In: CRC Press (2016)
26. Xin, Y., et al.: Machine learning and deep learning methods for cybersecurity. IEEE Access **6**, 35365–35381 (2018)
27. Aldweesh, A., Derhab, A., Emam, A.Z.: Deep learning approaches for anomaly-based intrusion detection systems: a survey, taxonomy, and open issues. Knowl. Based Syst. **189**, 105124 (2020)
28. Qiu, S., Liu, Q., Zhou, S., Wu, C.: Review of artificial intelligence adversarial attack and defense technologies. Appl. Sci. **9**(5), 909 (2019)

29. Alazab, A., Hobbs, M., Abawajy, J., Khraisat, A.: Developing an intelligent intrusion detection and prevention system against web application malware. In: Awad, A.I., Hassanien, A.E., Baba, K. (eds.) SecNet 2013. CCIS, vol. 381, pp. 177–184. Springer, Heidelberg (2013). https://doi.org/10.1007/978-3-642-40597-6_15

30. Khraisat, A., Gondal, I., Vamplew, P.: An anomaly intrusion detection system using C5 decision tree classifier. In: Ganji, M., Rashidi, L., Fung, B.C.M., Wang, C. (eds.) PAKDD 2018. LNCS (LNAI), vol. 11154, pp. 149–155. Springer, Cham (2018). https://doi.org/10.1007/978-3-030-04503-6_14

31. Ghazal, S.F., Mjlae, S.A.: Cybersecurity in deep learning techniques: detecting network attacks. Int. J. Adv. Comput. Sci. Appl. **13**(11) (2022)

32. Alghamdi, R., Bellaiche, M.: An ensemble deep learning based IDS for IoT using Lambda architecture. Cybersecurity **6**(1), 5 (2023)

33. Peterson, J.M., Leevy, J.L., Khoshgoftaar, T.M.: A review and analysis of the Bot-IoT dataset. In: IEEE International Conference on Service-Oriented System Engineering (SOSE), pp. 20–27 (2021)

34. Panwar, S.S., Negi, P.S., Panwar, L.S., Raiwani, Y.P.: Implementation of machine learning algorithms on CICIDS-2017 dataset for intrusion detection using WEKA. Int. J. Recent Technol. Eng. Regular Issue, **8**(3), 2195–2207 (2019)

35. Zoghi, Z. and Serpen, G.: UNSW-NB15 computer security dataset: analysis through visualization. In: arXiv preprint arXiv:2101.05067, (2021)

36. Stoian, N.A.: Machine learning for anomaly detection in iot networks: Malware analysis on the IoT-23 data set (Bachelor's thesis, University of Twente) (2020)

Author Index

Printed in the United States
by Baker & Taylor Publisher Services